compliments of

Institute
of the
Pennsylvania Hospital

Continuing Education
in Psychiatry

"The Use of Hypnosis
in Treatment"

January, 1984

*p103 - Induction Technique ———> entire chapter
22,3,4   "
23 Dental analgesia Trance
42. Discussion of hypnosis
49. Dealing ē physical sp.

HYPNOSIS
Trance as a Coping Mechanism

TOPICS IN GENERAL PSYCHIATRY

Series Editor:

John C. Nemiah, M.D.
*Psychiatrist-in-Chief, Beth Israel Hospital
and Professor of Psychiatry, Harvard Medical School*

HYPNOSIS
Fred H. Frankel, M.B.Ch.B., D.P.M.

THE FRONTIER OF BRIEF PSYCHOTHERAPY
David H. Malan, D.M., F.R.C. Psych.

THE PRACTITIONER'S GUIDE TO PSYCHOACTIVE DRUGS
Ellen L. Bassuk, M.D., and Stephen C. Schoonover, M.D.

SOCIOCULTURAL ROOTS OF MENTAL ILLNESS: An Epidemiologic Survey
John J. Schwab, M.D., and Mary E. Schwab, M.D.

SHORT-TERM DYNAMIC PSYCHOTHERAPY: Evaluation and Technique
Peter E. Sifneos, M.D.

HYPNOSIS
Trance as a Coping Mechanism

Fred H. Frankel, M.B.Ch.B., D.P.M.

Department of Psychiatry
Beth Israel Hospital
Harvard Medical School
Boston, Massachusetts

PLENUM MEDICAL BOOK COMPANY • New York and London

Library of Congress Cataloging in Publication Data

Frankel, Fred H
  Hypnosis: trance as a coping mechanism.

  (Topics in general psychiatry)
  Bibliography: p.
  Includes index.
  1. Hypnotism—Therapeutic use. I. Title.
RC495.F68   616.8'916'2   76-14856
ISBN 0-306-30932-7

First Printing — July 1976
Second Printing — June 1979

© 1976 Plenum Publishing Corporation
227 West 17th Street, New York, N. Y. 10011

Plenum Medical Book Company is an imprint of Plenum Publishing Corporation

Printed in the United States of America

To BETTY...
a rare person

Foreword

"Hypnotism," asserted Durand de Gros in 1860, "provides psychology with an experimental basis, from which point on it becomes a positive science and takes its place in the larger sphere of animal physiology."

At the time it was written, this pronouncement was perhaps more wish than fact, but it was accurately prophetic of many of the developments in clinical psychiatry in the decades that lay ahead. Charcot was the pioneering pathfinder. With his colleagues at the Salpêtrière in Paris, he employed hypnosis as an investigative tool to explore the psychology of patients with major hysteria. The discovery of the role of unconscious pathogenic ideas in the production of hysterical symptoms provided a basis for theoretical formulations that reached an apogee in the voluminous writings of Pierre Janet. For Janet, dissociation of mental functions became a central concept, and at the turn of the century, numerous clinical investigators in Europe and America were engaged in a study of its mechanisms and clinical manifestations.

Among those early investigators was Sigmund Freud, who after a visit to Charcot's clinic, initially turned his attention to dissociative phenomena. His interest, however, was soon drawn to the nature and source of the dissociated (repressed) mental contents and away from the mechanism of dissociation itself. In the emergence of psychoanalysis from Freud's early clinical observations, psychiatrists found a coherent body of fact and theory that provided useful explanations of psychiatric symptoms and a powerful therapeutic tool. It is not surprising, therefore, that analytic concepts and techniques have had a major influence in shaping twentieth century psychiatry, or that the modern psychiatrist is more concerned with psychological conflict than with dissociation, with free association than with the techniques of hypnosis.

The importance of psychoanalysis for understanding the human mind is incalculable. At the same time, its predominance on the modern scene has not been without its price. The decline of interest in hypnosis saw an early end to the work of the clinical investigators of nearly a century ago, and the attempt to elucidate the nature of dissociation was abandoned.

It is only in recent years that we have seen a revival of interest in hypnosis as a tool for clinical investigation, with a concomitant return to a study of the dissociative phenomena of which it forms a part. This volume is an outstanding example of that renaissance. With singular clarity Dr. Frankel provides the reader with a survey of the current facts and theories of hypnosis, and at the same time presents new observations of his own that suggest a close relationship between dissociation and psychiatric symptoms. His ideas help to revive the hope that psychology may, as Durand de Gros suggested, come closer to its neural roots.

John C. Nemiah, M.D.
Psychiatrist-in-Chief
Beth Israel Hospital
Professor of Psychiatry
Harvard Medical School

Boston, Massachusetts
April 29, 1976

Preface

In developing the ideas that are included in these pages, I have leaned heavily on numerous sources. In addition to those whose written works have been acknowledged in the bibliography, there are many whose comments, observations and attitudes have contributed richly to the work I have reported.

To my colleagues and very close friends of long standing, John Nemiah, Chief of the Psychiatric Service at the Beth Israel Hospital, and Peter Sifneos, Associate Director of the Service, I am deeply indebted for their warm and constant encouragement and scholarly interest in my work. To the former I owe my gratitude for the opportunity and time to work and report on the topic of hypnosis, and for the invitation to assemble my experience in a book to be included in this series of Topics in General Psychiatry. I am grateful to them both for reviewing the manuscript in its earlier stages, and for their frank and helpful comments.

While I bear the sole responsibility for the ideas expressed in these pages, Martin Orne's penetrating insights have been immensely helpful to me in formulating them. I am deeply indebted to him and to Emily Carota Orne, for their friendship, for the long hours of productive discussion, for enabling me to consider my ideas in the context of their wide experience with hypnosis, and for their helpful review of the manuscript.

My interest in hypnosis was first stirred by Herbert Spiegel, whose clinical approach is partially reported in these pages, and whose description of the grade 5 syndrome contributed to the ideas I have described. I am grateful to him for introducing me to the field, for his basic teaching, and for his encouragement.

Four of my friends and associates, who kindly agreed to read the manuscript in its preparatory stage, offered me invaluable suggestions which, I believe, have improved the format and the content of the first three chapters. I am especially grateful to Donald Fern, John Kihlstrom, Margarete Nemiah, and Stuart Wilson.

No review of my indebtedness would be complete without acknowledging the psychiatric residents and psychology interns who have elected to work with me in the past few years in the Clinic for Therapeutic Hypnosis at the Beth Israel Hospital. Their intelligent curiosity and our frequent discussions of clinical case material have led me to a greater understanding of the problems, and helped clarify my ideas.

For permission to reproduce copyright materials, I am grateful to the following: The Society for Clinical and Experimental Hypnosis for quotations from the *International Journal of Clinical and Experimental Hypnosis;* Springer Publishing Company for quotations from the chapter "Dissociation Revisited" in *Historical Conceptions of Psychology;* The American Medical Association for quotations from the *Archives of General Psychiatry;* and the *American Journal of Psychotherapy.*

Robert C. Misch was my associate in the treatment of one of the cases and Toni Greatrex worked with me in the treatment of another. Among the others presented, I have reported the histories of four patients treated under my supervision by the following trainees, who contributed to the preparation of their case reports: Meg Anzalone, Barry Claycomb, Sean Kelly, and Owen Robbins. I wish to acknowledge the assistance of all those mentioned.

In conclusion, I wish to express my gratitude to my staff assistant, Andrew Boxer, for his tireless, diligent and goodnatured deciphering and retyping of the manuscript; and to the many patients whose trust was sufficient for them to share their intimate thoughts and feelings. Without them, there would have been a few ideas, but no book.

FHF

Boston, Massachusetts
Spring, 1976

Contents

Introduction
1

Chapter 1
Landmarks in the History of Hypnosis: An Examination of the Concepts
5

Chapter 2
Investigating the Phenomenon
21

Chapter 3
Specific Theories
35

Chapter 4
A Clinical Critique
45

Chapter 5
Clinical Behavior and Hypnotizability: Part I
55

Chapter 6
Clinical Behavior and Hypnotizability: Part II
73

CONTENTS

Chapter 7
Clinical Behavior and Hypnotizability: Part III
89

Chapter 8
Hypnotizability and the Treatment of Phobic Behavior
99

Chapter 9
**Relationship of Phobic Behavior, Hypnotizability,
and Conditioning**
123

Chapter 10
Therapeutic Failures
133

Chapter 11
Hypnotizability and Related Physical Symptoms
143

Chapter 12
Hypnotizability and Unrelated Physical Symptoms
153

Chapter 13
An Unusual Trance
163

Chapter 14
Summary and Conclusion
169

Bibliography
173

Index
181

Introduction

The clinician newly acquainted with hypnosis is soon challenged by the controversies surrounding it, and surprised to discover that some of the most respected writers on the psychiatric use and understanding of hypnosis combine it so subtly with their treatment methods that, as an entity, it becomes lost. Some have even relinquished its use entirely. The reasons for this are probably varied, but one, at least, must lie in the different versions of what hypnosis is.

Some writers have placed such heavy emphasis on the importance of the relationship between hypnotist and patient, and on the intensity of the emotional involvement in the hypnotic experience, that they must have difficulty clearly differentiating the event of hypnosis from the manifestations of an intense transference. While it is recognized that hypnosis will probably not occur in the absence of a special interaction between therapist and patient, there is evidence in the following chapters to suggest that the interaction and hypnosis, while intimately related, are not one and the same, even though both lead to the production of useful material in the interviews. The use of hypnosis as an explorative and interpretative medium is one of the two major ways in which it has been applied clinically. The other major clinical use of hypnosis has been in symptom removal, which has led to the development of a vast literature not always discerning and sometimes apocryphal. If hypnosis as an entity has been lost in the uncovering process of hypnoanalysis or hypnotherapy, it has been more than amply compensated by the exaggeration of its quasi-magical properties and colorful rituals in symptom removal.

While acknowledging the value of both of these applications of hypnosis, my primary purpose in the following pages will be to work toward a greater understanding of the nature of the *trance experience* itself, and its clinical relevance. To appreciate the significance of the trance, we must refer not only to the clinical studies of altered states of awareness, but also to the work of the academic and experimental psychologists who have made exciting strides in the past few decades in the struggle to define hypnosis and to measure it. Basic to the problem, however, are the diametrically opposed orientations of research and treatment in the field of hypnosis. The former is committed to accuracy and skepticism, the latter to persuasion and credulity. Standardized procedures and searching questions in investigative work are a far cry from the general encouragement and concurrence that favor the development of the hypnotic experience in clinical situations. Not only the methods but the kinds of subjects differ, too. Most of the experimental research has reported the findings and experiences among college students who have a passing academic interest in hypnosis. Clinical efforts on the other hand are directed toward patients from several age groups, with varying degrees of physical and psychiatric distress; and reports on clinical work reflect a relationship with the therapist and a motivation to succeed with hypnosis that are not readily comparable to those of college students in their interaction with faculty. It soon becomes clear that the research findings we might consider as basic to an understanding of hypnosis cannot invariably be applied to the clinical situation. Inferences drawn from observations on individuals in one context have to be applied with the utmost caution to individuals in another.

Despite that caution, experimental research has provided some explanations, and has led to theories that are highly relevant to an understanding of the trance, the event that is believed to take place within the subject when hypnosis occurs. Traditionally, the term "hypnosis" implies the collaboration of the operator or hypnotist with the subject in the production of the ensuing trance, and its maintenance. But the trance can also be self-induced when the subject behaves toward himself like the hypnotist, and following the model provided by the hypnotist, purposefully creates the trance experience within himself. Moreover, close clinical observation suggests that the trance might occur even more independently, minus the assistance of an operator and without the conscious effort of the patient —in fact, spontaneously. Occasional symptoms or clinical pictures have qualities that resemble characteristics of the trance experience. Feelings such as depersonalization or dissociation; involuntary behavior that is recognized as exaggerated, irrational, but unavoidable such as a phobic attack; or disabling physical complaints such as pain or paresis in response to unconscious forces—all have similarities to the distorted perceptions, compelling ideas, and somatic experiences that can be introduced into hypnosis. Further clinical observation reveals that the clinical symptoms enumerated above occur in patients who are hypnotizable or highly hypnotizable. The suggestion follows that under such circumstances the trance occurs spontaneously, bringing with it one or a number of distorted perceptions. This means that it might, in fact, contribute to the development of the clinical picture. But under these circumstances it need not only be a liability leading to the development of symptoms; we can seek ways in which to make it an asset in the treatment context.

The occurrence of a sudden, spontaneous trance, or trancelike experience, can be expected to be confusing and frightening. If the patient can be helped to experience a trancelike event that resembles his distressing symptoms, but do so under controlled and comfortable circumstances, he can be provided with a coping mechanism, especially when he learns to achieve the trance on his own and without the assistance of his hypnotist. By repeatedly practicing such an exercise first in the presence of his hypnotist, and then on his own, he becomes familiar with and able to master the trance experience so that it loses its frightening character. This use of the trance can be integrated with a psychodynamically sensitive treatment plan that seeks, in addition to discovering what motivates the symptom, to augment a patient's coping mechanism.

In the pages that follow, an attempt will be made to explain from the relevant research data what we know about hypnosis, and to relate this to a series of clinical case reports involving patients with high or very high hypnotizability ratings. For such ratings I have depended largely on the Hypnotic Induction Profile, which is a clinical scale measuring a limited number of hypnotic responses. My routine use of the Stanford Hypnotic Susceptibility Scales or Harvard Group Scale in addition—scales that measure a wider range of hypnotic responses—did not begin early enough in my work for their inclusion in all cases. I have tried, in most instances where I have not used the broader scales, to rate the responsiveness again on another day by testing the separation of the clasped hands, under hypnosis. The importance of hypnotizability assessments will become clear to the reader as the clinical chapters unfold.

Speculation on the clinical relevance of high or very high hypnotizability is not new. An association between hypnotizability and hysteria was acknowledged at the turn of the century, and in recent years attention has again been focused on the distinguishable clinical behavior of patients who are markedly hypnotizable. This was challenged, however, by several reputable laboratory studies demonstrating that those who respond well to hypnosis are generally better adjusted than those whose level of response is lower. The apparent paradox fades when one realizes that those studies were of normal college populations, whereas the observations regarding hysteria were made on patients.

In drawing attention to the very positive value of being able to experience a trance, I will conclude with two cases where it is difficult to ignore the fairly obvious benefit of the use of the self-induced trance, even though the level of hypnotizability in both cases is average or unusual. Although their limited or unusual ability for trance experience could not be held responsible for the development of their symptoms, as might be the case in more highly hypnotizable patients, no account of the trance as a coping mechanism would be complete without them.

Landmarks in the History of Hypnosis:

AN EXAMINATION OF THE CONCEPTS

Although medical hypnosis is considered to have had its beginnings with the Viennese physician Franz Anton Mesmer (1774) in the latter half of the eighteenth century, most modern writers take pains to explain that hypnosis, or something very similar, has been practiced by religious and other healers in various ways since the dawn of civilization.

The subject of Mesmer's discovery became the focus of several controversial beliefs, one or two of which still are only partially resolved. It will be remembered that in 1774, Mesmer, an egocentric, flamboyant, and provocative man, used magnets in the treatment of his patients to promote in them an "artificial tide." His interest in the therapeutic use of magnets occurred at a time when magnetism and electricity were attracting increased attention. After having his patient swallow an iron-containing preparation, he attached magnets to her stomach and legs. She then reported feeling extraordinary streams of a mysterious fluid running downward through her body, and her many symptoms disappeared for several hours.

Mesmer's interest in the influence of the planets on human diseases preceded his therapeutic experiments with magnets, and his belief in the effects of the universal forces led naturally to his interpretation of what he observed. He concluded that the magnetic streams in his patient were provoked by a fluid accumulated in his own person, which he called animal magnetism. The magnets were merely an auxiliary means of reinforcing that animal magnetism and giving it a direction.

The events that ensued were surely influenced by Mesmer's personal style. Miraculous cures and treatment procedures designed with theatrical intent succeeded in attracting large numbers of patients, many of whom were influential. Within three years of his discovery, Mesmer moved to Paris where he was soon sought by patients from the highest social circles in such numbers that he initiated a group treatment method. As many as twenty patients sat around a wooden tub called a *baquet* in physical contact with one of the many protruding metal rods. Music was added to an environment designed to encourage high therapeutic expectations and the occurrence of "crises" that resembled hysterical fits, and from which the patients awoke cured. His extravagant methods and claims attracted not only considerable success, but also the concern and criticism of his medical colleagues.

One readily gains the impression from a review of the history of the subject that Mesmer's sense of the magical and histrionic, and the subsequent confrontation with his peers (to be described later), exerted a major influence on the course of events that took place in the two centuries that followed. It is not my intention to examine the history of animal magnetism and hypnosis in any detail, nor to trace the undulating fate of the discovery and of those who believed in it. A few brief comments will suffice.

Mesmer's disciples included people from several walks of life, and the skill of magnetizing, later described as mental healing, was taught by them to others far removed from the legitimate practice of medicine. The nineteenth century saw the development of groups dedicated to religious practices and the occult that were clearly derivatives of Mesmer's interpretation of his discovery. Prominent physicians of that period, using animal magnetism, found themselves castigated by their colleagues. Bramwell's review (Bramwell, 1903) of the history of the subject up to the turn of the century provides adequate testimony to that. To this day, doubts and eyebrows are not infrequently raised in medical circles at the mention of hypnosis. The problem has been compounded by the claims of professional hypnotists untutored in anything but the simple art of inducing a trance, and by their stage performances.

As I have already implied, I believe our purpose in this book will be better served by concentrating our attention at this point on the controversial concepts that grew out of Mesmer's original finding, than by a detailed examination of the magnetizing or hypnotizing practices over two centuries. This will permit me, eventually, to communicate intelligibly what I believe the term "hypnosis" means at this time, and to discuss it in the clinical context.

Mesmer was seduced into taking advantage of the magiclike properties of the phenomenon, as have many of those who succeeded him. This has hindered efforts to understand the events in hypnosis, and has contributed to the aggregation of controversial beliefs and dubious explanations of it. A closer examination of the ideas about hypnosis shows how they have arisen from observations, verbal comments, surmises, and hackneyed versions of previous reports, relating not primarily to clinical events but even more to stage performances and the imaginative themes in drama and literature. Few, if any, persons questioned about hypnosis claim never to have heard of it. All usually entertain some notion about magic or control, however inchoate or misinformed. Even by disclaiming it on the grounds that they do not believe in the irrational, they feed the faulty information back into the communication system, thereby reaffirming it and prolonging the legend.

Before proceeding to a consideration of the major controversial beliefs in greater detail, I will outline them briefly:

1. The Fluid Theory of Mesmer

This original controversy grew around Mesmer's concept of the physical existence of a magnetic fluid transferred by the magnetizer to the patient's body. It was this redistribution of the fluid that was assumed to account for the cure. As we shall see later, the magnetic fluid hypothesis was discredited early in the history of animal magnetism.

2. Somnambulism and Sleep

Among Mesmer's early followers was a French nobleman, the Marquis de Puységur, whose diligent observations of the marked responses of some of his subjects richly enhanced the understanding of magnetism. In describing such a response as artificial somnambulism, he lent support to the idea that hypnosis and sleep were the same, or closely related. The concept has become entrenched, and the term "sleep" has crept into the ritual of several present-day induction procedures.

3. The Essential Source of the Hypnotic Event

Another conceptual controversy has to do with *who* is primarily responsible for the events in hypnosis. Mesmer clearly attributed that function to the person of the magnetizer through whom, he believed, the fluid was conducted. Even though the fluid theory was discredited, the person or the mind of the magnetizer or hypnotist, and his special ability to influence the behavior and experiences of his subjects, was—and still is—considered by some to be central to hypnosis.

During the mid-nineteenth century the emphasis shifted to the importance of the subject, and his response to the rituals and induction procedures. Granted the importance of the subject's response, opinions have continued to vary regarding its nature. Some have favored a neurophysiological explanation for it, others a psychological.

4. Magic

For many the magic of hypnosis has persisted. It has been firmly believed and still is adhered to. Hypnotized subjects are assumed to be capable of transcending their usual physical and mental competence, which leads them to accomplish remarkable feats otherwise not attainable by them. The notion of magic extends somewhat to overlap with ideas already alluded to above, namely, the control of the subject by the operator, and the production of physiological changes as a result of suggestions and ideas. Where these are assumed to exist, they are accounted for in quasi-magical terms.

5. Hypnotic State Versus Social Interaction

Modern investigators have been caught in a struggle to decide how much of the event of hypnosis can be attributed to suggested behavior that results from social interaction, and how much is dependent on the occurrence of a specific psychological *state* that characterizes hypnosis as an experience that is different, and not adequately accounted for by the current general psychological theories.

6. Relaxation and Placebo

Interest in Eastern religious practices and mystical experiences, leading to investigations of the physiological concomitants of such events, has raised questions about the relationship of hypnosis to those procedures. Behaviorists have explained them in terms of relaxation and the placebo-response. They suggest that relaxation and the placebo-response are equally important, in achieving therapeutic success, to the rituals of religion and hypnosis, and that all the experiences referred to are closely related if not equivalent.

We can now return to a consideration of the several controversial beliefs in some detail.

1. Mesmer and the Fluid Theory

Mesmer's (1774) system can be summarized as follows: A subtle physical fluid fills the universe and forms a connecting medium between man, the earth, and the heavenly bodies, and also between man and man.

Disease originates from the unequal distribution of this fluid in the human body; recovery is achieved when the equilibrium is restored. With the help of certain techniques, this fluid can be channeled, stored, and conveyed to other persons. In this manner, "crises" can be provoked in patients and diseases cured.

It is clear that Mesmer considered himself the bearer of the powerful fluid, and capable of provoking the appearance and disappearance of symptoms by his physical presence or gestures. Every human being possessed the fluid, but to varying degrees. The sick had less than the healthy.

In 1784, as a result of the concern generated by Mesmer's activities, the king of France appointed two commissions to examine the practice of animal magnetism. The commissions comprised the foremost scientists of their day: One consisted of members of the Académie des Sciences and the Académie de Médecine; and the other, of members of the Société Royale. These commissions included the astronomer Bailly, the chemist Lavoisier, the physician Guillotin, and the American ambassador Benjamin Franklin. The principal issue was whether Mesmer had discovered a new physical fluid. The commissions were not primarily concerned with the therapeutic results attained by means of the magnetism. They concluded (Bailly *et al.*, 1784) that no evidence could be found of the physical existence of a magnetic fluid. The therapeutic effects were ascribed to imagination, suggestion, and imitation. The commissioners also pointed to the dangers resulting from the erotic attraction of the magnetized female patient to her male magnetizer.

The commissioners effectively put an end to any serious belief in the mysterious fluid, but not to the practice of magnetizing, which spread not only to other countries in Europe, but eventually also to England and America.

2. De Puységur, Somnambulism, and Sleep

Among Mesmer's disciples in France was the Marquis de Puységur. An astute observer, he recognized the characteristics of the "perfect crisis" with its subsequent amnesia, and compared it to somnambulism, the act of sleepwalking. He also realized that in this state of artificial or induced somnambulism, his patients were able to talk freely about topics they might otherwise not be prepared to discuss (Puységur, 1784). He considered the real agent in the cure of magnetism to be the magnetizer's will, and stressed the importance of the magnetizer's belief in himself.

Although the available evidence that we will discuss later points to the importance of the subject's responsivity rather than the magnetizer's powerful determination, de Puységur's emphasis on the latter resembles

Mesmer's inflated interpretation of his own role in animal magnetism, and leads naturally to the belief, still prevalent in some circles, that the hypnotist controls the will of his subjects.

Despite this fallacy in de Puységur's notions, it was his recognition of the somnambulic crisis as a valuable opportunity for the therapeutic uncovering of painful feelings that helped to lay the groundwork for the development of dynamic psychotherapy.

Less fortunate consequences of the sleepwalking analogy are these: (a) The magnetized or hypnotic state is still often equated with sleep, despite contradictory electroencephalographic evidence. (b) Fantasies in hypnosis are often referred to as dreams. Some investigators, having lost sight of the metaphorical allusion to sleep, have equated the fantasies in hypnosis with the dreams of sleep. (c) Artificial somnambulism inherited some of the magic associated with sleepwalking. Sleepwalkers were considered capable of miraculously avoiding catastrophe when moving about in dangerous areas, and those magnetized into the somnambulic state were seen as having special diagnostic and clairvoyant skills when deeply magnetized. (d) The more modern term "hypnosis," a misnomer, is derived from the Greek word meaning sleep.

3. The Essential Source of the Hypnotic Event

Braid. Both Mesmer and de Puységur had emphasized the special gift or powerful will of the magnetizer as crucial to the occurrence of mesmerism. An English physician, James Braid, is generally credited with being the first to document his view that the skill essential to the event is that of the patient (Braid, 1843). He was impressed by the psychological responsiveness of the subject, not the influence of the operator, and observed how a single suggested idea could monopolize the attention of the subject when it was presented to him under special circumstances. Under the term "hypnotism," which he coined, Braid made magnetism acceptable in some medical circles.

In the interest of history, it is worth noting that the Abbé Faria, a Portuguese priest, contended earlier than did Braid that the essential process of magnetization was due less to the magnetizer than to the subject (Faria, 1819). It is also worthy of comment that Braid acknowledged his regret at having created the term "hypnotism" once he recognized the powerful influence of the suggested idea. He realized, too late, that the event was not akin to sleep but largely the opposite, a near-total absorption of the attention by an idea. The parallel had been drawn, the term introduced, and over a century later we still struggle with its controversial connotation.

Charcot and Janet. By the end of the nineteenth century, hypnosis had attracted the attention of the distinguished French neurologist, Jean Martin Charcot, who taught at the Salpêtrière in Paris. Having created order out of the confusion that had previously prevailed in neurology, he then turned to an investigation of the clinical entity of hysteria (Charcot, 1886). This led to his interest in hypnosis, which he interpreted as a neuropathological event closely associated with hysteria, the explanation for which, he believed, was to be sought in neurophysiological principles. His student, Pierre Janet (1907), similarly emphasized the association of hypnosis and hysteria, but laid greater stress on an underlying psychological mechanism, namely dissociation, than he did on the supposed neurophysiological changes. (Janet's contribution to the understanding of hysteria and its relation to hypnosis will be developed in a later section.)

Bernheim and Liébeault. Hippolyte Bernheim and Auguste Ambroise Liébeault, physicians of vastly different temperament, were drawn to work together in Nancy by their interest in hypnosis. They proclaimed that hypnosis was not a pathological condition found only in hysterics, but was the effect of suggestion. They defined suggestibility as the aptitude to transform an idea into an act. As time went on, Bernheim made less and less use of hypnosis, in the belief that the effects that could be obtained with hypnosis were equally attainable by suggestion in the waking state. Needless to say, a bitter struggle ensued between Charcot, on the one hand, and Bernheim and Liébeault, on the other (Ellenberger, 1970).

Despite Bernheim's commitment to the uncomplicated concept of suggestibility, his uncertainty was apparent in at least one of his reports. Hilgard, in his introduction to the 1964 reissue of the Bernheim studies (Bernheim, 1884) comments on how Bernheim's wide clinical exposure to hypnosis eventually prevailed. Having stressed suggestion as the keystone of the arch of all hypnotic manifestations, he then later stated: "I define hypnotism as the induction of a peculiar psychical condition which increases the susceptibility to suggestion." In this statement he came close to Janet's view of a specific psychological state of dissociation as the essential mechanism in the hypnotic event.

4. *Magic: Three Basic Assumptions*

To many the magic implied by the term "hypnosis" has rested on a poorly organized system of three basic assumptions, the essence of which is that (a) hypnosis involves the control of one person by another; (b) it enables the subject to transcend his normal physical and mental capabilities; and (c) it influences organic structure by means of neurophysiological mechanisms.

Whatever is achieved by the subject in (b) and (c) above is attributed to the inescapable influence of the operator. Where subjects use self-hypnosis to transcend their normal capacities, they ascribe to themselves the magical skills otherwise associated with the operator.

(a) Control Magnetizing and hypnotic induction procedures require the operator to be assertive, to take the initiative, or to direct the behavior and subjective experiences of the patient by means of suggestions. The inexperienced or uninitiated observer often fails to recognize that this occurs because the subject permits it to happen. The result is an illusion. The operator appears powerful and in control. Theatrically inclined magnetizers and hypnotists have taken advantage of this with the use of gestures and glances, often serious and even sinister, thereby enhancing the illusory character of the event, and their own reputations. They behave as if they are in indisputable control of the patient's actions, attitudes, and how he perceives his world; and accomplish this so effectively that many observers and patients are convinced. Dramatists and writers, by adding their own fantasies to the widely held assumptions, have reinforced them (du Maurier, 1895; Mann, 1931). Clinicians learn readily that in reality they direct the experiences of their patients in hypnosis only to the extent that they remain sensitive to what the patients communicate they are prepared to follow. Attempts to gain control over behavior or symptoms by means of simple posthypnotic suggestions generally fail, and the therapist who believes he can recover memories, in hypnosis, when the patient is poorly motivated to share them, soon has to retrace his steps.

Despite the recognition that a clinical operator has no absolute control over the behavior of his patients, a difference of opinion does exist in the general ethical context regarding the more dangerous influence of an unscrupulous operator on the behavior of a deeply hypnotized subject. The logical question seeks to know whether under those hypothetical circumstances the subject could be influenced to commit antisocial acts against his will. Some maintain that if he, in fact, does commit such acts, we still cannot immediately hold the hypnotic state to be primarily responsible. We must first rule out the effect of the relationship, and the situational context in which the request is made.

This aspect was neatly demonstrated by Orne and Evans (1965) in a study of social control in the psychological experiment. They exactly replicated a study conducted by Young (1952), which in turn replicated a study conducted by Rowland (1939) in which deeply hypnotized subjects were asked to handle snakes and throw nitric acid at the experimenter's assistant, tasks from which they normally would have recoiled. Orne and Evans confirmed that in deeply hypnotized subjects such dangerous and antisocial behavior could be elicited. (Completely unknown to them, the subjects were protected from harming themselves or others by the use of a concealed pane of glass between them and the snake, and by the covert substitution of the acid with an identical beaker containing a harmless colored solution.) However, Orne and Evans also demonstrated that similar antisocial behavior could be elicited in the control groups of nonhypnotizable persons treated in an identical fashion to the group of hypnotized subjects. This finding indicates that the dangerous tasks are within the broad range of activities that are perceived as legitimized by the nature of the experimental situation; they were requests made by experimenters viewed by the subjects as responsible scientists, in the context of a psychological experiment.

The question whether a hypnotized subject is likely to perform antisocial behavior exceeding that which is legitimized by the experiment (and perceived by him as truly dangerous or antisocial) remains unanswered. Orne and Evans believe that it may not be possible to test the antisocial question in an experimental setting because of the problems of finding tasks that are not seen as legitimate, and sanctioned by the experimental context.

These extreme circumstances are not strictly comparable to general clinical situations. It is also clear that the answer to the question about hypnosis providing the means to antisocial acts is a matter of opinion. The varied views that prevail, however, testify to the ambiguities that still hover over our understanding of all the aspects of hypnosis and control (Conn, 1972; Kline, 1972; Watkins, 1972; Orne, 1972b).

(b) Transcendence of Normal Physical and Mental Capabilities. The concept of transcending the normal captures the spirit and the flavor of Mesmer's posture, the analogy of sleepwalking with its miraculous avoidance of danger, and de Puységur's assumption that his somnambules acquired insight into the diseases of others. Stage hypnotists have fostered this belief by having subjects exhibit exceptional physical feats after hypnosis has been induced, claiming the prowess is attributable to the hypnosis. The fallacy lies in the *post hoc ergo propter hoc* reasoning. Holding an arm up for interminably long periods of time, or holding one's body as rigid as a board and suspending it between two chairs with the head on one and the heels on another, do not require hypnosis. But the use of a hypnotic induction procedure before requesting such behavior leads to the assumption that there must be a causal relationship. Suggesting to male college students that strong, healthy, well-motivated young men can suspend themselves in like manner between two chairs accomplishes the same results without hypnosis. Provided that the setting is appropriate, and the subjects are motivated to carry out the task, they will perform in the waking state to the same degree that they will in hypnosis (Barber and

Calverly, 1962; Orne, 1966). Orne points out that this does not entirely eliminate the possibility that hypnosis may actually increase the range of behaviors that people are willing to carry out. It merely demonstrates, again, that subjects tend to do almost anything that might conceivably be required of them in an experimental setting (Zamansky, Scharf, and Brightbill, 1964).

Feats demanding exceptional mental skill and insights have been reported anecdotally, but have not been unequivocally demonstrated experimentally. However, in the area of memory, the evidence in both the clinical and experimental reports suggests that hypnosis is associated with increased memory skills and the increased ability to forget or repress (Evans, 1968).

(c) Somatic Changes. Clinical reports abound with anecdotes of somatic alterations following the use of hypnosis. These range from the rapid disappearance of warts to the development of blisters on his skin after a hypnotized subject was touched by the blunt end of a pencil presented to him as the burning tip of a cigarette. With Misch, I, too, have reported the marked improvement in a case of psoriasis following the use of hypnosis (Frankel and Misch, 1973).

While it is not possible to interpret clinical cures with the certainty that can be applied to experimental procedures, after examining many of the clinical accounts the reader is still left wondering whether hypnosis really occurred, or was even possible. He must ask what other factors might have been present in the situation that could, equally well, have accounted for the improvements. Strict controls are generally unavailable, and the physiological effects of ordinary relaxing and calming procedures (to be considered further in a later section) are rarely, if ever, taken into account. In the clinical literature, measurements of hypnotizability are scant and usually unreliable.

The production of blisters on the skin by the blunt end of a pencil has never been demonstrated in a strictly controlled experiment that precluded the use of artifice and deception; the report that a Babinski-response was elicited in subjects who were age regressed to infancy, when in hypnosis (Gidro-Frank and Bowersbuch, 1948) was not supported by subsequent studies (O'Connell, Shor, and Orne, 1970; Barber, 1962); evidence that age regression in hypnosis entails any true neurophysiological or physiological alteration is lacking; and whatever evidence there is that structural alterations are achieved clinically with hypnosis remains unsubstantiated and controversial. A comprehensive survey of experimental work with hypnosis by Sarbin and Slagle (1972) concludes that there is at present no convincing evidence that deeply hypnotized subjects produce any observable behavior or physiological changes that highly motivated nonhypnotized subjects in the usual waking state are not capable of producing or mimicking, if willing.

And yet, despite the above, we cannot ignore the clinically documented cases of structural change after the use of hypnosis in previously persistent pathological states. For example, cases of ichthyosis, a chronic and stable skin condition without remissions, are occasionally treated successfully with hypnosis. Clinical events can rarely be brought into the laboratory, and in such circumstances good controls other than the known natural history of the condition, are lacking. There is sufficient clinical evidence to justify an open mind, and continued clinical investigation. Indeed, rather than seeking to explain the remission of somatic disorders following the use of hypnotic suggestion as a quasi-magical event, or denying the occurrence of such remissions, we ought, instead, to look upon such circumstances as evidence of psychosomatic relationships where the neurophysiological mechanisms are as yet obscure. If and when these can be explicated, it is likely that we will find hypnosis to be one of several ways in which they can be activated.

5. Hypnotic State Versus Social Interaction

The concept of the *hypnotic state* as a special and different event presents a challenge to those students of the subject who interpret it within the context of their preferred general psychological theory. They have developed and presented very formalized accounts of hypnosis within the framework of their chosen perspectives. Among them are included the theories of (a) the psychoanalysts exemplified in the writings of Schilder and Kauders (1927) and Gill and Brenman (1959), (b) the social psychologists presented by the role theory of Sarbin (1950; Sarbin and Coe, 1972), and (c) the neobehaviorists expounded by Barber (Barber, Spanos, and Chaves, 1974).

Despite their major differences, these theories have in common the rejection of the explanation that a special mental state occurs in hypnosis.

(a) The Psychoanalytic Explanation. In brief, the psychoanalytic explanation involves the concepts of transference and regression. The phenomenon of hypnosis is defined in terms of a primitive, regressive transference in which passive dependent longings and magical expectations are displaced onto the person of the hypnotist. This regression in the service of the ego is viewed as involving only a subsystem of the ego, leaving a more autonomous part of the ego still able to observe and monitor events.

The psychoanalytic perspective describes the passive and expectant transference in hypnosis as primitive and archaic, and the fantasies of the hypnotist as omnipotent. These ideas, loaded with innuendo, have discouraged many psychoanalytically trained therapists, already reluctant to use hypnosis, from ever considering it. We will return in a later section to a consideration of the heavy emphasis placed on the transference aspects of hypnosis, by psychoanalysts who use it as an adjunct to their treatment methods.

(b) Sarbin and Role Theory. Sarbin and his students view concepts such as hypnotic trance or hypnotic state as misleading, and have tried to demonstrate that the events of hypnosis are not unique or isolated from other kinds of social psychological phenomena. Sarbin's formulation pivots around the concept of *role.* He sees the role as defined by the instructions and suggestions of the hypnotist, superimposed on the subject's general conception of how a hypnotized person is supposed to behave. The subject strives to take the role of the hypnotized person.

The analogy used by Sarbin is that of the actor striving to take the role that is assigned to him. When involved in his role—crying, laughing, and experiencing the feelings—the actor focuses his attention and concentration on such a narrow range that he might tend to lose an awareness of himself. Similarly, the hypnotized person involved in his role, focusing his attention narrowly, might also tend to lose self-awareness.

The subject's success in taking the role of the hypnotized person depends on the following variables: (a) his role expectations (how he expects to behave in the hypnotic situation); (b) his role perception (his interpretation of the statements describing what he is to experience and how he is to behave); (c) his role-relevant skills (for example, his capacity for vivid imagination); (d) his self-role congruence (whether his idea of himself as a person who behaves in certain ways meshes with his understanding of what is required of a hypnotic subject); and (e) his sensitivity to role demands (for example, recognition of the fact that he will embarrass the hypnotist if he fails to respond to his suggestions). The different responsiveness among subjects is seen as a function of these variables.

In the understanding of Sarbin's role theory and its application to psychopathology, it should be clear that he conceptualizes the idea of role in a far broader way than would be apparent on casual reading. For example, he views schizophrenia as a role. Similarly, when he conceptualizes hypnosis as a form of role-playing, he is not merely describing someone as play-acting, but rather conceives of it as a believed-in role. Indeed, he speaks of role-playing at a nonconscious level.

Whereas the importance of role-taking in hypnosis is interesting and persuasive, and is included in a more embracing theory to be reported later (Shor, 1959 and 1962), role theory as presented to date uses a metaphor sufficiently alien to the clinical context to be easily misunderstood and therefore difficult to incorporate clinically.

(c) Barber and the Neobehaviorist View. In presenting the neobehaviorist viewpoint, Barber and his associates (Barber, Spanos, and Chaves, 1974) have gone to great lengths to account for hypnotic behavior in terms of its antecedent events. They cite variables such as: (a) a subject's attitude toward the test situation; (b) a subject's expectations concerning his or her own performance on assigned tasks; (c) a subject's motivation to cooperate, not to resist, and to try to perform the suggested effects; (d) the tone and wording of the specific suggestions administered by the operator; and (e) the tone and wording of the questions that are designed to elicit reports of subjective experiences. The five sets of variables specified above were conceived as similar to those that operate in many, and possibly all situations in which specific tasks are to be performed. Barber is critical of the concept of a hypnotic *state,* and eager to strip hypnosis of its aura, mystery, and separate status. He believes that in the final analysis all hypnotic behavior can be accounted for in terms of its antecedent events, thereby making the concept of hypnotic state redundant. In addition to the emphasis on attitude, expectation, and motivation in the production of hypnotic behavior, Spanos and Barber have recently stressed the importance of goal-directed imagination and cognitive strategies used by subjects to help them experience the behaviors suggested to them; e.g. imagining the arm as hollow in order to experience the light feeling in the arm and the levitation that have been suggested. Barber believes that most of the achievements in hypnosis are within the range of normal human capabilities, and considers as unnecessary the postulate that a person carries out the cognitive processes more proficiently when he is in a hypnotic trance. He claims that individuals can be taught to respond to the suggestions of hypnosis within the context of "training in human potentialities."

Here again, the treatment of the topic of hypnosis severely limits its relevance clinically. The very two-dimensional explanations offered by the neobehaviorist viewpoint provide no place for the clinical concepts of dissociation and altered states of consciousness, without which some clinical behavior is virtually impossible to understand.

Investigative studies in the experimental setting lend support from that sector, too, to the idea that hypnotic phenomena cannot be accounted for simply in terms of suggestibility. They show quite convincingly that hypnosis adds something (Evans, 1967; Evans, 1968). In a comparison of scales that measure hypnotic responsivity and suggestibility, Ruch, Morgan, and Hilgard (1974) demonstrate that the total domain of hypnosis is more than simply suggestibility.

6. Relaxation and Placebo-Response

When hypnosis is viewed in psychological terms as a behavioral phenomenon, it is interpreted, as shown above, from the particular vantage point of the observer. Other behavioral perspectives include those of relaxation and the placebo response.

(a) Relaxation. Despite the generally held belief that relaxation is essential to hypnosis, subjects experience hypnosis while sitting, standing, or even walking about. Authors aware of the very different styles of response have classified them into active and passive responses (White, 1937), the active being less relaxed. There is no question that the great majority of induction procedures include relaxation, and some subjects rarely if ever proceed beyond a degree of considerable relaxation. Whether this is the same experience as hypnosis is questionable. Many find it difficult to be persuaded that it is.

The relaxation that is an integral part of the exercises in the self-hypnosis of autogenic training (Schultz, 1932; Schultz and Luthe, 1969), and the relaxation that permeates the hypnoidal state of Meares (1960) are indistinguishable behaviorally from the relaxation associated with Progressive Relaxation (Jacobson, 1938), Yoga, Zen, Transcendental Meditation, and other ritualized practices. Benson and his co-workers (1974) and Benson (1975), having recently investigated the literature reporting physiological change associated with some psychological or religious experiences, use the term "relaxation response" to describe the basic characteristics shared by them all. The techniques all include four basic elements: (1) A mental device such as a fixed gazing at an object, or the silently or audibly repeating of a phrase, word, or sound. The purpose of these procedures is to shift from the logical externally oriented thought; (2) a passive attitude in which thoughts that distract should be disregarded—one should not worry about how well he is performing the technique; (3) decreased muscle tonus, a comfortable posture so that muscular work is not required; and (4) a quiet environment with decreased environmental stimuli.

When the different techniques that appear to produce the "relaxation response" are used, the physiologic parameters alter in comparable fashion. Although all parameters had not been reported for each technique, in almost all oxygen consumption, respiratory rate, and heart rate were reported as decreased. Alpha waves, not measured in hypnosis, were reported as increased when measured, as was skin resistance. Blood pressure shifts were inconclusive.

Because further work is both indicated and planned in this area, it would be hasty to conclude at this stage that all the relaxing techniques reported lead to equivalent states, but their similarities are impressive. When the hypnoidal or relaxed level of hypnosis (that aspect most readily achieved by most patients even when unresponsive to the other suggestions on the hypnotizability scales) is considered and compared with the lighter stages of the other modes, the evidence for the widespread occurrence of the relaxation response seems persuasive. Despite these similarities, however, hypnosis involves other elements as well as the relaxation response; indeed it is quite possible to induce hypnosis in the absence of relaxation, or when the subject is encouraged to remain mentally alert. A recent study dramatically demonstrates the successful induction of hypnosis in subjects performing at peak capacity on an exercycle (Banyai and Hilgard, 1974). Another by Vingoe (1973) illustrates the use of an "alert-type" induction procedure in which concurrent suggestions for body relaxation and mind alertness are made. Furthermore, hypnosis includes subjective experiences and memory changes (to be considered in later chapters) that are not part of the relaxation response.

(b) Placebo-Response. Strong suggestion, explicit and implied, and the confident anticipation that the method will be successful, account for the positive response of a patient to the prescription of a placebo (a pill or other form of treatment presumed by the patient to be effective, but lacking pharmaceutical or other known specific therapeutically effective ingredients). Attempts have been made to explain hypnosis in similar terms. In other words, those who favor the placebo-response as the explanatory model of hypnosis regard the increased tolerance for pain in hypnosis, for example, exclusively as a result of the attitudes, expectations, and reduced anxiety inherent in the hypnotic situation.

One study to determine the difference between hypnosis and placebo has been reported. The effects of hypnotically induced analgesia and placebo response were investigated (McGlashan, Evans, and Orne, 1969). Two groups of highly motivated subjects, one very responsive to hypnosis and the other essentially nonhypnotizable, were given a task that led to ischemic muscle-pain. Plausible expectations had been established in *both* groups of subjects that the ingestion of a "powerful analgesic drug" on one occasion, and on another occasion the induction of hypnotic analgesia, would effectively reduce the intensity of the experimentally induced pain. Subjects were told that they would receive the strong pain-killing drug on the one occasion so that the effects of the hypnotic analgesia on the other could be properly evaluated. Unknown to the subjects and the experimenter administering the remedies, all subjects received and ingested an inactive placebo. It was found that increased pain tolerance following the ingested placebo was similar for both hypnotizable and nonhypnotizable subjects; in the nonhypnotizable group the procedure of hypnosis produced increased tolerance only to the extent of that achieved by the ingested placebo; but pain tolerance exceeding that produced by the placebo response occurred only during hypnosis for those who were highly hypnotizable. Highly hypnotizable subjects experienced relief over and above that obtained through the placebo response, and the concept of the placebo response can serve to explain only what the hypnotic procedure does for the nonhypnotizable person.

While further work of this kind will help to confirm the above findings, those just described suggest that response in hypnosis and placebo-response are not one and the same. This does not mean that a large quantity of the published clinical material claiming to demonstrate the effect of hypnosis might not in fact have resulted from the placebo-response. A large proportion of it is probably the result of placebo, precisely because those reporting the cases have failed to differentiate between hypnosis and placebo, and recount little or no attempt to measure adequately the hypnotizability of their patients.

SUMMARY

We have reviewed the major concepts that have been employed in the attempts to understand hypnosis. As the event of hypnosis itself has been the subject of doubt and disbelief, it comes as no surprise that the explanations offered have all been, and in some instances still are, the center of controversy. Although the fluid theory of Mesmer was laid to rest, and the subject, not the operator, is now recognized as the essential reason for the hypnotic response, persistent use of the sleep metaphor continues to defy negative electroencephalographic findings, and the unexplained structural changes reported clinically tempt us to understand how people came to believe in magic. Argument still prevails over the justification for a separate theory of hypnosis to account for the concept of a hypnotic state, and those interested in social interaction theories continue to coax the events in hypnosis into their favored conceptual molds.

CHAPTER 2

Investigating the Phenomenon

The previous chapter carries references to important experimental studies that have contributed in a major way to the understanding of hypnosis. Modern quantitative research into the subject began with Hull (1933), and has made considerable strides over the past two decades. The work has been enriched by the contributions of several outstanding laboratory studies too numerous to review in a work of this nature. From the perspective of the clinician, however, seeking a basic science from which to practice and develop his concepts, work of two investigators with their associates and students is of major importance.

Hilgard (1965) reported one phase of a long-range collaborative investigation of hypnotic phenomena. In studying the nature of hypnotic responsivity as exhibited by some one thousand college students, Hilgard and his associates developed several scales for the quantitative assessment of that responsivity. The scales, in turn, provided criteria for the study of individual differences in hypnotizability and the parameters and correlates of hypnosis.

Orne (1959) demonstrated the unsuspected complexities inherent in the study of hypnosis by drawing attention to what he called demand characteristics. In an elegant yet simple investigative procedure he was able to illustrate how the essential elements of hypnosis become confused and enmeshed with artifacts created by the circumstances of the experimental situation. An investigator failing to take into account such spurious elements is readily led to false conclusions. Orne, with his associates, developed the idea of the nonhypnotizable control subject simulating what he (the control subject) perceives as hypnotic behavior (Orne 1959, 1972a).

The concept of the nonhypnotizable simulator has had a major impact on the methodology of the experimental study of hypnosis.

We will return to consider the work referred to in some detail, but only after we have inspected an example of hypnosis.

DESCRIPTION OF HYPNOSIS

Typically a subject is seated comfortably opposite or alongside the operator. They generally have already had a conversation during which the topic of hypnosis was discussed. The subject is encouraged to talk about his attitudes regarding hypnosis and the operator, and any previous experience of hypnosis. If the situation is a clinical one, then a full psychiatric history and evaluation will already have been completed. For an enriching experience of hypnosis to occur, we require a comfortable and trusting relationship between subject and operator, a willingness of the subject to undergo the experience, and a sensitive, observant, and supportive attitude on the part of the operator. Not all subjects are hypnotizable, but most, under appropriate circumstances, can respond to the simpler suggestions.

The induction procedure can be one of many types (Weitzenhoffer, 1957), ranging from directions to the subject to close his eyes and think of a peaceful scene, to having him gaze at a spot on his hand, a shiny object, or a swinging pendulum until his eyelids become heavy and close. The object is to lead the subject, carefully but confidently, to redistribute his attention so as to withdraw it from his general surroundings and focus it on a circumscribed area. Meanwhile he is encouraged to relax and let happen what will happen. This induction procedure is sometimes followed, or even replaced, by what are described as deepening techniques. He is directed to imagine himself descending gradually on an elevator or staircase, or drifting on a boat past a slowly shifting landscape. Counting forward or backward is another deepening or induction technique. Throughout this procedure the operator fosters the illusions by offering his comments in a slow, repetitive monotone, exhorting the subject to feel relaxed and calm, or to float and drift.

After a period generally lasting from one to several minutes, the operator introduces ideas of a motor and sensory kind. He suggests to the subject, for example, that as he concentrates on the feelings in his fingers and his hand, the small muscles in his fingers will begin to twitch and his hand and forearm will begin to feel light. They will eventually feel so light that they will lift up off the arm-rest of the chair, and continually floating upward, will ultimately reach the side of his face. The operator might add the comment that the higher the hand floats, the deeper the hypnosis will become, and the deeper the hypnosis becomes, the higher the hand will float. He adds, too, that when the hand reaches the side of the face, the subject will be deeply hypnotized.

When this point is reached, and the hand and arm have "levitated," the operator assumes that the subject is well hypnotized, and then adds whatever other suggestions are appropriate to the situation.

Before leaving the induction procedure and the introductory phase, I would like to emphasize that the initial procedures can be as simple or as complicated as the operator prefers them to be. They can be delivered with a dramatic flourish, or offered very simply. The use of gadgets such as shiny objects, spinning disks, and metronomes is not recommended. The simpler the procedure, the better. The type of suggestions and their sequence is left to the operator's preference. A useful principle, however, is to proceed from the suggestions that are easily experienced to those that are more difficult. Success in the early stages enhances the likely success of the suggestions that follow. As twitching movements in the small muscles of the fingers and the hand are more readily experienced in the early stages of hypnosis than levitation of the hand and forearm, the suggestion of the small movements and sensations should precede the other. Failure to experience the ideas that are offered early in the hypnosis procedure tends to interfere with its progress. Exhortatory comments are made as the subject progresses from step to step.

Returning now to the point at which the operator considers the subject is hypnotized, we will consider some of the possibilities that are available. If the purpose is merely to demonstrate the experience of hypnosis to students, the operator can suggest to the subject that the light feeling in the hand is beginning to fade, and is slowly being replaced by a feeling of heaviness that will cause the forearm to lower itself back onto the arm-rest. He is told that at that point he will open his eyes and be wide awake; and will notice that the usual feelings and control have returned to the hand and the forearm. He is told that he will continue to have a comfortable feeling of well-being.

If the purpose of the procedure is to induce dental analgesia, for example, the operator instructs the patient, whose hand is still touching his face, to concentrate on the feelings in his fingers, to feel the numb and tingling feelings intensify in his fingertips, and then feel the numb and tingling feelings drain from his fingers into his face and teeth, which will then be surrounded and permeated by the numbness. He is then advised that the numb sensation will screen out any hurt or pain from the dental procedures he is about to experience. For the relief of pain in other sites, transferring the numb feeling from the fingertips to other parts of the body is readily accomplished by suggesting that the hand can move to touch the appropriate areas.

Other procedures are, of course, also possible. If the operator is assessing the range of a subject's responsivity, or a therapist plans to demonstrate to his patient that he, the patient, does indeed have the capacity to experience hypnosis and therefore to use it in the alleviation of his symptoms, other suggestions can be useful. The simplest is to suggest to the subject that his arm will continue to feel weightless and remain in the levitated position; that when he opens his eyes (which he will be instructed to do, shortly) the operator will lower his arm onto the arm-rest; and that the arm will then move upward again into the levitated position. The execution of a posthypnotic suggestion as simple as this one is a persuasive experience for both the subject and those who witness it.

More complex suggestions can be tried with the more hypnotizable subjects. They include the following, in which the subject can be told:

1. To interlock his fingers tightly, so tightly that it is doubtful whether they can be separated; he is then asked to try and separate them.

2. That he can hear a fly buzzing about him, and that it will become so bothersome to him that he will be obliged to shoo it away.

3. That he will have a dream, and that he will be able to report it vividly as it occurs.

4. That he is no longer an adult but a small child in school; he is then expected to engage in a dialogue as if he were indeed at the age to which he is regressed.

5. That he cannot recognize certain letters in the alphabet; when asked to read aloud from a well-known book, he is not expected to be able to do so, nor to be able to comprehend the passage he is examining.

6. To consider a simple statement as hilariously funny, and is expected to laugh uproariously at it.

7. That when he comes out of the hypnotic experience (which he will do shortly after appropriate instructions from the operator) he will be wide-awake and feel fine, but will remember nothing of certain items, or events that occurred during the experience of hypnosis, until he is given a signal by the operator or is told that he can now remember everything; he is expected, on awaking, to remember only vaguely and very little of the events in hypnosis, until given the appropriate cue.

The above description is not intended as an exhaustive report of the varieties of experience possible in hypnosis, but includes a sufficiently large number for our purposes. Good hypnotic subjects are able to respond positively to many or most of the suggestions listed.

SUSCEPTIBILITY SCALES

As has been stated above, not all subjects respond to hypnosis to the same extent, nor at the same rate. In order to study the phenomenon and its value in the treatment of a specific person, it becomes important to learn how individuals respond to it. Nineteenth-century students of hypnosis recognized this. They categorized the depth of hypnosis experienced by their patients according to the manifestations of drowsiness, amnesia, catalepsy, and other variables. Despite the uncertainty about borderline states, and the confusion attributable to the nonstandardized methods of inducing hypnosis and giving suggestions, the nineteenth-century scales have enough in common to make possible some relevant comparisons among the findings of the various authorities.

The twentieth-century interest in measurement scales began with the publication in 1930 of a scale by M. M. White (1930). He made use of specific responses to suggestions given in hypnosis as a means of arriving at scores, and thus began the practice adopted by most of the later scales. The Davis and Husband Scale appeared in 1931, and the well-known Friedlander and Sarbin (1938) Scale seven years later. Weitzenhoffer and Hilgard, by essentially expanding and refining the Friedlander-Sarbin Scale, developed the first of the Stanford Hypnotic Susceptibility Scales (SHSS) (Weitzenhoffer and Hilgard, 1959). One of these was adapted for use among groups by Shor and Emily C. Orne (1962), and is known as the Harvard Group Scale (HGS). This and the Stanford Scales are now probably the most widely used of the tests for hypnotic responsivity.

The development of the scales to measure a person's hypnotizability or hypnotic responsivity (terms now preferred to susceptibility, which implies a weakness) depended on the use of the representative hypnotic behavior described above, organized and administered in a manner that adds some precision to the quantification of hypnotic experience. In essence the scales measure the number and the extent of the subjects' responses to suggestions of classic hypnotic behavior, given in hypnosis. While the scales depend on behavioral criteria, there is a high association between what the subjects experience and how they behave. The scales include a finite number of test items, namely twelve, given following an induction procedure, and the administration is carefully standardized. The induction procedure and directions to the subject are read by the operator from a prepared text; those who plan to use the SHSS, are advised to read them thoroughly before administering them to subjects, to familiarize themselves with the procedural details. The extent of the subject's response is measured over a precise time interval, and the use of a mechanical timer is recommended.

An example of the items in the SHSS (A and B) and HGS is the following:

The subject, hypnotized and with his eyes closed, is asked to hold his hands out in front of him, palms facing each other, about a foot apart. He is then asked to imagine them moving closer and closer together. From the end of the verbal instruction he is observed for exactly ten seconds. If at the end of this period, his hands are as close as six inches, he passes the test. If his hands are still separated by more than six inches, he fails. Were the operator to wait an additional twenty or thirty seconds, the hands might indeed move to within an inch or two of each other, or even touch. The aim of the scale, however, is to measure how close the hands are at the end of the allotted period of ten seconds. With this standardized method, individual responses can be compared with others, and studied in relation to factors such as age, sex, educational level, etc.

The Harvard Group Scale is administered by means of a recorded tape in which time intervals are carefully observed. The measurement of the responses is carried out by the subject in a self-rating questionnaire that he completes when the hypnosis has ended.

The scales contain twelve items, and the final score is between zero and twelve, depending on the number of items satisfactorily completed in the allotted time intervals. The test-retest reliability of the scales is high, of the order of magnitude of well-standardized intelligence tests. The scales include the five general categories of hypnotic behavior, all of which were covered in the description of hypnosis earlier in this chapter. They are:

1. Ideomotor Suggestions. Ideas, for example, that an outstretched arm becomes too heavy to maintain in that position, or that an arm resting on the subject's lap is too heavy to lift.

2. Challenge Items. In these the subject is exhorted, simultaneously, to follow two contradictory messages. For example, he is told that his extended arm will become as rigid as a bar of iron, too rigid in fact for him to bend. He is then told to try and bend it.

3. Hallucinations. The subject is told that he can hear a bothersome fly or mosquito buzzing about him.

4. Amnesia. The subject is told that after he awakes he will be unable to remember the events in hypnosis until he is told that he can.

5. *Posthypnotic Suggestion.* The subject is told that when he awakes he will make some move with his body (e.g., move to another chair, rise and stretch, or touch his ankle) when the operator taps his pencil on the desk, but will not remember that he was told to do so.

For the measurement of special hypnotic abilities such as agnosia, age regression, and dreams, special profile scales have been devised (Weitzenhoffer and Hilgard, 1963). These provide an interesting assessment of a subject's profile of scores, rather than a single score, and have special relevance for experimental research in hypnosis. Any detailed consideration of them here will take us further in this direction than we need to go.

CHARACTERISTICS OF HYPNOTIC RESPONSIVITY

What have we learned about hypnotic responsivity from an extensive use of the scales?

1. Hypnotizability Is a Relatively Stable Attribute

The ability to experience hypnosis is a relatively stable attribute of the person. In a review of the research into the modification of hypnotizability, Diamond (1974) concludes that there is little evidence to indicate that behavioral-situational factors or observational learning procedures can meaningfully enhance hypnotic responsiveness. The evidence is consistent with Hilgard's (1965) assertions that there are multiple pathways into the hypnotic experience, and that the use of diversified methods can meaningfully increase the responsiveness of subjects initially resistant to hypnosis as well as those less resistant. Thus, environmental alterations only appear to increase the ability to absorb oneself in hypnotic suggestions. Diamond suggests that *specific* techniques might be more effective in enhancing responsiveness to *particular* suggestions for *certain* subjects under *varying* conditions.

Gur (1974) described an attention-controlled operant procedure for enhancing hypnotic responsiveness. The procedure consisted of instructing the subject to press a button every time the word "relax" was mentioned in the hypnotic instructions in order to avoid an electric shock. This ensured that he would listen attentively to the instructions. Repeated measurements were conducted to assess the effect of this procedure, as well as its durability and generalizability, on subjects varying in initial responsiveness to standard hypnotic inductions. It was found that subjects who cannot, or who are not willing to respond to hypnotic suggestions, are not affected by this procedure. Furthermore, even those subjects who respond to the procedure are still unable, by and large, to display the wide array of hypnotic responsiveness that can be observed in very highly susceptible subjects. The view of hypnotic susceptibility as a stable personality characteristic rather resistive to change remains unchallenged by these results. The study indicated that hypnotizability is largely determined by factors other than situational manipulations.

Children are consistently found to be more hypnotizable, overall, than adults (London and Cooper, 1969). It is possible, therefore, that all people are born hypnotizable, but that the demands of reality on the maturing personality discourage the freedom of imagination that our society encourages only in children. But all children are not hypnotizable, and some adults retain their hypnotic abilities despite maturing influences. This suggests that there may be predispositional factors that determine the degree to which the individual develops his hypnotic abilities within his own particular environment. Such a predisposition could be in part genetic. This perspective (that the stable individual differences in hypnotic responsiveness might in part be inherent) led to a study of the hypnotizability of twins and their families from a behavior genetics approach (Morgan, 1973).

Morgan tested 140 pairs of twins and their families on the SHSS (Form A). A significant heritability index for the scores of the twin pairs and a significant correlation between the midparent score and the mean child score support a genetic component in hypnotizability. Morgan also found a statistically significant interaction between parent hypnotizability and the child's hypnotizability, conditional upon the resemblance of the child to the like-sexed parent in personality. This was interpreted as a consequence of environmental influence, either through social learning or identification.

2. Distribution of Hypnotizability in the Population

Hypnotizability is distributed in the population in essentially the same manner as any other skill, along a normal curve, with some positive skew (Hilgard, 1965). A study of the nineteenth-century measurements generally supports the consistency of that observation.

In a review of 519 cases tested in six separate studies between 1931 and 1958, Hilgard and his associates found the following:

The mean of percentages of those who were refractory or nonresponsive was twenty; the range of percentages was from three to thirty-seven.

The mean of percentages of those who were lightly responsive was forty-seven; the range of percentages was thirty-seven to fifty-nine.

The mean of percentages of those who were moderately responsive was twenty; the range of percentages was fifteen to thirty.

The mean of percentages of those who were deeply responsive was thirteen; the range of percentages was three to twenty-nine.

It is of great importance to note that despite observations by some clinicians to the contrary (to be discussed later), repeated laboratory investigations indicate that not all persons are hypnotizable; that those who are, are not all hypnotizable to the same degree; and that some persons are markedly hypnotizable. These data, in conjunction with the finding that a person's hypnotizability is a relatively stable attribute, bear directly on some of the work by Orne and his associates with nonhypnotizable simulators (to be considered at the end of this chapter) and on the clinical use of hypnosis.

3. Not All Hypnotic Experiences Are Equivalent

Items included in the scales vary in difficulty. They are not equivalent nor are they equally important. Most people are able to experience ideomotor suggestions, but only some are able to experience compelling positive and negative hallucinations. A score of six therefore on the SHSS or HGS may include all the relatively easy items, or may include a difficult suggestion, such as the hallucination of a buzzing fly. In the latter instance, which is unusual, we would be right to conclude that the subject is probably clinically more hypnotizable than the average person with a score of six made up of easier items. The final score is therefore not a reliable reflection of the individual's responsivity in all instances. As mentioned above, the profile scales could be of assistance in learning more about such an individual's special abilities.

4. Factorial Complexity of Hypnosis

A contribution of the psychometric approach to hypnosis is the growing volume of evidence that hypnosis is not a unitary or homogeneous phenomenon. Factor analytic studies have indicated that there are several types, or clusters, of hypnotic phenomena (Evans, 1968; Hilgard, 1965), and that at a given level of hypnotic responsivity, not all people can have the same experiences. In concrete terms, even some deeply hypnotized subjects will be unable to respond to suggestions for analgesia, or for age regression, etc. This is important in the interpretation of investigative studies. It is possible that inconsistent results occur because different investigators measure different clusters of hypnotic phenomena.

5. Correlates of Sex and Age

There are no sex differences in hypnotic responsivity, but there are some systematic changes with age (Hilgard, 1965; Morgan and Hilgard, 1973). In general, children are more hypnotizable than adults; a peak of hypnotizability appears in the age interval nine to twelve years, with a gradual decline thereafter; adult levels of responsivity are established by about age sixteen; and responsivity diminishes somewhat in post-middle and old age.

6. Hypnotizability in Relation to Cognitive and Personality Traits

Hypnotizability is a trait that is virtually isolated from other cognitive and personality traits. It is not related to intelligence or cognitive style, although there may be some relationship with the way in which the subjects deploy their attention (Graham, 1973; Krippner and Bindler, 1974). There may also be a relationship with enduring aptitudes for vivid imagery (Sheehan, 1972) and creativity (Bowers and Bowers, 1972).

In normal populations, the usual personality trait measures have shown no relationships with hypnotizability. However, recent work using intensive interviews (Josephine Hilgard, 1965, 1970, 1974) or specially constructed questionnaires (Shor, Orne, and O'Connell, 1962; Tellegen and Atkinson, 1974) have shown that those who can experience hypnosis also have a capacity for sustained, absorbing, and imaginative experiences in the ordinary course of everyday living. Josephine Hilgard's findings are specially interesting to the clinician. She sought to relate the contemporary personality to its longitudinal history and development within the family, in order to gain an understanding of the development of hypnotizability. She uncovered several pathways that seemed to lead to hypnotizability, including deep involvement in reading, dramatic arts, aesthetic experiences, religious dedication, and adventure. The characteristics of these activities such as the blurring of fantasy and reality, the involvement in "pretend games," the enjoyment of sensation, and the feelings of omnipotence are part and parcel of childhood, and intricately bound up with the hypnotic experience. Parental identification in and support for such activities permits them to be free of conflict.

7. Correlation with Hypnosislike Experiences Outside Hypnosis

Shor (1960) and Ås (Ås, O'Hara, and Munger, 1962) have sought to find in ordinary experience the kinds of behaviors that are called for in hypnosis. Personal experience inventories were devised to gather data on the incidence of hypnosislike experiences outside hypnosis. The experiences sought in the inventories included altered states that occur when things become strange as one looks at them, unwitting role-talking such as being convinced by one's own embellishments of a story, dissociative experiences such as part of one's body moving seemingly involuntarily, and so forth. No correlation was found between a high incidence of such experiences and increased hypnotizability. Hilgard (1965) concludes that there is little doubt, however, regardless of the pencil-and-paper results, that there are many continuities between experiences outside hypnosis and those inside. These give plausibility to the notion that the contents of the experience inventories cannot be ignored in favor of a purely response-style interpretation. Clearly, further work in this area remains to be done.

8. Hypnotizability in the Presence of Neurosis and Psychosis

Evidence here is not firmly established. As this aspect of hypnotic responsivity will be fully discussed in later chapters dealing with clinical issues, I will not pursue it further at this stage.

PROGRESS IN METHODOLOGY

1. Recognition of Demand Characteristics

Investigative studies in the behavioral sciences have been challenged by the need to develop appropriate methodologies. Nowhere has this been more urgent than in the efforts to learn about hypnosis. The complexities of the phenomenon were epitomized by the findings of Orne (1959), referred to earlier in this chapter, when he demonstrated what he called the demand characteristics. Let us now consider the procedure he used. He compared the responses to an induction procedure in two groups of undergraduates who had attended two separate lectures on hypnosis that were identical apart from one important item. The difference between the lectures lay in the demonstrations of hypnosis that were offered. The very hypnotizable subject used in the demonstration of hypnosis at the first lecture had received a posthypnotic suggestion on a previous occasion that the next time he was hypnotized he would develop catalepsy of the dominant hand. This suggestion was carried out in front of the group. The subject used to demonstrate hypnosis at the lecture for the other half of the class had received no such suggestion, and demonstrated a good but unembellished trance. When the members of both groups were subsequently hypnotized, the majority of those attending the first lecture where catalepsy was demonstrated did indeed show catalepsy of the dominant hand when in trance. None of the students in the other group showed it.

Orne thus clearly demonstrated that much hypnotic behavior results from the subject's conception of the role of the hypnotized person as determined by past experience and learning, and by explicit and implicit cues provided by the hypnotist and the situation. Previous conclusions reported in the literature were reconsidered and in some instances revised as a result of this finding. Investigators now prevent the demand characteristics of the experimental procedure from influencing subject behavior, only by being constantly aware of the possibility that they may. When they do, they create artifacts that are mistaken for the essentials of hypnosis.

2. Controls and Nonhypnotizable Simulators

The introduction of effective controls into the study of hypnosis was, similarly, an original and imaginative step that has few parallels in its influence on our concept of hypnosis.

It is clearly essential to be able to compare the effects of identical procedures on hypnotized and nonhypnotized subjects, if we are to learn about the effects of hypnosis. Orne (1959, 1972a) introduced the idea of the nonhypnotizable controls or simulators, who, submitted to procedures identical to those experienced by the hypnotized subjects in the experiment, were asked in several studies to behave in a manner that they believed would be appropriate for a hypnotized person. They were accurately informed that the experimentor would not know who among the subjects were hypnotized and who were not. They were instructed to do all that they could to make him believe they were.

Orne considered the introduction of nonhypnotizable simulating subjects a safeguard against the situational demands that were unwittingly introduced into the investigative procedure by the experimentor. He had observed, in comparing the responses of hypnotized and nonhypnotized subjects, that it was difficult for an operator not to give instructions to hypnotized individuals with greater intensity and conviction than that associated with his instructions to subjects he knew were in the waking state. Furthermore, it was thought to be impossible to know whether or not control subjects who were hypnotizable had in fact been unwittingly hypnotized. If, however, controls known to be nonhypnotizable are subjected to the experimental procedures, and the experimentor is blind to those among his subjects who are hypnotized and those who are nonhypnotizable simulators, he will interact with them all in the same way. In other words, he will be prevented from treating the two groups differently, and they will both respond to cues that have crept into the interaction and the situation whether by design or by coincidence. The experimentor is thereby prevented from concluding falsely that a certain behavioral response is attributable to hypnosis when it is not, and also becomes aware of methodological flaws that he could not possibly have detected otherwise. Orne emphasizes that the crucial issue in the experimental work is not the information explicitly provided to the subject, but how the subject perceives he is expected to behave in the experiment.

This use in research of nonhypnotizable simulators is made possible by the fact that all people do not respond to the same extent nor in the same manner to procedures that induce hypnosis, and because responsivity is a stable attribute. Furthermore, even highly competent hypnotists with remarkably wide experience in hypnosis can often not tell who is and who is not hypnotized when the nonhypnotized group is encouraged to behave as they believe hypnotized subjects would.

SUMMARY

In the first chapter, we reviewed the discovery of animal magnetism, which was the precursor of hypnotism, and examined the controversial beliefs and theories that attempted to explain it. In this chapter we have had an opportunity to observe hypnosis happening, and have become acquainted with the measurement scales by which the phenomenon can be quantified. We have also learned of the complexities inherent in the study of it, and now know something of its parameters. At this stage we can return to the theory, and consider three important theoretical positions in the light of what we have learned about the event. We will then consider a working definition of hypnosis before proceeding to a critique of its clinical use.

CHAPTER 3

Specific Theories

THREE DIMENSIONS OF HYPNOTIC DEPTH

Publications by Shor (1959, 1962) are important because they expose both the commonplace and complex aspects of hypnosis, and advance formulations that draw together many useful distinctions embedded in several theories of hypnosis. They are also important because they succeed in emphasizing the difference between the experiences of trance and hypnosis, and the relationship between them. Shor analyzes the experience of *trance* with painstaking attention to detail, indicating that it can occur unobtrusively as when one is absorbed by listening to music; deliberately as when one studies intensively; or spontaneously as when drowsiness leads to sleep or in pathologic conditions such as fugue states. *Hypnosis,* on the other hand, requires an interaction with another person to whom responsibility for inducing the trance is ascribed.

Shor's first paper describes two fundamental cognitive processes assumed to underlie hypnotic phenomena, and is presented as an elaboration of the dual-factor theory of hypnosis (White, 1941). White had explained hypnosis as the result of two intertwined processes, namely, *goal-directed striving* that takes place in an *altered psychologic state.* The goal was ". . . to behave like a hypnotized person as this is continuously defined by the operator and understood by the subject . . ." Although the altered psychological state received little more than peripheral attention from White, the number of widespread references to it in his work helped to reconstruct his conception of it. Shor develops the concept of the *altered* psychological state in his first paper (1959) by commencing with an examination of the *usual* state of consciousness and tracing the changes that occur as hypnosis takes place. He views the usual state of consciousness as "characterized by the mobilization of a structured frame of reference in the background of attention which supports, interprets, and gives meaning to all experiences." This wide orientation to reality, described as the "generalized reality orientation," is sustained by numerous perceptual supports, i.e., constant sensory input with minimal and subliminal acknowledgement, resulting from active mental effort not usually consciously directed, but contantly devoted to its maintenance. ". . . Consciously directed [effort occurs] when we study, i.e., when we deliberately try to structure our mind with various ideas. Most of the time, however, the direction is essentially nonconscious and seemingly automatic (as when we drive our car or play tennis or comprehend a social situation)" . . . "Whenever its supportive energy diminishes, the generalized reality orientation fades into the more distant background of attention and becomes relatively nonfunctional."

Shor explains that the generalized reality orientation is developed slowly throughout the life cycle, and that the concept is not equivalent to the many processes that derive from it nor is it a mere sum of them. It goes beyond reality-testing, body image, critical self-awareness, and cognition of the self, world, other people, etc., all of which have meaning, however, because they are embedded within the wider orientation to reality. The generalized reality orientation is also seen as having a shifting character with many facets, not as an inflexible entity. What enters into the central background of attention depends on the special cognitive requirements of the immediate situation; and in normal waking life, even though only some aspects of the wide orientation to reality are in central focus, the rest of it remains in close communication at all times. *"When this close communication is lost, the resultant state of mind may be designated as a trance"* . . . "Any state in which the generalized reality-orientation has faded to relatively nonfunctional awareness may be termed a trance state."

Shor cites an illustration of how he was absorbed in a book and had not known clearly that a second person had spoken to him, although he had been aware in some dim way of something intruding. An instant later, when he had reinstituted into his mind's immediate background of attention an orientation to generalized reality, everything became clear to him. He then knew that the jumble of something that had occurred a moment before was indeed words spoken to him by the other person. In his illustration he refers not only to an extensive fading of the usual generalized reality orientation, but also to the presence of the special small task orientation, namely, reading, which functioned in relative isolation. He concludes that the experience of the trance contains more than one fundamental process. The first is the construction of a special, temporary orientation to a small range of preoccupations, and the second is the relative fading of the generalized reality-orientation into nonfunctional unawareness. It should be noted that in this example of the trance the generalized reality orientation does not just inadvertently slip away but is voluntarily and deliberately suspended.

Shor then emphasizes that although these two processes are cited as the fundamental core of the trance, they are not exhaustive of the variables relevant to understanding hypnosis. He views them as referring only to the underlying skeleton, the fundamental cognitive basis of hypnosis that may be assumed universal to all human beings. "The flesh and blood of hypnosis—its multidimensional clinical richness and variation—only appear when hypnosis is viewed in terms of the dynamic interrelationships between real people." He sees no inherent antagonism between his conceptualization and more psychodynamically oriented formulations, and feels they must supplement each other for a complete theory.

Within the special human interaction, and where the task is a personal preoccupation with a small range of interests, the result is labeled absentmindedness, daydreaming, or intense meditation. The distinction between trance and hypnosis becomes clear. "Trance is the superordinate concept used to refer to states of mind characterized by the relative unawareness and nonfunctioning of the generalized reality-orientation. *Hypnosis is a special form of trance* developed in Western civilization, achieved via motivated role-taking, and characterized by the production of a special, new orientation to a range of preoccupations" directed by the hypnotist. The new special orientation becomes temporarily the only possible reality for the subject who, in White's terms, is motivated to behave like a hypnotized person as this is continuously defined by the operator and understood by the subject. This is considered to be identical with what Sarbin has called role-taking from the standpoint of social psychology (Sarbin, 1950; Sarbin and Coe, 1972).

As stated above, Shor devoted the major portion of his earlier publication to synthesizing theoretical viewpoints relating to the *altered psychological state* in hypnosis, simultaneously acknowledging the importance (stressed by other authors previously) of the *motivation to be involved in the roles* of hypnosis; or, in other words, of the striving to behave like a hypnotized person. His development of the concept of the generalized reality-orientation fading spontaneously under nonpathological *and* pathological conditions, or when it is purposively diminished as in the hypnotic interaction, explains in a novel and lucid manner what is generally meant by the altered psychological state or altered state of consciousness, and points to a major distinction between the trance, and hypnosis that is the induction of trance with the help of another.

In a later publication, Shor (1962) felt it necessary to synthesize the psychodynamic explanation of hypnosis with the more cognitive approach, and extended his dual factor theory to include the *transference*. The importance of the transference in hypnosis was originally described by Schilder and Kauders (1927). Reference is made by them to a relationship in hypnosis between two portions of the subject's personality: the first entering into suggestive rapport with the hypnotist, while the second is described as the more highly developed central portion of the ego. Only the first portion can be said to be hypnotized while the central portion assumes the role of observer, continuously controlling and supervising the hypnotized portion. When a large proportion of the central personality unreservedly consents to the hypnotic rapport, it is because that central personality is profoundly involved in the subject's interpersonal attachments to the person of the hypnotist. Shor incorporated the transference into his theory, considering it a third dimension of hypnotic depth that may vary independently of the other two.

The three dimensions of hypnotic depth thus elaborated by him include: (a) the dimension of hypnotic role-taking involvement; (b) the dimension of trance; and (c) the dimension of the primitive relationship or archaic transference.

The three dimensions of hypnotic depth can now be reviewed together:

"(a) Hypnotic role-taking involvement depth is the extent to which the complex of motivational striving and cognitive structurings regarding the role of the hypnotized subject has sunk below the level of purely conscious compliance and volition, and has become nonconsciously directive."

It should be noted that "when role-taking involvement deepens, a compulsive and involuntary quality derives from it . . . the task of being a hypnotized subject has become not a consciously controlled choice." The new special orientation to reality becomes temporarily the only possible reality for the subject who is brainwashed to behave like a hypnotized person as this is continuously defined by the operator and understood by the subject.

"(b) Trance depth is the extent to which the usual generalized reality-orientation has faded into nonfunctional unawareness."

"(c) Depth of archaic involvement is (i) the extent to which during hypnosis archaic object relationships are formed onto the person of the hypnotist; (ii) the extent to which a special hypnotic transference relationship is formed onto the person of the hypnotist; (iii) the extent to which the core of the subject's personality is involved in the hypnotic processes."

When depth along all three dimensions is roughly equivalent, it is likely that the observer will not be able to disentangle the separate entities. When the depth is not in relative balance, however, the resultant hypnosis will have characteristics corresponding to the imbalanced configuration. Different ways of experiencing the event of hypnosis can thus be more fully understood than they would be if considered only in terms of a single dimension, namely, trance depth.

Shor has, by means of his formulations, demonstrated the commonplace quality of the trance, recognizing that it is neither special nor rare. He has at the same time drawn attention to the complexity of the event of hypnosis, which resists any attempt to explain it as simply the result of this entity or that. His formulations pave the way to further investigations into hypnosis and related conditions.

ALTERED STATES OF CONSCIOUSNESS (ASC)

Support for the emphasis that Shor places on the importance of the trance comes from other authors who have attempted to investigate what is described as an altered state of consciousness. Because of the limited interest shown by the Western world in the concept of a nonpathologic altered state of consciousness, we have as yet no dependable definition nor neatly conceptualized notion. There can be little doubt, however, that those who speak of trance and altered state of consciousness are referring to the same or greatly similar subjective experiences. The very subjective nature of the event accounts for the difficulties experienced by the investigators. Tart (1969) strongly encourages the acceptance of the essentially subjective nature of the experience under discussion, and presents logical argument that if we accept the ability of people in the usual waking state to describe themselves as being in a normal state of consciousness at any moment, we should acknowledge their capacity to recognize when they experience a state of consciousness that is different, namely, an altered state of consciousness. He argues that our knowledge of altered states is too incomplete at this time for tight conceptualization, but presents a simple sort of definition as a beginning. He describes the normal state of consciousness as the one in which an individual spends the major part of his waking hours, and the altered state of consciousness for a given individual as one in which that individual clearly feels a qualitative shift in his pattern of mental functioning; that is, he feels not just a quantitative shift (more or less alert, more or less visual imagery, sharper, duller, etc.) but also that some quality or qualities of his mental processes are different. Ludwig (1966), for the purpose of discussion, regards altered states of consciousness as any mental state(s), induced by various physiological, psychological, or pharmacological maneuvers or agents, that can be recognized subjectively by the individual himself (or by an objective observer) as representing a deviation in subjective experience or psychological functioning from his or her general norms during alert waking consciousness. This deviation may be represented by a greater preoccupation than usual with internal sensations or mental processes, changes in the formal characteristics of thought, and impairment of reality testing to various degrees.

The attention paid by Tart and Ludwig among others to altered states of consciousness points to the relevance of Shor's close examination of the event of hypnosis, and his disentangling of the trance from its other components. Despite the conceptual and semantic challenge, it is reasonable to assume that the subjective experiences described by those writers are the same. Furthermore, all three refer to the ability of an individual to experience the state independently and voluntarily. In his comprehensive overview of the altered states of consciousness, Ludwig also refers to its defensive function in conditions such as fugues, depersonalization, and other clinical conditions. In these circumstances the nature of the alteration is spontaneous. The resultant situation for the subject is likely to be strange, novel, poorly understood, and fearsome. To what extent such an event creates its own anxiety can be imagined, and is well worth considering. I will attempt, in a later chapter, to return to a discussion of this very point.

A NEODISSOCIATION THEORY

In the speculative reasoning that seeks to understand how such alterations in the state of consciousness might take place, one cannot but be fascinated by the idea of a neodissociation theory tentatively presented by Hilgard (1973). In a relatively brief essay he adds to his monumental contribution to the study of hypnosis by paving the way to a theory that has its roots in the writing of Janet (1907).

After first focusing on the multiple mechanisms whereby a person controls his behavior and his thoughts, Hilgard reexamines the earlier attempt by Janet to discuss some of these problems by way of the concept of dissociation. He indicates that although the processes controlling behavior and experience in hypnotized subjects can be considered as involuntary compared to voluntary, as subconscious compared to conscious, and as the result of a regressed compared to normal ego state, none of these pairs of distinctions completely accounts for what happens. This incompleteness has to be supplemented either by further distinctions, or by some alternative formulation. It is here that Hilgard is led to reexamine the concept of dissociation.

We are reminded that Janet's interpretation of dissociation is that systems of ideas split off from the major personality and exist as a subordinate personality, unconscious but capable of becoming represented in consciousness through hypnosis. Janet regarded the dissociated system of thoughts as *completely* independent, and attributed the dissociation to an enfeebled state in which there was insufficient mental energy to maintain the integration of ideas.

Hilgard finds the concept of dissociation inviting because, as he points out, although our normal ego controls take care of our needs enabling us to behave in socially acceptable ways and to make sensible choices, there *are* processes that are carried on outside of such normal controls, which occasionally also operate simultaneously with them. Because he prefers not to defend all that has been claimed for dissociation in the past, Hilgard states the case for a neodissociation theory. He reminds us that:

1. "The human behavior and conscious control apparatus is not highly unified and integrated. It is a weak and not strong Gestalt." Dissonance exists between behavior systems, and discrepancies exist among the divisions of feeling, thinking, and doing.

2. "The stream of consciousness flows in more than one channel at a time, or to put it differently, there are more than one concurrent streams." This is illustrated by the participant in an intelligent conversation who listens, watches, and formulates a reply at the same time.

3. "Habitual control mechanisms can often operate in behavior with a minimum of conscious attention, freeing conscious processes to reflect other kinds of cerebration." This is illustrated by the driving of a car while carrying on a spirited conversation.

4. "Conscious processes take place that in their nature and sequence are relatively independent of normal ego control." The night dream, daydream, and fantasy are presented as illustrations.

Turning to hypnotic and posthypnotic phenomena, he asserts that posthypnotic amnesia, posthypnotic automatic writing, age regression, positive hallucinations, and challenge motor items, when examined closely, provide considerable support for the concept of a dissociative process. The amnesia exists because although the memories are not destroyed, they are temporarily unavailable. Automatic writing indicates a kind of independent cerebration, and in age regression it is apparent that the observing ego watches the childlike regressed behavior. A positive hallucination is sometimes differentiated from true object (for example, when the subject is told that he sees two lights when there is only one) by noting which one has the reflection in the polished surface on which the object stands. In challenge motor items, the subject is told, for example, to bend a rigid arm or other suggested motor response, while given the contradictory suggestion that he will be unable to do so. Here the conflict is created between the two relatively independent control mechanisms, one producing the response and one attempting to break it.

Hilgard tells us that he chooses not to propose a neodissociation theory in any detail at this time. He indicates only something of the nature of a theory that includes, among other ideas, the notion that complete functional independence between structures that are considered to be dissociated is not required; and that all dissociation is best viewed as a matter of degree. This differs from Janet's explanation (1907) in which he considered the dissociated system of thoughts as completely independent. Furthermore, in his reexamination of Janet's theory Hilgard makes no specific mention of Janet's view that dissociation occurs because of insufficient mental energy to maintain the integration of ideas, clearly a consequence of an enfeebled and pathological state. This notion would not be included in a theory of hypnosis as it is conceptualized at this time. Hilgard, does, however, refer to the cognitive effort that is needed to maintain the dissociative process, and the consequent cost to cognition of holding a task out of awareness (Stevenson, 1972). We cannot leave the topic of dissociation without noting the historical justice that is inherent in a reexamination of Janet's work.

HYPNOSIS: WORKING GUIDELINES

From the concepts and theories discussed thus far, we can consider the following as a brief summary of our current understanding of hypnosis.

Hypnosis is an event developed in the Western world, involving a subject and an operator, and dependent for its occurrence on the trance capabilities of the subject, his or her motivation, the situation, and the relationship between the subject and the operator. When these are appropriate, the subject can be guided or directed to experience reality differently.

This experience includes distorted perceptions of various kinds; and unusual achievements of memory such as hypermnesia or amnesia can be part of it. The experience has a beginning and an end, and includes a tolerance for logical inconsistencies. During the event, at some level, an awareness of reality persists, e.g., a subject who does not see a chair in the middle of the room will nevertheless walk around it.

The changes result in part from the effective use of suggestion and imagination by which the subject is encouraged to relegate his or her usually wide perceptual awareness to a position of relative unimportance and to replace it with a specific and narrow range of preoccupations, which creates a different experience of reality. The ability to effect this change is referred to as trance capacity, and varies from person to person, even though fairly consistent for each individual. The motivation to be deeply involved in the role of a hypnotized person, the circumstances in which the event occurs, and the degree of total trust and dependency on the operator all influence the extent to which the changes are subjectively experienced.

There is no evidence to support the widely held view that the operator in hypnosis is able to control the experience and behavior of the subject against the latter's wishes. It is the subject's motivation and preparedness to behave in accordance with the wishes and directions of the operator that create the erroneous impression. There is similarly no evidence to support the idea that a hypnotized subject can transcend his normal volitional capacity because of the hypnosis; and despite persuasive clinical reports of altered somatic structure in hypnosis, no physiological changes uniquely associated with hypnosis have yet been demonstrated.

We would do well to remember the receptivity of the hypnotized subject to situational cues that may be purposively or inadvertently introduced by the operator and that shape hypnotic behavior. These demand characteristics reflect the responsivity of the well-hypnotized subject and have been responsible in the past for several faulty notions about what happens in hypnosis. Hypnosis is not so much a way of manipulating behavior as of creating distortions of perception and memory.

Easy explanations of the phenomenon, which include ascribing it to simple concepts such as that of suggestibility or relaxation, fail to take into account the complex nature of the event, which clearly includes not only the trance, but motivation and interaction between the subject and the operator. We are tempted to consider seriously some mechanism such as dissociation to account for the major characteristics of the event.

CHAPTER 4

A Clinical Critique

At this point we turn our attention to the use of hypnosis and the importance of hypnotizability in the clinical area. Despite the availability of a considerable number of clinical case reports praising the use of hypnosis, few include more on the hypnotizability of the patient than the therapist's clinical impression. In the light of what has been learned from the well-organized laboratory investigation of hypnosis in recent years, we have little alternative but to reexamine closely any assertions that are made about hypnotic behavior in the clinical setting. Furthermore, although authors generally seem to be in agreement that normal subjects are more hypnotizable than those who border on the neurotic or are frankly neurotic (Ehrenreich, 1949; Hilgard, 1965), clinicians have been enticed for close to two centuries into suspecting marked hypnotizability in patients displaying certain clinical features. This aspect will be developed in some detail as it lies at the heart of what I hope to convey, but before doing so I would like to discuss the clinical use of hypnosis to date.

THE DIAGNOSIS OF HYPNOSIS IN THE CLINICAL CONTEXT

Many or perhaps even most of the clinical reports alluded to above have displayed a minimal awareness of the complexities of the hypnotic response; of the wide variations in the ability of different people to experience trance; of the effects of placebo, relaxation, and demand characteristics; of the major importance of the transference; and of the marked influence of the patient's motivation to be hypnotized or to comply with the therapist's wishes. The difficulty experienced by expert hypnotists in trying to differentiate a true hypnotic response from a pretended one, as reported by Orne (1959), seems never to have been conceded by large numbers of clinicians, although they must many times have been at least partially aware of that possibility in their own practice. Hypnosis depends for its success on the readiness to be receptive to ideas, a readiness that could, at times, be subtly influential in the hypnotist as well as in the hypnotized.

The question that should be important in any clinical encounter involving hypnosis is one that asks whether the therapist, after shaping the behavior of his patient, is likely to draw false conclusions regarding whether or not hypnosis occurs. The behavior is shaped by the induction procedure or an equivalent series of signals, and subsequent encouraging directives. It is easy to lose sight of the fact that the presence of hypnosis should not be presumed from the actions of the therapist, but should be diagnosed from the experience and behavior of the patient. The fact that the former induces hypnosis cannot be taken to mean that the latter is experiencing it. He may merely be very relaxed or be complying with what he considers to be the wishes of his therapist, and be doing so sincerely.

THE USE OF RATING SCALES

By comparing the patient's ability to respond to a standard hypnotic procedure with the responses of many thousands of subjects who have been rated on the same hypnotizability scales in the laboratory, we are able to employ the term "hypnosis" according to a formula acknowledged both by clinicians and research workers. The loose use of the word to date in clinical circles has contributed to the repeated decline of hypnosis in the medical and scientific community. Even though standardized tests could also be influenced by the factors of motivation and compliance, the availability of repeated assessments by means of the different but related tests, and the opportunity for the patient to focus specifically on the test responses (unencumbered for that circumscribed period of time by issues that arise in therapy), allow for a more accurate measure of hypnotizability than informal clinical evaluation. The responses enable us to check our clinical impressions against a valid and reliable scale, and permit the growth of our understanding of what happens in hypnosis.

Despite contrary opinions, research findings testify to the constancy of the hypnotizability level in the great majority of individuals who have reached adolescence or early adulthood. Claims that all persons are ultimately hypnotizable to the degree desired by their therapists have not been supported by acceptable studies. Empirically it seems that repeated exposure to induction procedures may increase the rate at which hypnosis occurs, but the evidence for a greater depth or intensity of hypnosis being achieved is lacking.

The susceptibility scales widely used in experimental work, although clearly influenced by the clinical experience of those who helped to develop them, are probably more suited to the laboratory. Like most tests and assessments, they do have a somewhat intrusive quality. There seems at present to be no way of circumventing this unless a scale is devised that provides access to aspects of hypnosis that have not yet been discovered, or fully understood.*

In keeping with this, Spiegel has constructed an interesting scale, the Hypnotic Induction Profile (HIP) (Spiegel and Bridger, 1970) based in part on his observation that markedly hypnotizable individuals when experiencing hysterical symptoms often display large areas of the sclera as they roll up their eyes. The profile measures, in the waking state, the amount of sclera displayed on upward gaze accompanied by closure of the eyelids; then it measures the responses to instructions given after an induction procedure, encompassing forearm levitation and posthypnotic suggestion. It is a rapidly administered test lasting five to ten minutes, and includes an assessment of the eye roll and two aspects of hypnotic behavior, namely, the ideomotor and posthypnotic responses. Amnesia for the signal that terminates the posthypnotic suggestion increases the rating. The nature of the eye roll and the relevance to hypnosis attributable to the quantity of the exposed sclera have not yet been settled. They deserve close study, however. Meanwhile, the profile serves as an interesting and useful way of introducing the hypnotic experience into the clinical situation and gaining a rough estimate of the likely responsiveness of the patient.

EVALUATION OF CLINICAL TECHNIQUES

Use of hypnosis in the clinical context has been directed largely (1) at symptom removal, and (2) at aiding the explorative and interpretive aims in psychotherapy and psychoanalysis. Symptom removal, most often involving emphatic and specific suggestions following an induction procedure, has been widely reported in medical and scientific publications, and seems to be the logical heir to the therapeutic method used by Mesmer in his practice of animal magnetism. Regarding the use of hypnosis as an ex-

---

* A new clinical measure of hypnotic responsivity has been introduced by Hilgard and Hilgard (1975), too recently to have been used in the cases reported in this work.

ploratory aid in psychotherapy and psychoanalysis, Wolberg (1945), one of the few psychoanalysts using hypnosis, states, "I have become increasingly convinced that hypnosis conservatively employed can contribute greatly to psychoanalytic process, particularly instances where resistance impedes free association, blocks dreaming, masks transference, and nurtures impenetrable amnesia."

Let us now look, in a somewhat more critical manner, at these major clinical uses of hypnosis. In applying it to the removal of symptoms, use is made of the relaxing effects of an induction procedure in addition to the more specifically hypnotic element of perceptual distortion, depending on the directives of the therapist and the hypnotizability of the patient. By encouraging patients to focus on calm and relaxed bodily sensations or on visual images of a peaceful nature, we enable them to achieve a hypometabolic state consistent with decreased sympathetic nervous system activity and a consequent reduction in tension. This is a state similar to that achieved by means of Jacobson's relaxation (Jacobson, 1938), the self-hypnosis involved in autogenic training (Schultz, 1932; Schultz and Luthe, 1969) and the meditative exercises of philosophies such as Zen, Yoga, and Transcendental Meditation. We also have evidence of the physiological changes achieved in the relaxation response (Benson, Beary, and Carol, 1974; Benson, 1975). Such relaxation is conducive to the alleviation of symptoms arising from general tension or localized spasm that occurs, for example, in asthma or hypertension. But when the patient, in addition, experiences an appreciable distortion of perception, the diagnosis of hypnosis is possible. The distortion is used either to mask the physical discomfort or to displace it with a more tolerable sensation such as tingling or numbness. It is this specific effect, namely, perceptual distortion, that we regard as belonging uniquely to hypnosis as we understand the term at this time. In other words, hypnosis is a trance phenomenon, and shares important characteristics with other trance states that may be achieved in a variety of ways, and that in other respects, e.g., hypersuggestibility, may not be identical with the hypnotic trance state.

A few illustrative clinical methods will follow:

1. Techniques with Physical Symptoms

In a previous paper I reported the effects of brief hypnotherapy in a series of psychosomatic problems (Frankel, 1973). The therapy included the use of hypnosis to achieve muscular relaxation, to distort perception purposefully and strategically, or to influence attitudes in a beneficial and therapeutic way. Several of the patients had gastrointestinal symptoms including difficulty controlling bowel action. Some responded favorably to one or two interviews that entailed an investigation of the history, a rapid assessment of the response to hypnotic induction, and instructions in how to relax. They were encouraged to concentrate on the right or left hand and forearm until they became aware of a very light or relaxed feeling in that limb, and to permit that limb then to move across to rest on the abdomen to enable the relaxed feeling in the fingers and hand to spread through the abdominal wall to the bowel, which would then also become relaxed. They were advised that if they wished they could also permit the appropriate sphincters in the gastrointestinal tract to contract gently and securely in a manner that would provide reassurance to them when they experienced a pressing urge to defecate.

The relaxation technique was made part of a self-induced exercise that the patients practiced with regularity. One thirty-nine-year-old man had feared to move any distance from a toilet since a humiliating punishment for soiling during school hours at the age of five years. He had previously refused psychotherapy even though the need to move his bowels was so great when he was any distance from a toilet that he had bought a camper with bathroom facilities to drive to and from his place of work. Despite a limited education he had made considerable progress in the firm he worked for, but further promotion was hampered by his refusal to journey away from the main depot on business trips. His ability to dispel the urgent need for a bowel movement by placing his hand on his abdomen to induce a sense of relaxation contributed immensely to his growth in self-confidence and his ability to travel without hindrance. Previous occasional use of pharmacological relaxants and antidiarrheal agents had been of little or no help. A follow-up questionnaire six months after his two interviews revealed that his improvement had continued. The procedure had depended on only average responsiveness on his part to the induction of hypnosis. He would probably have responded to any relaxation technique, including religious meditation, had the circumstances and the interaction with his mentor been favorable, and in my opinion, regardless of whether he had been encouraged in calming and persuasively reassuring tones to enter "deep hypnosis" or merely "deep relaxation."

Meares in his publication on medical hypnosis reports effective treatment in a lighter stage of hypnosis, which he refers to as the hypnoidal state (Meares, 1960). This too, it would seem, is yet another way of describing the same relaxation phenomenon.

The masking or displacement of physical discomfort and pain by means of perceptual distortion is similarly dependent on the interaction between patient and therapist, but as indicated above, it is a function of the capacity of the patient to achieve such distortion, and to experience hypnosis. Where the nature of the pain is clear and physical in origin, such as in the presence of obstetrical and dental surgery, or malignancy, the use of sedative and hypnotic drugs have been considerably reduced or even eliminated when perceptual distortion has been possible. August has recorded this both on film and in published reports of obstetrical surgery (August, 1960). When the usual dental anesthetic agents were precluded by a patient's allergic responses, Owens (1970) produced glovelike anesthesia under hypnosis, and then had the patient touch his face to enable the anesthesia to drain from the hand to the mouth area. The effective use of hypnosis in the relief of pain in patients with cancer has been well described by Sacerdote (1966, 1970), Crasilneck and Hall (1973, 1975), and Hilgard and Hilgard (1975).

Where physical symptoms are in part or wholly attributable to psychological factors, their enduring removal either by means of relaxation or perceptual distortion can be complex. Attention must be paid to the psychodynamically based need that such patients have for developing symptoms in the first instance. Even though very often responsive to hypnosis, they generally have great difficulty relinquishing the secondary gain from symptoms, and require face-saving techniques and environmental manipulation based on a psychodynamic understanding of the problem. Controversial opinions compete around the issue of removing such symptoms with direct suggestion of perceptual distortion, under hypnosis. Some claim excellent results and others insist that these efforts are ineffective and even dangerous. In the absence of acceptable follow-up studies, we can conclude that both these positions are somewhat exaggerated, and that the truth lies somewhere in between. A cavalier attitude toward the psychodynamic demands is considered as ill-advised as one that precludes the use of hypnosis altogether. As symptoms not infrequently remain unaffected by psychotherapy even though patients might gain much in other ways from their treatment, alternative and ancillary methods are needed. Such symptoms, no longer nourished by the unresolved unconscious conflict that originally gave rise to them, not infrequently continue because of habit and learning. Should hypnosis be selected as treatment in such cases, care in establishing and maintaining the relationship between hypnotist and patient is essential. Suggestion and persuasion are gently offered even if authoritatively, and continuous or repeated contact on the day of treatment and subsequently are often necessary. A useful procedure that provides for the superordinate need of the patient to retain the symptom includes the introduction of autohypnosis and the prescription of routine exercises each day, aimed at either relaxation or that plus the production of altered sensory perception. In this way the option is clearly with the patient to omit the practice or to engage in it. Hypnosis is thus likely to be more effective when it forms part of a larger psychodynamically sensitive treatment plan.

2. Techniques with Psychiatric Symptoms

The removal of psychiatric symptoms, whether fears, phobias, feelings of depression, or schizophrenic behavior, by means of exploration or suggestion during hypnosis has been reported. It is difficult to present a consensus regarding the reasons for the success or failure of this use of hypnosis, but one widely held view is provided by Gill and Brenman (1959). It is representative of the opinions, and commands the respect of many psychoanalytically oriented therapists. Those authors concluded that there was no correlation between the depth of hypnosis obtained by a patient and the therapeutic result. They describe case histories in which it appears that some patients with a marked hypnotizability benefited not at all from the introduction of hypnosis into the treatment program, while others who were poor hypnotic subjects responded well to the use of hypnosis. Their results with hypnotherapy appeared to be in no way dependent on the degree of hypnotizability. At first sight this is disappointing to those who have witnessed a different clinical picture.

On a subsequent occasion Gill (1974), speaking to the same issue, expressed the view that evidence supports a correlation between the responsivity to the *hypnotic situation* and responsivity to therapy, rather than between *hypnotizability* and responsivity to therapy. To understand this, let us consider it in the light of Shor's three dimensions of archaic transference, motivation to experience the role of a hypnotized person, and ability to experience the trance. It is clear from their comments that to Gill and Brenman the relationship with the hypnotist is of the essence of hypnosis. The nature of that relationship in association with the patient's motivation to be hypnotized for therapeutic purposes comes close to constituting what Gill refers to as the hypnotic situation.

Given a positive transference and good motivation, there is no doubt that a patient can enter a state of marked relaxation or one in which defenses and vigilance are reduced, regression occurs, associations are freer, and greater access to primary process material occurs. Associated with these circumstances the patient is deeply involved emotionally in the event. The question to be answered, however, is whether all this includes the experience of the trance.

Here we move to the heart of the issue. Opinions continue to vary on what hypnosis is. The situation just described, namely, one of an intense involvement with the therapist leading to regression and a facilitated uncovering and working through of deep-seated problems, does *not* constitute an event of hypnosis for all students of the phenomenon, although the strongly psychoanalytically oriented therapists consider it to be one.

Those who have studied and reported on the experience of hypnosis among healthy college students have leaned toward establishing the presence of other criteria before diagnosing hypnotic trance. As emphasized above, evidence of distorted perception with potential changes in memory must be present, too. Furthermore, they agree that a positive transference and strong motivation are necessary for it to be induced. Shor (1962) suggests that strong motivation and positive transference alone may enable a subject to approach close to the experience of hypnosis, but do not permit him to achieve it in quite the same way as a person who also has trance capacity. The capacity to experience the trance is seen to provide the dimension essential for the full experience of the event of hypnosis.

It should be remembered that the view of hypnotic behavior expressed by Gill and Brenman has been influenced by the fact that most of the subjects seen by them in the hypnotic state were also in therapy, and the hypnotic situation referred to is not easily separated from the therapeutic situation. An examination of the case histories presented by them to illustrate their viewpoint reveals that their criteria for diagnosing the presence of the hypnotic situation do not necessarily include presence of the trance as defined above. If oriented differently to hypnosis, one has difficulty discerning what belongs essentially to hypnosis in the therapeutic events they report, and what belongs to the psychotherapy. Furthermore, among the very hypnotizable cases reported as having derived no benefit from hypnotherapy are two patients with psychotic disorders, one probably melancholic and the other schizophrenic. These cases were treated with psychotherapy and hypnotic suggestion in an era when many therapists still placed their hopes on the effectiveness of psychotherapy as a single method of treatment in the psychoses. In retrospect, it seems that psychotherapy was on test in those situations rather than hypnotherapy.

Painted in strokes as bold as those used by Gill and Brenman, the dimensions of transference and motivation tend to obscure the relevance of trance capacity. It is the major thesis of this book that if we overlook the importance of the trance, we miss what is an essential aspect of hypnosis and the opportunity to study clinical events in a light that can ultimately enhance our understanding of them. The emphases in the orientations of those who work with hypnosis determine the subjects they study, what they observe, and what they ultimately conclude. What appear to be major disagreements may turn out to be literally different points of view, which are not necessarily irreconcilable.

As we move to an examination of other authors, also strongly interested in hypnosis from the psychoanalytic perspective, we find affirmation of the views expressed by Gill and Brenman. We find hypnotic induction procedures and signals to enter hypnosis woven into and out of the treatment course with the sole intention of furthering the treatment strategy of uncovering, exploring, and developing insight into the psychodynamic issues. Little or no attempt is made to measure the depth of hypnosis objectively. Hypnosis is used primarily to subserve the needs of the therapy or the analysis. This is very evident in Wolberg's writing (1945), and Schneck (1965) makes the following comment regarding depth:

> ... the increasingly accepted view among hypnotherapists [is] that the usual concept of trance depth based on descriptive phenomena alone must give way to a more psychologically dynamic view of depth in terms of emotional involvement of the patient in the trance state itself and in the psychological content of the hypnotic setting. The latter involvement may obtain even when this setting is described in traditional terms as light or medium. The hypnosis may be viewed as deep if significant emotional involvement is present.

Schneck and Wolberg have contributed significantly to the literature. Their comments help to demonstrate the different emphases that have been laid down by various students of the subject.

Kline (1963) too reminds us of the need to be aware of the regressive components in hypnosis when using it clinically, and encourages increased attention to the interaction process rather than the behavioral responses alone, in order to shed light on the essential nature of hypnosis and help in expanding its therapeutic applications.

The majority of other authoritative clinical comments regarding the use of hypnosis in psychiatry have followed the lines indicated by the authors quoted above. This has come about as a result of the importance of the transference in psychoanalytically oriented therapy, and as an attempt to balance the attention to behavioral responses and descriptive phenomena that prevails in experimental work. The view espoused in this book favors the development of as much valid measurement as the clinical situation can tolerate, measurement of subjective experience as well as behavioral response. At the present state of our knowledge we recognize that hypnosis neither appears to be a single process, nor does it seem to be governed by the all-or-none principle. Dialogue and a spirit of tolerance should prevail among those interested in understanding it, regardless of the divergent positions from which we approach it. I must add that, for myself, I find it difficult to defend the use of a special term like hypnosis in the continuing absence of a way to differentiate that concept from an event that merely combines a marked transference with a strong motivation to cooperate and regress constructively. A greater emphasis on the study of the trance experience and associated clinical behavior will increase our understanding of it and pave the way to improved treatment methods. The following chapters will, I hope, illustrate the point.

ERICKSON

Before leaving this section on the psychiatric use of hypnosis, it must be stated that no consideration of hypnotherapy is adequate without reference to the phenomenal achievements of Milton Erickson, whose therapeutic interventions with hypnosis have become legendary. He is widely acknowledged as one of the great practitioners of medical hypnosis, and an authority on techniques of induction. He has explored the possibilities and limits of the hypnotic experience, and investigated the nature of the relationship between hypnotist and subject. He has a unique approach to psychotherapy that he combines with hypnosis, often in the absence of formal induction procedures. As so often happens with charismatic leaders, to his followers must fall the task of separating in his procedures that which is part of a system, and that which is part of the man. Those interested in traveling a fascinatingly instructive clinical course involving hypnosis should not fail to read the reports of his work (Haley, 1967).

CHAPTER 5

Clinical Behavior and Hypnotizability:

PART I

There is little certain evidence regarding the hypnotizability of neurotic and psychotic patients. Results with psychotics are somewhat contradictory; and findings generally have suggested that normal subjects are more hypnotizable than neurotics, whereas among the neurotics those who are hysterical are more hypnotizable than those who are not (Ehrenreich, 1949; Hilgard, 1965). This assertion that normals are presumed to be more hypnotizable than hysterical patients is somewhat puzzling if compared with the comments of the late nineteenth century, when specific clinical pictures were regarded almost as evidence of marked hypnotizability. Different diagnostic criteria at this time could partially account for the discrepancy. However, the persistently imprecise definitions of clinical terms such as hysteria and neurosis, the paucity of acceptable hypnotizability ratings in most clinical work, and evidence of the casual diagnosis of hypnosis in some clinical reports continue to cloud the issue. The disappointing results in the use of hypnosis to help suggest away psychiatric symptoms have added to the confusion. It is a short, even if illogical, leap to assume that the patient is not hypnotizable when hypnosis fails to bring about symptomatic improvement.

We do well to examine recent opinion more carefully, while we also revisit experiences and views that prevailed throughout the last century and in the early part of this one. In doing so, we will find it difficult to ignore the observations of those earlier clinicians and their conviction that specific clinical conditions were associated with marked hypnotizability and were successfully treated by hypnosis—or animal magnetism. Granted the need to be circumspect when considering the evidence for their conclusions, it still should be recognized by us that they were enticed into assuming an affinity between some psychopathological states and hypnosis for good reason. We might ultimately be tempted to do so, too, if we make our observations freely, without first refining them through our favorite conceptual grid.

It will be remembered that in the eighteenth century the Marquis de Puységur (1784), a follower of Mesmer, was the first to describe the resemblance of behavior in the deeply magnetized state with its subsequent amnesia to somnambulism, the act of sleepwalking. Somnambulism was not the only clinical condition seen to resemble the experience of magnetism. According to Ellenberger (1970), it was not long before other clinical conditions showing close affinities to somnambulism were classified with it in a group sometimes called magnetic diseases. These included lethargy, a deep and prolonged sleep at times appearing as death; and catalepsy, which is dominated by a passive and total acceptance of postures imposed on the limbs and body by the manipulations of others or by chance. These conditions, bearing traces of suggestibility and the histrionic, were seen to have characteristics that appeared in the magnetized or hypnotized state, and could be artificially produced through hypnotic maneuvers. Ecstasy and ecstatic visions were also subsequently included as were multiple personalities and fugues.

HYSTERIA

This whole fascinating group of clinical pictures dominated by the bizarre and the dramatic, by rapid changes and multiplicity of forms, came to be included in the category of hysteria. The ease with which they were reproduced in hypnosis and modified by suggestions in hypnosis persuaded Charcot (1886) and later Janet (1907) to recognize them as a result of the same pathological process, albeit Charcot emphasized the physiological and Janet the psychological. In preparing to offer his personal opinion, Janet commenced by asking, "Is this hypnotism something distinct from hysteric somnambulism? Is it something peculiar, an abnormal state independent of hysteria?" He then proceeded to supply five principal reasons for his opinion that they are the same. First, he believed that considered in itself the hypnotic state never has any character that cannot be found in natural hysterical somnambulism. Second, he considered subjects in whom hypnosis could be induced to be mostly hysterical patients who have had somnambulism in some form or other, or who have presented other hysterical symptoms. He believed that they all demonstrated the mental state characteristic of hysteria. Third, he believed that subjects troubled with diseases other than hysteria are not hypnotizable, and that one will never be able to reproduce in them a real somnambulic state with complete consecutive amnesia. Fourth, he believed that a subject whose hysteria decreases, who moves toward recovery and whose mental state changes, ceases to be hypnotizable. Fifth, he believed that the two states are so analogous to each other that you can pass from the one to the other by imperceptible transitions. In summary he commented that there is no reason for making special place for the hypnotic state; it is somnambulism analogous to the naturally occurring condition, and differs from it only in that it is produced artificially instead of developing spontaneously.

Janet's emphasis on the identical nature of the two experiences; his all or none approach to both, ignoring the possibility of degrees of hypnotic responsivity, degrees of hysterical symptomatology, and degrees of relatedness; his conviction that subjects troubled with diseases other than hysteria are not at all hypnotizable; and his belief that those in whom the hysteria disappears cease to be hypnotizable, capture the sweeping quality of his conclusions. This in turn has drawn an emphatic response from his critics, but it is likely that they, too, have overreacted to the extent that his careful observations seem to have been ignored, let alone his interpretations rejected.

Even in a climate inhospitable to Janet's ultimate conclusions, hysterical patients have been considered to be more hypnotizable than other neurotic patients, and psychotic patients have been viewed by many as either difficult to hypnotize or unhypnotizable. Furthermore, observations by others (Sutcliffe and Jones, 1962) confirm that hypnosis has beeen used clinically to gain access to the dissociated states that occur with fugues and alternate personalities. Although these observations are in keeping with what Janet reported, they lack the wide sweep of his conclusions.

There are several clinical pictures that seem to resemble events in hypnosis, and to share the mechanisms that operate in hypnosis. They include cases of multiple personality, fugues, hysterical behavior, hysterical symptoms, phobic behavior, and an unusual syndrome related to an identifiable configuration of personality traits, described as the grade 5 syndrome (Spiegel, 1974). I will commence with a consideration of multiple personality.

FUGUE AND MULTIPLE PERSONALITY

The numerous cases reported during the nineteenth century and since depict very clearly a close association between multiple personality and hypnotizability. In some instances, the alternate personalities were unintentionally evoked during hypnosis; and in many, hypnosis was used to provide access either to previously unavailable memories of events that occurred during the supremacy of other personalities, or to call forth the other personalities purposefully. The responsivity to hypnotic induction was most impressive in virtually all cases where it was attempted.

Among those cases reported and discussed were some of limited duration involving brief or longer periods of ambulatory automatism and better known as fugues or flights from reality, and others that were increasingly complex cases of enduring and at times perplexing multiple personalities. In the absence of an adequate clinical history, we are often left guessing the psychodynamic etiology of the clinical picture. In several, the use of hypnosis in the treatment and resolution of the problems is dramatic and effective, and although there is as yet no generally accepted explanation of the mechanism sustaining the condition known as multiple personality, any theory that attempts to account for the condition will also have to provide for the effectiveness of the therapeutic hypnotic procedures.

In discussing fugues and some forms of somnambulism, Janet spelled out a series of laws about fugues (Janet, 1907). It should be remembered that although his contribution to the prevailing philosophy of his time was vast, he recognized and declared that he had built on the foundations laid by those who preceded him. In fact, he exhorted students to search for and learn about the achievements of the past in order to define their own direction. Janet's laws conveyed the predominant viewpoint that had grown from several important sources during the latter half of the last century. As fugues and multiple personality are closely related, we may consider Janet's laws of fugues, with minor modifications, to be relevant for both. His observations are noteworthy:

1. During the abnormal state, thoughts other than those that have assumed disproportionate significance and have absorbed all of the subject's attention appear to be suppressed. They are thoughts relating to the former life, the family, the social position, and the personality. Affected persons may assume false names, create for themselves fictitious personalities, and have no memory of their real personality.

2. The recollections of the fugue vanish to an extraordinary extent when the individual is no longer in the abnormal state. The thoughts and

feelings connected with the idea that predominated during the fugue disappear more or less completely.

3. During the state considered as normal, the psychological phenomena that were suppressed during the alternate or abnormal period are recovered. They include recollection of the entire existence, perception of all present occurrences, and a clear idea of identity.

4. The somnambulistic or abnormal state may be artificially reproduced by means of hypnosis, and in this artificially induced state the memory of the first abnormal state reappears entirely.

In the enunciation of his laws Janet again states the case in terms perhaps too fixed for our modern comfort. Today we look for degrees of amnesia or of recollection, and tend to avoid terms such as "entire," "all," and "completely." As we reexamine the case histories of that period we are struck by the importance assigned by those authors to a rigid structure and by their efforts to find it. Prince (1905) in his case report of Sally Beauchamp reveals how the alternate or several personalities were ranked. Schematically, personality A was seen as not knowing of the existence of B but B knew all about A; B knew nothing of the existence of personality C, who in turn knew all about both B and A. A close examination of the details of other case histories fails to support such an established structure, even though the findings vaguely suggest it at times.

Enlightened by an awareness of the importance of the demand characteristics in a situation and of the importance of cultural influences in any epoch, critics have raised questions about the verity of multiple personality. Questioning its existence and independence as a pathological entity, observers have considered other possible explanations. Sutcliffe and Jones (1962) focus on these, in a review of the cases in the literature and a discussion of personal identity, multiple personality, and hypnosis. They draw attention to the high incidence of the diagnosis during the latter part of the nineteenth century when compared with the preceding and succeeding periods, and consider the effects of a diagnostic fashion trend. They examine the part played by a therapist prejudiced in favor of the diagnostic entity, as he proceeds in therapy to shape the clinical picture by his responses to ambiguous comments. They examine it as merely the product of hypnosis because of its frequent association with hypnosis, and also raise the question of its being the result of simulation or pretense.

They then offer the following conclusions:

1. Although some of the cases reported in the literature were probably misdiagnosed as a result of the fashion that had overemphasized the category of multiple personality, many of the cases could not be dismissed as merely wrongly diagnosed.

2. Although multiple personality behavior might have been "shaped" by a prejudiced therapist when the picture developed during the course of treatment, "shaping" required an amenable subject as well as a prejudiced therapist. Furthermore, many of the cases exhibited their first signs of personality alteration without the aid of therapy. Shaping did not therefore fully account for the condition.

3. Although multiple personality cases were produced during hypnosis, there were instances where they arose apart from the hypnotic condition. The category could therefore not be dissolved away in hypnosis. The facility with which multiple personality could be brought about in hypnosis suggested there was something in common between the two. Features of the multiple personality might be indicative of, or coincide with features of the hypnotizable personality.

4. Regarding simulation on the part of the subject, it was felt that deliberate pretense could not be held responsible for multiple personality. Rather, it represented a true delusion on the part of the individual.

5. As a final comment, those authors felt that the contrast between multiple personality and certain behaviors of normal people was probably too strongly drawn. Normals might be expected to exhibit multiple personality behaviors to some degree.

My own experience with a case of multiple personality to be described shortly illustrates several of the conclusions reached by Sutcliffe and Jones. There was clear evidence of her marked hypnotizability and the separate existence of a portion of her personality. The latter was acknowledged by her before any clinical investigation had begun. Regarding the shaping of the clinical picture, the strong impression was gained that treatment procedures could readily have exaggerated the split in the personality, or have minimized it. Other authors have also made this observation (Bowers *et al.,* 1971).

CASE HISTORY I

Martha and Harriet

A thirty-six-year-old married woman, Martha, was referred for psychiatric assistance in evaluating her puzzling physical symptoms, and because she herself, at the prompting of her husband, wanted help in understanding an angry voice that spoke out of her mouth periodically, offending those around her with insults. She claimed no knowledge of the source of the voice, an inability to control it, and no responsibility for the utterances.

The physical symptoms had been present in varying degrees for the previous three months, and included general malaise, headaches, pain in her back, a swollen painful right leg, and an inconsistent inability to move either of her lower limbs, to stand or to walk. The symptoms had fluctuated in their intensity since their onset shortly after the patient was a passenger in a car that was involved in a collision. She was not obviously injured at the time of the accident, and was admitted to a hospital for the first time a few weeks after it had happened, where she was thought to be suffering from thrombophlebitis. Her discharge after a few weeks was succeeded by her remaining in bed at home, increasingly dependent on the nursing care provided by her husband. With little or no response to bed rest and administration of anticoagulant therapy, she was readmitted for a second time and referred shortly thereafter for a psychiatric consultation.

It is of interest to note that examination of her previous records in other hospitals revealed that during the previous six years she had undergone a surgical procedure in which her inferior vena cava had been tied off to control multiple emboli, and she had had a hysterectomy and other surgical procedures. She had had brief admissions to another hospital for investigation of different symptoms and had paid numerous visits to its emergency ward for minor ailments. On each visit and admission her complaints appear not to have been completely explained, objective findings were equivocal, and the medical opinions recorded were frequently perplexed.

When first interviewed psychiatrically by our consulting team, she was in a wheelchair, her miserable and dejected posture accentuated by a scarf amply wound around her neck in an attempt, she explained, to oppose the pressure of a voice inside her moving up into her mouth. In addition to the physical symptoms that had led to her admission, she complained of a voice periodically insulting those around her. She would have no recollection of most of its statements, but would find herself having to explain them or deal with the consequences. Regarding her physical complaints, she described an inability to walk or even stand with confidence because her legs felt numb, and because she was in pain, and weak.

Reporting the constant struggle to keep the voice down inside of her, she was encouraged in the interview to permit it to emerge, reassured that we were confident of being able to deal with the remarks that would be made. After cautioning us about the unattractiveness of those remarks, she closed her eyes and for about sixty seconds grimaced, tensed her muscles, and jerked her limbs. She then opened her eyes and angrily asked why we were staring at her. Her demeanor had dramatically altered from one of dejection to one of hostile assertiveness. She explained that her name was Harriet, and that she was weary of Martha's constant complaints, illnesses, religious commitments, and churchgoing. She criticized her for wanting people to approve of her constantly, and for acquiescing to her husband who objected to smoking, dancing, and drinking, although previously he himself had drunk excessively. He had been persuaded by Martha in recent years to follow a righteous course, and having made the switch, had become much more conscientious than she was. Harriet attributed Martha's constant illnesses to her having to behave appropriately all the time, and somewhat arrogantly referred to the fact that she, Harriet, was well, had no pain, and was able to walk perfectly well. With encouragement, she then demonstrated this by standing up, declaring that she felt like dancing. She then walked across the room and returned to her wheelchair.

In answer to questions, she related that she had been a childhood friend of Martha, that she had become ill and died, and that she had then become a part of Martha. The age at which this had occurred was reported initially as four years, and on subsequent occasions as six and five. She felt that although she was gaining power, Martha was still able to maintain control. She believed that Martha did not know of her (Harriet's) origins, felt it would be inadvisable for her to know, and claimed that although Martha was often unaware of her actions, she, Harriet, was more or less constantly aware of Martha's thoughts and behavior. After half an hour of this sort of revelation, Harriet was persuaded reluctantly to return to where she came from and permit Martha to reappear. The transition was again accomplished by means of eye closure, tension, twitching movements of the limbs for about a minute, at the end of which period we were greeted in an unusually friendly manner by Martha with a sheepish apology for having fallen asleep during our discussion.

After an explanation to her that hypnosis was at times of value in resolving problems like hers, her hypnotizability was assessed using the Eye Roll Levitation Method (Hypnotic Induction Profile). Her response was immediate and dramatic, earning a maximum rating. In a subsequent interview she very convincingly demonstrated a negative hallucination (following a posthypnotic suggestion that she would not be able to see a member of the company in the interviewing room until a specific signal occurred) and was capable of age regression to infancy, experiencing the events most realistically and showing considerable emotion as she did so.

She was interviewed on seven subsequent occasions, her husband was interviewed, and her personal history was reconstructed with gaps and inconsistencies, as she was unable to recall all the relevant periods of her past. She was the fourth of eight siblings born and raised on a farm in the South. Her childhood was strict, with religion playing an important role. Memories of her childhood and age regression to early childhood were associated with deeply sad feelings that were not clearly accounted for. Very little information about the members of her immediate family was offered. She claimed to have worked on the farm from the age of nine years, and to have given birth to a baby girl as the result of a rape when she was sixteen years old. The daughter was twenty years old at the time of the interviews, herself now the mother of an infant and living near the patient. At the age of eighteen she moved north with her family and later had settled in Massachusetts. About the age of twenty-five she lost a newborn infant. She remembered being grief-stricken at the time and admitted to having taken infants from baby carriages left outside stores, with only very dim memories of the details. Her late mother had told her husband that the patient had been in a hospital on one occasion because of a nervous breakdown, and the patient believed, although she was not certain, that it may have followed the loss of her child. She claimed to have been aware of the extraneous voice within her from the age of twenty, and her husband, an apparently reliable man, claimed to have known that she was occasionally bothered by it when he first met her some ten years prior to her interviews with us.

Their marriage of six years was marked initially by considerable party-going and drinking, which he had now foregone at her insistence, and which had been replaced by regular attendance at religious services. Although he made no specific mention of the fact, it is clear from the examination of her medical records that the serious physical symptoms leading to major surgery had commenced about the time of her marriage. In recent years her life had seemed to be marked by a sense of loneliness and relative isolation when her husband was away at work. She attended church services regularly, sang in a church choir, and sewed clothes for herself and others in the church community. She had little or no contact with her siblings, and her parents had died prior to her marriage.

Clinical Course

During the course of the seven interviews, some of which took place after her discharge from the in-patient service because of the marked improvement in her physical symptoms, efforts were made to reconcile the differences between Martha and Harriet. The interviews were spent initially addressing one or the other, attempting whenever possible to convey the impression that they were in reality inseparable. The induction of hypnosis was used to strengthen suggestions that the different wishes of each were reconcilable, and was also employed to gain access to Harriet and to forgotten memories. Early in the treatment program both personalities agreed to cooperate and to try and accept and live with the other's contradictory wishes. On each succeeding interview the differences in their manner of speaking and interacting were less noticeable. They gradually became more like each other. On one occasion Martha's mixed feelings in the transference were used to illustrate to her that she could entertain both warm and hostile feelings toward another person simultaneously, and that many fine and successful people often did just that. It is always difficult to evaluate the effectiveness of various therapeutic techniques and maneuvers, but it seemed that in the three interviews that followed the discussion of ambivalence her mood was decidedly brighter. She then spoke convincingly of how she had come to recognize that Harriet was really a deep part of her mind, and not another person. Because she continued to remain symptom-free, the therapy aimed at resolving the alternate personality was ended, and plans were drawn up for her to be supported when necessary in the out-patient clinic. She reported twice within the following three months and since that time has attended the emergency ward once or twice a year for minor physical ailments.

A review of this case history in the light of the conclusions drawn by Sutcliffe and Jones follows:

1. There was little in the diagnostic milieu that favored the creation of the multiple personality. Although the presence of a voice inside or outside of a patient is usually considered a sign of schizophrenia, that diagnosis was never considered in this case by any of the four experienced psychiatrists and clinical psychologists who interviewed her. Her history of puzzling physical symptoms and her behavior during the interviews were more typically those of the classic hysterical patient. She also was clearly depressed.

2. As the picture of the multiple personality was in evidence years before her interviews with us, it clearly was not shaped by events in our interviews. We cannot, it is true, be certain that her previous psychiatric contacts might not have influenced her behavior somewhat. We have very little useful information about that period, but the gaps she reports in her memory of that time and of other periods in her life are similar to the blocks of amnesia that are prevalent in the histories of others who have presented with multiple personalities.

Whether or not our interviews with her influenced the nature of her symptoms should also be considered. Although we assumed from the first encounter that the conflicting parts of her personality were reconcilable and ultimately would be, we initially addressed one or other part in keeping with her presentation of herself as two personalities. It seemed reasonable to utilize the avenues of approach that were available in order to gain the ultimate end, which was fusion, rather than to insist from the outset that she was one person and was expected immediately to function as such. It was implied, however, that she eventually would. When she on occasion talked of both Martha and Harriet simultaneously in the third person, even though she was ostensibly one or the other at the time, we did not assume there was yet a third personality to contend with. One cannot but ponder what the effect might have been had we have asked her at those times whether we were now addressing a third personality.

We at no point interacted with her as if we assumed a rigidly structured relationship between the two personalities, or as if her comments about the relationship were binding. There were several inconsistencies that we overlooked in the interests of the final outcome. She had said, for instance, that although Martha knew very little about Harriet's existence, she, Harriet, knew everything about Martha. At one interview, when the physical medicine personnel who had been treating the physical symptoms were present, as Martha she recognized them but failed to do so when she was Harriet. There were also inconsistencies in her reports about the ages at which Harriet died and when her voice first became apparent, and also in the way in which she experienced these events in age regression.

3. There was no evidence of hypnosis prior to the onset of her symptoms, and neither she nor her husband recalled her having been exposed to hypnosis previously. However, her very dramatic response to hypnosis was most impressive. Hypnotic induction by the interviewers was used at times to gain access to forgotten memories, and at others to make contact with the alternate personality. It was also noteworthy that in her voluntary transition from one personality to the other, she displayed a determined refocusing of attention, much like a subject experiencing hypnotic induction. The refocusing was embedded in a ritual of grimacing and muscle twitching, the origins of which we can only guess.

4. Regarding the question of simulation, there seemed little doubt that although the patient's delusion about her two personalities was malleable to an extent and open to some influence, she was caught up in a false perception rather than in a game of pretense. It would be difficult to accept that she consciously and purposefully set out to deceive others into believing what she herself did not. The analogy of secondary gain might be usefully employed here to amplify the last comment. Although we recognize that secondary gain can unconsciously account for the perpetuation of symptoms, we do not equate its presence with malingering, which is deliberate deception.

5. We must note how the sharp lines of demarcation between the personalities faded as the underlying conflicts were attended to, reminding us that multiple personality behavior might represent a difference in degree rather than in kind when compared with other neurotic, or even normal behavior.

One question arises directly out of J. Hilgard's finding (1970) that an unexpectedly large number of very hypnotizable subjects report imaginary playmates in childhood. We had no way of knowing with certainty whether Harriet had in fact existed in reality. Given J. Hilgard's work, we should wonder whether Harriet was not, from the very outset, the product of a richly imaginative mind.

CASE HISTORY II

Hysterical Fugue

A twenty-nine-year-old black male was brought to the emergency ward of a city hospital in a police ambulance, following a fall down a flight of stairs in his place of work. He had lain, apparently concussed, for several minutes after the fall and when roused could recall nothing of his identity or his past. He complained of a diffuse headache, tenderness over the back of his neck, and an inability to tolerate bright light.

When examined in the emergency ward he appeared initially to have a left hemiparesis and impaired sensation on the left side although his deep tendon reflexes were present and equal bilaterally, his plantar responses were normal, and there was no evidence of any bruising or injury to his head, body, or limbs apart from a soft tissue swelling around his right elbow. Observation of the neurological state over the ensuing two hours revealed a changing picture with each examination and the ultimate disappearance of any weakness or impaired sensation in his limbs. He continued, however, to appear to know nothing of his identity, his family, his work, or his past. When first seen in psychiatric consultation he was lying on the examining couch, moving his limbs in a flail-like fashion and displaying mostly sclera as he rolled his eyes upward and moved them from side to side. When quieted down he could give no account of himself whatsoever other than that he had found himself at the foot of the stairs in a building, in the midst of a group of people he failed to recognize, and that the ambulance ride to the hospital had been a bumpy one. He was slightly perturbed by questions about himself, his family, and his work, which he was unable to answer.

First his employer and then his wife arrived at the hospital to provide the following information: Immediately prior to his falling down the stairs, he had been interviewed for about an hour by the representative of his former employers who were threatened by the loss of a few thousand dollars as a result of the patient's alleged mishandling of funds. He had worked for only a short period of time for his present employer. According to his wife who had known him for ten years, he had had an unstable work record as a result of his erratic behavior and his proclivity for borrowing company funds. He also tended to place himself in awkward positions by attempting to hold more than one job, committing himself to one or the other beyond his capacity, and then creating pandemonium by withdrawing at a critical point in time. One company had apparently set up an expensive sales program with him as the key person. After considerable expenditure by the firm, the patient grew anxious and withdrew with no explanation to his employers, who lost what they had invested in the program and were forced to discharge several employees. On most occasions he would develop a warm social relationship with the people he worked for, and had held some of his jobs for two years or more.

Although their marriage had been strained by his unreliability and the need for his wife or her father to come to his assistance on several occasions, he was considered by her to be a good and loving husband and father. They had been married for eight years and had two young sons.

His father was a skilled artisan, somewhat passive, who rarely played a part in his life. His mother was a large and very controlling woman, who had objected to his marriage because she felt he was too young. He had three sisters younger than he. After graduating from high school, he had worked as an office clerk, and later in different sales jobs.

On two occasions since his marriage he had been referred to a psychiatric clinic for his tendency to complicate his life by unnecessary involvements and his repeated ingenuous and minor frauds. Treatment had lasted no longer than a few weeks on each occasion when he lost interest. His physical health had been good. He had, however, had a loss of consciousness following a fall several years prior to this admission, at which time he had spent a week in the hospital. The exact nature of that episode was unclear.

During the psychiatric consultation, having failed to provide any information on his past, he was told to roll his eyes up, to close them, to breathe deeply, hold it, breathe out, relax, imagine he was floating, and then feel his hand and forearm become as light as a feather and float upward into an upright position. Within seconds of this instruction his whole arm was suspended midair as he lay motionless, waiting, I believe, for the next instruction. He was then regressed in time, and referred to business difficulties that he had experienced earlier that day and in recent weeks, which he preferred not to discuss. As the age regression was pushed further he recounted earlier events in his life, reaffirming some of the information we had already gained from his wife and employer. When the age of sixteen was reached he petulantly refused to discuss the events. At the age of five he found himself looking at twenty-two steps leading upstairs, while he was being beaten by his mother with a flyswatter. He became extremely upset by the memory of that experience. The years were then rapidly retraced back to the present. He was told that he would remember whatever would be comfortably tolerated by him, and the hypnosis was terminated.

Clinical Course

Having been admitted to the hospital for observation and further neurological investigation, if necessary, he was seen in psychiatric interviews almost daily for the following week. After the initial interview including age regression he displayed an increasing, if inconsistent, awareness of his past, and by the fourth day of his admission was able to discuss his most recent and very clumsy financial entanglements, which consisted largely of taking sums of money on the unrealistic assumption that he would soon be able to replace them. The events of his past were neither dramatically or clearly recalled; the memory of them seemed to seep in slowly, and in blocks. Although hypnosis was used to gain access to them, there appeared to be no logical sequence to the order of their appearance, and the impression was gained that occasionally what was clearly recalled one day was less vividly remembered the next. He volunteered that his peeks at the past were painful and made him draw back.

He recounted being severely punished and beaten as a small boy by his mother, but protected and charmed by a kindly grandmother who lived in an upstairs apartment, which was reached by a flight of twenty-two stairs. He would try to spend time with her as frequently as he could, especially when in trouble, and was noticeably emotionally stirred when he remembered the warm relationship and pet name with which he used to summon her. He described himself as very prone to spinning yarns about himself and easily able to imagine himself in important and heroic positions. At those times he saw himself as two people. He told lies and wondered simultaneously why he was lying. He knew that he was successful in winning friends and influencing others.

During the interviews his responsivity to other factors in hypnosis were assessed. In addition to the impressive responses to sensorimotor suggestions and age regression, he produced negative hallucinations and scored well on challenge items such as the handclasp, during which he was increasingly incapable of separating his fingers, the harder he tried to do so.

Once his memory had returned seemingly fully, discussion in the last two interviews prior to his discharge led to a consideration of the reasons for his loss of memory and the mechanics of it. He understood that it was an escape from a very uncomfortable and unpleasant reality. He talked of his inclination to escape into flights of fantasy in which he was usually the hero. While pondering *how* it happened, he recalled vividly—for the first time since his childhood, he claimed—how he had coped with the numerous beatings he received as a child. His mother would frequently threaten and beat him with a flyswatter. He remembered that to him it seemed as if he turned a switch somewhere within himself as the punishment began. This helped him block out the feelings and make it painless. He had no recollection of how he had learned to do this, or of anyone instructing him in it. He then excitedly remembered how a blow to his head from a swinging beam on one occasion was rendered painless by him when he "turned the switch inside" as he saw the beam approaching.

Once the members of his family and he had reconciled themselves somewhat to the events that had taken place, he was discharged to the care of his local community mental health center with a plan for continued family support and help in finding other employment. Neurological investigation, including a cerebrospinal tap, brain scan, and electroencephalography, had failed to reveal any identifiable organic pathology, and he was discharged with the diagnosis of hysterical amnesia one week after his admission. Contact with the mental health agency six months later revealed that the family situation had further improved during the week he remained with them, at which point he left to take a job.

A year after his discharge from the hospital he was invited to return to report his progress. He had made a success of his new job of being responsible for over twenty sales representatives. He had also taken on a second job four nights a week as a barman in an exclusive club. Concerned about dishonest practices among his fellow workers there, he had found himself rapidly involved at one stage in gang rivalry that sounded like a movie script. His wife confirmed that fear of retaliation had forced the family to move out of their home for a month. About a year later he and his wife requested an appointment to discuss his ouster from the firm that had initially welcomed and promoted him. His honesty had not been impugned. From their account it appeared that he had become the victim of his own unrealistic planning and credulity.

Discussion

A review of this case report raises several questions:

1. He claimed a total amnesia for events prior to finding himself on the stairway landing, but retained his full knowledge of the English language and the significance of his office building, the ambulance ride, and

the hospital. The nature of the amnesia was such that he could remember the language symbols but had blocked out all associations leading to the situations in which he had learned them. This inconsistency did not seem to bother him. In some case reports, notably that of Reverend Hanna, described initially by Sidis and Goodhart (1905), the amnesia was reported as total, and the patient assumed the global ignorance of the newborn, including the inability to talk. It is well known that hysterical symptoms follow no anatomical or physiological consistency. The finding that the patient was in no way upset by the illogic of retaining his knowledge of speech while losing all knowledge of his past reminds us of the illogic described in hypnotic trance, where inconsistencies are comfortably tolerated. We might consider this as adding to the support of the opinion, firmly held and then questioned, that there is a similarity between hysterical symptoms and hypnosis.

2. He talked of seeing himself at times as two people, deeply involved in lying and simultaneously wondering why he lied. He could discuss his withdrawal from painful memories of the truth, and his flights into fantasy in which he was the hero, with the objectivity of a second person. The question is raised whether this experience of judging and being judged simultaneously is qualitatively different from the interaction between the alternate persons in multiple personality. One recognizes, too, that it resembles the kind of self-examination that is an everyday occurrence in the lives of normal people. This seems to support the assertion of Sutcliffe and Jones (1962) that the contrast between multiple personality and certain behaviors of normal people is generally too strongly drawn.

3. Nine years prior to this event he had been in the hospital for concussion following a fall. We have no way of knowing whether he had been concussed severely enough at that time to warrant a week in hospital, or whether that event had elements similar to those we were witnessing on this occasion.

4. He was consistently remarkably responsive to hypnotizing procedures displaying evidence of a somnambulistic response. He denied any previous experience with hypnosis and this was confirmed by his wife. Despite the defensive nature of his amnesia, he moved rapidly on our first meeting into a pattern of behavior identical with what we consider hypnotic behavior, and within a minute or two of claiming amnesia for his past, began to recount incidents in it. It is this immediate trust coupled with his conscious concern about his misdemeanors that identify his behavior as being different from that of the psychopath. Furthermore, his problems were not all due to his acts of dishonesty, which, unlike those of the psychopath, had a childlike and dream-fulfilling character. A not in-

considerable share was due to his unrealistic commitments and impractical promises from which he was later forced to back away, or which led him into dangerous situations without any real chance of reward. The readiness with which he was persuaded by his own imaginings, the illogic of his schemes, his flexible identity, and his preparedness to trust have their counterparts among the hallmarks of the hypnotic experience. Hypnosis was readily entered by him on each of the several occasions that it was applied, and easily integrated into the clinical interaction and the treatment. It is questionable whether the manifestations of this patient's psychopathology can be considered apart from his marked hypnotizability. The ways in which denial prevails in a negative hallucination and in hysterical amnesia are strikingly similar.

THE GRADE 5 SYNDROME

Consideration of this case leads directly to a discussion of the grade 5 syndrome (Spiegel, 1974). Spiegel uses this term to describe behavior in a group of highly hypnotizable persons who tend to exhibit a clinically identifiable configuration of personality traits. The descriptive title reflects the very high score they attain on the Hypnotic Induction Profile (HIP). Although they are the same group described by previous authors as somnambules, Spiegel has redirected our attention to them, and has added to our understanding of them by recording their behavioral characteristics in the absence of hysterical symptoms and when not in hypnosis.

As indicated above, their scores are consistently very high on the HIP. They display a trust and faith that go beyond reasonable limits, and even tend to suspend critical judgment. They affiliate extremely readily with new events, and tend to have a relatively telescoped time sense focused almost exclusively on the present and not on the past or future. This enables them to disregard the lessons of past experience and the implied warnings of the future. They can be strikingly unaware of even extreme logical incongruity. They have excellent memories capable of total recall, which is evidenced by their rich responses in age regression. They have an intense capacity for concentration, and despite their surface malleability, tend to cling to certain ideas or behavioral patterns that are of deep importance to them. Because of the contradictions in their makeup, they easily experience role confusion.

He reminds us that the group comprises not more than 10 percent of the population, and that although these features are most obvious in those who score at the levels of grade 5 on the HIP, they are not exclusive to the most hypnotically responsive group. They appear to taper off as hypnotic responsivity decreases to the grade 3 level. He notes further that he is discussing the characteristics of individuals who have presented themselves for psychiatric treatment; some of their characteristics may or may not be as evident among those highly hypnotizable subjects who do not seek psychiatric help.

Recognition of the grade 5 syndrome provides another context in which to view the apparent relatedness of psychopathology to marked hypnotizability. Spiegel has provided the modern impetus for a reexamination of that relationship, and has enlivened the clinical scene with his rich observations. An examination of the history of Case II in the context of Spiegel's description adds to our understanding of that patient's immensely trusting, illogical, and erratic behavior. It also leads to a better appreciation of what terms such as "somnambulism" and "classical hysterical symptoms" imply.

CHAPTER 6

Clinical Behavior
and Hypnotizability:

PART II

The clinical behavior of the two patients presented in the previous chapter was dramatic, as were their responses to hypnosis. The observation that the abnormal clinical states and the behavior in hypnosis were closely related in each case—if not at times even identical—cannot be avoided, even though the meaning of that resemblance is not yet quite clear. It might be helpful to our understanding of the relationship between clinical behavior and hypnotizability were we now to consider a few less dramatic clinical examples and the extent to which *they* are associated with hypnotizability. A consideration of other clinical behavior might reveal patterns that are less remarkable than multiple personality and hysterical fugue but nonetheless unusual, and perhaps predictably associated with high (for the most part) rather than very high hypnotic responsivity. This is in keeping with the accepted fact that hypnosis is not an all-or-none phenomenon, and that hypnosis is experienced to varying degrees by different persons on different occasions.

In the cases that follow, one is struck by the episodic nature of the disturbed behavior, its limited duration, and its repeated occurrence. Furthermore, during the episodes the patients appear to be impervious to logical argument and overwhelmed by the events, which run a relentless course, which are clearly ego-alien, and which are maladaptive even though some secondary gain might accrue. Again it is difficult to avoid

recognizing the similarities between such events and the seemingly autonomous, illogical, disconnected preoccupation in the behavior of hypnotized
persons. This idea that spontaneous trancelike events can occur in the clinical context is supported by work with healthy subjects in the experimental
sector, where subjective experiences presumably related to hypnotizability
have been reported (Shor, 1960; Ås, O'Hara, and Munger, 1962).

CASE HISTORY III
A Fear of Driving

A rather plain and unimaginatively dressed forty-year-old married
mother of four children sought help for incapacitating panic attacks that
had increasingly bothered her for approximately six months. Although attacks of intense anxiety were not entirely new to her, the disruptive effect
of these recent symptoms had left her incapable of running her home or of
attending adequately to the needs of her children.

The attacks of panic occurred primarily when she was driving a car,
but also appeared on a few occasions when she was a passenger or when
she was taking coffee with friends. The more she grew to expect the symptoms while driving, the more frequently they occurred at home on the
mornings she was scheduled to do so, even before she entered her car. On
occasions the panic occurred without any apparent precipitant. During the
attacks she would suddenly feel different, and the world around her would
appear to be strange and flat as if it were a two-dimensional picture. She
would be aware of a very rapid heartbeat at those times, and would be
seized with the fear that she would go through the picture to find that
everything had disappeared on the other side, or that she was blind. On
several occasions she had had to draw over to the side of the road to wait
for an attack to pass. This could take from minutes to a half-hour or
more. Although the details of the various attacks might differ somewhat as
might the intensity, the overall picture was one of episodic panic associated with distorted perception. The impact of this was so disorganizing to
the patient that she had found herself avoiding or rearranging car pools,
shopping trips, and even brief social encounters with other mothers over
coffee.

As mentioned previously, panic attacks were not unknown to this patient. This particularly severe phase, present for about six months prior to
her seeking help, had been heralded by a very severe episode that had occurred while driving as a passenger in her husband's car, about the time
they had been negotiating the purchase of their own home. The urgency of
the purchase had resulted from an eviction notice by the former landlord,

who intended rebuilding his property. Although the patient had at first considered the humiliation and chagrin associated with the eviction notice as the cause of her distress, subsequent exploration revealed other more likely factors that will be better considered at a later stage in this report.

She had had a troubled history of similar symptoms since the age of about thirteen years. Although she had experienced a fairly constant level of mild anxiety and discontent for much of her life since that time, the troublesome panic attacks seem to have reached peaks of frequency and discomfort at specific points in her history. At the age of twenty-three she had sought psychiatric help that had continued for a year, but provided little relief. At the age of twenty-six she had again been troubled, and had been trained in special eye exercises, the purpose of which was to correct faulty eye movements held to be responsible for the distorted perceptions. The symptoms had on each occasion abated some when she was given six or seven meprobamate (400 mg) per day.

Closer examination of the history revealed that although she could remember no crisis of symptoms prior to the age of thirteen, she could re-call playing solitary games as a child of about six, in which she could create perceptual distortions. By thinking about them in a specific way, she could cause objects to appear puffed out and fat, or lean and thin. Since that time she could not tolerate complete darkness, and always slept with a night-light. At the age of ten or eleven she had woken in terror on one occasion and confused her dream with reality to the extent that she had run out into the street in her night clothes. As indicated above, the trou-blesome symptoms began when she was thirteen. Spending a night in her girl friend's house at that time, she panicked when she was unable to see her hands in the dark. She recalled struggling through the night in terror lest by morning she would find that she had been blinded. She knew that her mother disapproved of her friend. On another occasion about that time, while in a bowling alley with the same friend and two somewhat older boys, she experienced panic when the world about her began to ap-pear strange and flat. Again she feared the onset of blindness. For a few years after that, she had fairly frequent similar spells lasting from minutes to an hour or more. They were always associated with intense feelings of anxiety, unpleasant cold feelings in the pit of her stomach, some trembling and the thought, repeatedly troublesome, that as she moved through the two-dimensional world she would have no vision on the other side. The episodes interfered with her schoolwork, and during one of them her par-ents were called by the school authorities to take her to the local hospital. She was deeply ashamed by the doctor's diagnosis of anxiety neurosis. At the age of twenty-three, shortly after taking employment in a large commercial firm, the symptoms again became troublesome, precipitated by her trying to focus on the clock in the large hall in which she worked. The recrudescence of the symptoms at the age of twenty-six coincided with the time of her marriage.

Her personal history is interesting and relevant. She was the oldest of three siblings, with two brothers, one seven years younger, and the other ten years younger. At the time of her initial visits to me, her parents were in their mid-sixties, her father an architect and her mother a musician. She was able to recall a distinct change in her life at the time of the older brother's birth that marked the onset of her discontent. Memories prior to that time were vague but pleasant, including the warm recollection of ice-skating with her father, whom, she perceived as friendly and kind but weak and lacking in character in his dealings with her mother. Her parent's marriage had been tempestuous for years, according to the patient, but improved since she had moved out of the house after graduating from college at twenty-three. She related a virtually unending series of tirades against her father and herself by her mother, whose utterances made a deep impact on her. She was told, among other things, that she was the cause of the problems in her parents' marriage, that she was angry and evil, that her mother would have been all right had the patient not been born, and that the hospital must have confused the babies in the nursery and sent home the wrong one. She was also told that she would be returned to the hospital because she was bad.

Her father would not infrequently leave the house at the height of a quarrel with his wife, who would then displace her anger onto the patient with comments such as those just quoted. Through the stages of latency and puberty she felt herself the victim of her mother's fury without ever fully knowing what her alleged wrongdoing was, other than that she disliked and quarreled with the brother she resented. In her view he was clearly the mother's favorite and never the object of her criticism.

Details of the house in which they lived prior to her sixteenth birthday along with many other facts of that period were either remembered with great difficulty or not at all, even though some were recalled under hypnosis. She remembered her low self-esteem and lack of popularity among her peers, her utter defeat in a class election, her struggle to achieve any friendships with other girls and her mother's disapproval of the few that she did persuade to come to her house. To use her own phrase, she felt she was a rotten person.

She recalled that her parents had slept in separate bedrooms for some years prior to her sixteenth birthday; she thought that her father had shared a bedroom with her brothers; and she remained uncertain at the end of her eighteen months of treatment where, precisely, her bed had been for the greater part of puberty and adolescence. She remembered a weekend at about twelve years of age when her mother determinedly left the house, demanding a divorce. The absence was cut short when the patient developed bronchopneumonia. She recalled, too, that her father would not infrequently permit her to do things in opposition to her mother's wishes.

She was forced by her parents to follow the nonacademic courses at high school, despite her expressed wish to attend college. She worked in a junior office role for three years, saved her earnings, and then attended college achieving a BA degree at the age of twenty-three. At twenty-six she married a man five years older than herself. He was an accountant, somewhat passive, but very supportive of her in dealing with her symptoms, in the raising of their four children, and in her interaction with her parents, especially her mother. The success of their sexual relationship fluctuated but was fairly reassuring to both of them.

Clinical Course, Use of Hypnosis, and Psychodynamic Formulation

The direction of the initial interviews constantly returned to the disabling symptoms of panic associated with feelings of depersonalization and derealization. Because of the urgent nature of the symptoms and the long history of perceptual distortion, the suggestion was made that hypnosis might be of value. She had had no experience of hypnosis prior to that time and entertained the generally held misconceptions about it. Her responses to the Eye Roll Levitation Method (HIP) were very good, but not outstanding. She seemed highly hypnotizable with good arm levitation, a positive posthypnotic response, and amnesia for the signal that terminated the posthypnotic suggestion. In her first comment on emerging from the experience, she drew a comparison between her discomfort in the trance and the strange and frightening feelings she had in association with her panic attacks. Subsequent use of the hypnotic trance was directed toward increasing her familiarity with it, and was accompanied by the repeated suggestion that she could and would be comfortable during the event and would learn to use it to hasten her improvement. She gradually acquired the skill of inducing the trance voluntarily, and though reluctant, she practiced on her own at home between her visits to me and learned to deal with the feelings of dissociation with greater confidence. This was reflected in her reactions to the symptoms of derealization and panic, which became less frequent and less overwhelming in the subsequent months as she became accustomed to the similar experience of the trance under controlled conditions.

Hypnosis was also used in the clinical interviews to aid in the recall of the memories of her youth and childhood. As indicated above, this was helpful in exploring the period of her life between the time of the older brother's birth when she was seven and the time she left high school. Among the first fantasies to emerge under hypnosis was one of herself at an unknown age delightedly holding her father's hand. Discussions under hypnosis of how she favored her father in his arguments with her mother made her very uncomfortable. Among the memories she recalled often was that of herself running around the house to escape her mother brandishing a strap.

During the course of the treatment, which consisted of weekly interviews for a period of eighteen months, it became apparent that the phases of acute symptoms occurred at the time of puberty, later when she moved out of her parents' house at the time she began working in a large commercial office, again at about the time of her marriage and now at the age of forty. It is clear that much of her psychopathology was intricately woven into her relationships with her parents and the resultant Oedipal problems. Her mother's near-psychotic outbursts and her father's passive-aggressive approach to the difficulties did much to aggravate the conflicts. In addition, she struggled with a mean and lowered self-esteem with serious questions about her worth and her right to a reasonable marriage and a home in a pleasant suburb. Her clothing and general appearance were not only low-key, they reflected a studied self-effacement.

Her defenses were primarily denial, repression, and dissociation in dealing with her intense feelings of anger, sadness, and guilt. Initially, she not only failed to cope with her feelings but seemed for the most part even not to recognize their existence. As she became increasingly aware of how she handled her feelings, she was able to describe how she would detect her mind "disconnecting" from her body when her feelings became too strong for her to tolerate. Examining her responses to strong negative sentiments within herself, she recalled her mother's repeated admonition in childhood that she was angry and evil, and that a child's duty included respect and love for parents, but never anger. She became aware during treatment, more than ever before, of how much she really craved her mother's praise. When symptoms without an obvious precipitant were closely considered in subsequent interviews, it was discovered that they not infrequently arose in the wake of uncomfortable telephone conversations with her mother, which she had failed to appreciate fully when they were in progress. She discovered, too, that the first severe panic attack that had heralded this present phase of her symptoms had occurred when she and her husband were returning from a visit to her parents who had just given them a sum of money to use as a deposit on their new home. A confused sense of guilt, anger, and entitlement swept over her as she recalled the event. Her recollection of it, after a year of repression, followed her admission in the transference that a part of her secretly believed she was entitled to, and should have, her therapy without having to pay a fee.

Her strengths included a good intelligence, strong motivation and interest in improving her situation, and the tenacity to endure the hardships she encountered on the way. The achievement of her college degree and other special skills bore testimony to this. She had also been fortunate in her choice of a husband who was very supportive and intuitively aware of her needs.

With the passage of the months she had learned to discuss the real issues while the number and intensity of the panic attacks diminished. She worked well in the treatment, examining several of her problems and resolving some of them very satisfactorily. Her sense of self-worth increased as did the quality of the care she gave to her appearance. She talked at times of her surprise at discovering, during the treatment, the extent to which she had played games with her interpretation of sensory stimuli as she was growing up. She recalled how, as an adolescent, she would purposefully concentrate on the physical feelings in her head and body when she was emotionally upset. In this way she had been able to change the sound of voices in her ears so that they sounded flat rather than shrill. This included her own speaking voice as well as her mother's. She remembered that she would think of a sensory distortion, and then experience it. The significance of her preoccupation at age six with having objects around her appear alternately very puffed up or very lean was not discussed with her, but it seems logical to wonder whether this was in some way related to her mother's pregnancy. She had remained convinced since her childhood that the birth of the elder brother had created a major crisis in her life. She seemed to be describing the development of consciously distorted perceptions as a defense.

Discussion

1. While the therapeutic use of hypnosis in this partially successful case history is an interesting aspect that will be developed in a later chapter, the nature of her symptoms, the resemblance of the panic attacks to hypnotic trance, and her childhood games of voluntarily and successfully distorting perception are especially relevant and noteworthy. Her clinical behavior was less dramatic than that reported for the first two cases, and her response to hypnosis was similarly less impressive, but she also volun-

teered that for her the experience of the symptoms and the experience of hypnosis were subjectively similar. The symptoms of dissociation occurred spontaneously when feelings became stressful. It is reasonable to assume from the history that as dissociation had been used repeatedly—and at times consciously to defend against anger, anxiety, sadness, and guilt—it must initially have been, or subsequently been developed as a readily accessible mechanism. Considering how skillful and practiced this patient was since her early childhood in dissociating and distorting perception, one wonders whether she discovered that she had such a special skill, or whether she purposively developed it with practice. In either event, by the time her symptoms appeared in early adolescence, it was established. It is reasonable to ask about the relationship between the ease with which she distorted perception, the overwhelming part played by it in the clinical picture, and the high degree of hypnotizability she consistently demonstrated.

2. While I can claim no immunity from the bias that hounds most observers with a point of view, and conceding that my responses to the material produced in the interviews must have shaped their subsequent content to some extent, the memories of her games of perceptual distortion came as a complete surprise to me. She was excited at the discovery of clues in her past, and of explanations in her own past behavior that could account for her remarkable problems resulting from her perceiving the world in so strange a way. Her description of her head feeling disconnected from her body when she began to grapple with her emotions during an interview was a sincere report of a new observation, and one remarkably similar to that made by subjects trying to describe what they experience in hypnotic trance.

3. Her behavior during the driving panics, probably reinforced by her experience, was to draw over to the side of the road, to concentrate on a single familiar object in her surroundings, and to sit and wait. On one occasion she tried to persuade her husband to take her to the hospital for help. All these responses were based on her knowledge that the episode would end, and that although the two-dimensional world seemed real, it really was not and would pass. This suggests that through it all there was some observing ego, much as a portion of the ego persistently maintains its autonomy even in the midst of a deep hypnotic trance.

CASE HISTORY IV
A Marital Crisis

A thirty-five-year-old European on a study visit to the United States sought help for a crisis in his marriage. He had been married for fourteen years to a woman two years younger than he and had three young children. The crisis was precipitated by his wife's withdrawing her affection during the previous months, refusing sexual intercourse, referring openly to her fantasies about other men, and talking about the advisability of a divorce. Disturbed as he was, the patient found that he grossly aggravated the situation by his apparently uncontrollable responses to her rejection. Although he could cope with the day's activities at work and the family interaction at home fairly successfully, he reacted to her rejection of his advances at night with intense sadness, followed by an overwhelming emotional outburst during which he would weep uncontrollably, plead in a helpless childlike manner, feebly assault her, and on occasions—brandishing a knife—threaten suicide. The episodes would last from a half to a few hours, generally but not invariably ending with her acquiescing to his wishes. Their increasing frequency in the two months prior to his first visit led to his decision to seek psychiatric advice. He described the episodes as being out of his control. He felt he could sense their onset, yet knew that he was incapable of containing them.

The disruptive effect of these outbursts, and the man's subsequent remorse and humiliation can be appreciated only by recognizing how grossly incongruous this behavior was when compared with his achievements, his life-style, and his background. He had outstanding professional accomplishments to his credit and was highly esteemed by his senior colleagues and peers. He was warm, friendly, and well-liked socially, and according to both his wife and himself, he was considerate and effective as a husband and as a father. His self-assured manner as he presented his history contrasted noticeably with the unusual behavior he was reporting. Although their early marriage had been preceded by a somewhat stormy courtship, the years prior to the onset of the present crisis had been relatively smooth.

He was the second of two siblings, with a sister six years older than he. His father had been a successful and wealthy industrialist who had died in his early fifties when the patient was seventeen. His mother was an attractive but rather inept and dependent person who had been overwhelmed by her husband's death. She had remarried a few years later. The patient was visibly moved as he discussed his parents and his childhood, which he remembered as sad and lonely. He felt that his father had demanded unusually high standards from him, and that neither of his parents had been available to him emotionally. He had been raised by a series of governesses, none of whom had had any emotional impact on him as he had continued to crave affection from his mother and approval from his father. His supposedly free hours were filled by private tutors, and while engaged in his studies he frequently heard the adult parties taking place in the house from his room.

Despite his considerable achievement at school, he constantly sensed his father's criticism of him. The home was authoritarian and strict as was the school selected for him to attend. Bullying and bigger schoolmates terrified him as did some of the stricter schoolmasters. Although he claimed he did not want to blame his father, he realized that the man was neither able nor willing to understand his childhood fears. He perceived his mother, despite her fussing over him, as constantly aloof and distant, and although he craved her affection he considered her praise of his scholastic achievements worthless. It was his father's approval he longed for. In retrospect he resented his mother's failure to intercede on his behalf when his study schedule had been made far too rigorous for a child. He believed this to be the consequence of her unquestioning admiration for, and devotion to, her husband without whom she appeared to be helpless.

He suffered frequent attacks of asthma as he grew up. These occurred usually at bedtime and would draw his mother to his side to comfort him. His father rarely, if ever, responded in that fashion. One of his warmer memories of childhood was that of attending a small gym class, where he enjoyed the friendly interest, praise, and attention of the instructor. When reporting his relationship with his father and his grief at the time of his death, he was surprised at the depth of his reaction. He sobbed unashamedly, was bitter at the lack of emotional support he had had from both parents, and felt resentful at the lack of any further opportunity for establishing a better relationship with his father. He recounted that he had dreamed for quite a few years after his father's death that he would return, and had on one occasion sought to communicate with him through the services of a spiritualist.

The bereavement period had been complicated by his mother's overwhelming grief reaction, which had placed an undue burden on him. It was during this time that he met his wife, who was then sixteen. They had a stormy courtship, which ended in marriage when he was twenty-one and she nineteen. She had reached early adulthood with very confused feelings about her parents, who had constantly directed the course of her life, including the choice of a husband whom she claimed she liked but had never loved. She realized that her parents saw in this very eligible, highly intelligent, and affluent young man all the prestige and success that her lackluster academic career had failed to provide. The parents had suffered a dull relationship throughout their marriage with little exchange of affection. Her father had been distant and absorbed by his rather menial work, her mother artistic and temperamental. From the reports of the mother's actions, she seems to have been intensely flattered by the attentions of her daughter's boyfriends, especially our patient. He in turn reacted very positively to the warm support and affection shown him by her. Although he and his wife had had a somewhat rough courtship, there were no emotional outbursts of major proportions. There had been one mention of suicide by him when she talked once of canceling their marriage plans.

Progress after the marriage seemed very satisfactory. She was delighted with her role as a mother, which she occupied increasingly with the birth of her three children. His professional promise more than fulfilled itself with impressive achievements at an early age. Without much warning, after some months in the United States she first disclosed her loss of interest in him, her preoccupation with fantasies of other men, and her decision that were she to remain married it would be only for the sake of the children.

Clinical Course

It became rapidly apparent that no adequate understanding of the crisis would be possible without interviewing his wife, and also discussing it with both of them together. As they were due to return to Europe some months later, the goals of the intervention were necessarily limited. It was important for them both to be able to communicate their needs to each other at this time and to avoid precipitous or hasty decisions while away from their native land. We were not intending to resolve extensive neurotic conflicts. The impact of the increasingly frequent hysterical behavior in the bedroom at night was such that unless attended to, no progress was likely in any area. One episode was of such severity that the wife feared to continue sharing the bedroom with him. His remorse and humiliation were heightened by knowing that his children had overheard that disturbance. He repeatedly referred to the uncontrollable nature of the episodes and to the experience, when they occurred, of feelings of sadness associated with some pleasure. The attention that he gained during these episodes, and the extent to which the threatened loss of his wife and his marriage reactivated the sad and angry feelings associated with the unequal struggle in his childhood to win the affection of either of his parents, were discussed on a few occasions. This had little impact on him emotionally, and contributed little to the improvement of the symptoms.

Because of the apparent autonomy of the episodes, the irrational and inappropriate character of the behavior and the manner in which he appeared to disclaim full responsibility for those actions, hypnosis was mentioned as a possible therapeutic approach to providing some control. He expressed an immediate interest in hypnosis and demonstrated very good response when assessed on the Eye Roll Levitation Method (HIP). Arm levitation, posthypnotic suggestion, and amnesia for the signal to terminate were all present. In addition, after he had been told in a subsequent episode of hypnosis that he would not be able to separate his clasped fingers, he was unable to do so, regardless of how hard he tried. He did not achieve a negative hallucination and fell just short of somnambulism. When in trance, he was readily able to expand on the feelings associated with his hysterical outbursts, and he then vividly recognized the similarity between them and feelings experienced by him in childhood during bouts of uncontrollable behavior. He also then recalled quite spontaneously how between the ages of four and eight he would have uncontrollable tantrums of weeping, fits of laughter, or bouts of terror precipitated by relatively minor stimuli. He had been convinced as a child that he could not control them but simultaneously had recognized in them something of an "act." On one occasion his sister had frightened him by hiding in a closet, and on another he accidentally damaged a valuable chair. He dramatically recalled being roused into a state of increasing terror by those events, a terror that appeared to engulf him, but one that he nonetheless could recognize as not being quite the same as other very fearful experiences.

He was excited by his discovery during the trance, and in subsequent discussions, that his outbursts followed some sort of consistent pattern, and that hypnosis had provided him some access to childhood memories. He displayed considerable skill in learning to induce the trance himself, and found that he was able to prevent the onset of a tantrum by entering a trance and persuading himself to relax when he recognized that he was about to lose control. His confidence grew with the removal of the threat that he would inexorably humiliate himself. Whatever secondary gain he might have achieved from the attention-demanding behavior, he had never doubted that he had much to lose by it nor that it was maladaptive. This symptomatic improvement allowed us to pay more attention to other relevant issues. After a few months they returned to their home country, where they seem to have made a satisfactory adjustment.

Discussion

This case history has not been presented with the intention of emphasizing the therapeutic effectiveness of hypnosis, although there is little doubt that the intervention was useful. It has been reported rather to draw attention, again, to the resemblance between a demanding clinical symptom and hypnotic behavior, and to the high trance capacity consistently shown by the patient. His disclaiming responsibility for the clinical behavior, the perception that it was autonomous, and the ambiguity about controlling it are all reminiscent of comments made about the trance experience. His immediate and emotionally laden recall during his first hypnotic trance of similar previous episodes in childhood adds an interesting dimension to any consideration of the nature of the present symptoms.

While stressing the above, I also recognize that the therapeutic impetus of the supportive relationship in the therapy should not be overlooked. We are obliged to ask whether that relationship was not in itself responsible for the clinical improvement, with hypnosis merely acting as a face-saving device. On the other hand, did hypnosis offer him an effective means of controlling himself? Even though I suspect the latter, I realize that hypnosis could not have been used successfully without the continued support of the therapeutic relationship. Had I have given him instructions in the use of the trance on his own, and told him to practice it and return in three months' time, would he have followed the directions and used it diligently? I am inclined to think not.

Considered further, hypnosis allowed the symptom into the therapeutic hour; it also helped to bring the therapeutic hour to the symptom. In a sense, it made the therapist available to him at the times of his crises.

CASE V

Flight Phobia (1)

A twenty-eight-year-old white married woman requested treatment for "terror" associated with flying. She arrived in the company of her husband, specifically seeking hypnosis for her problem, which consisted of an overwhelming fear, not only when she boarded planes but also when she watched them in flight, that they would explode throwing people out in all directions. She immediately followed with the report that her mother had been terrified of flying all her life, and claustrophobic. She continued that she herself disliked any form of violence and was very disturbed when the news media reported it in any detail.

This concern with violence was immediately smothered by her comments on the extent of her anxiety and its totally immobilizing effect. She was a bright, colorful, and imaginative person who related to the interviewer very warmly even if somewhat anxiously. She recounted how she had never flown in a plane prior to the time of her marriage five years earlier, and that she had flown only once since then. Despite her having been raised in a large city, her mother's great fear of flying had prevented any members of the family from taking air trips. She had been convinced that she would be terrified on a plane before she ever boarded one, but was persuaded by her husband at the time of their marriage that they should fly home from their honeymoon. The experience was a dismal failure as was a repeat flight a year later, which she took in order to prove to herself that it could be done. Her anxiety for a few days prior to the flight had mounted as the time approached for boarding. Once on the plane she was seized by a need to sit as close to the exit as she could, and having done so, was engulfed by a sense of terror that lasted the whole of the trip. She pressed close to her husband for comfort and spent almost the entire journey in tears, clutching his arm, oblivious of anything but her panic. She was inaccessible to logic, was convinced it was all hopeless, and behaved as if catastrophe was imminent. The vivid descriptions of both journeys were provided by the patient and her husband. It is of interest that despite the apparent anguish of the first trip she had attempted a second, and now came for treatment in anticipation of a third. She and her husband had been planning a summer trip to Europe that would be possible in the time available only if they made arrangements to fly.

The patient was the younger child of a couple now in their sixties. Her father was a physician who had agreed throughout his marriage to travel to the various congresses in his field by train, because of his wife's overwhelming anxieties about plane travel. Her mother had had psychological problems for several years and had had several lengthy periods of treatment. From the description, it seemed that she had a hysterical personality and suffered recurrent depressions. The patient was keenly sensitive to the notion of psychiatric treatment, and fearing that she, too, might be handicapped by prolonged emotional illness and lengthy treatment, emphatically preferred the direct removal of her symptoms by means of hypnosis to any other form of therapy. She denied having sought psychiatric treatment in the past, and reported that her one exposure to hypnosis by a dentist several years earlier had failed because she did not want to be hypnotized.

She had graduated from college at the age of twenty-two and had worked as a schoolteacher for a few years. She had married at twenty-three to a professional man ten years her senior. He was good-humored, warmly sympathetic, and protective of her. They had two small children.

Her response to the Hypnotic Induction Profile was impressive. Arm levitation and posthypnotic suggestions were accomplished convincingly and well, and she was amnesic for the signal that terminated the posthypnotic suggestion. She experienced a marked feeling of dissociation in her levitated arm. Subsequent to that test she failed, in hypnosis, to separate her clasped fingers when advised that she would not be able to do so, regardless of how hard she tried. She was not able to achieve a negative hallucination, and though marked, her hypnotizability appeared to fall short of somnambulism. It was agreed that the treatment program would avoid exploration and would be centered on hypnosis.

Clinical Course

She was instructed in how to induce self-hypnosis, and in how to relax deeply and completely during practice sessions at home. At her second appointment she reported considerable success in her exercises, even to the extent of feeling somewhat strange for a few minutes after an especially successful practice. The strategy then woven into the exercises included suggestions that involved an image of floating. She was to think of the plane floating, of herself floating, and if the image of an exploding plane were to impinge on her mind's eye, she was to think of all the passengers floating down to safety. She was able to imagine that the noise at the airport, about which she had concerns, would float over her and leave her undisturbed.

After the second interview she visited the airport in the company of her husband, practiced a hypnotic exercise in the departure lounge, and felt more comfortable about the problem than she had before. She continued to practice at home, to attend interviews for reassurance and updating of the strategy, and to make fairly rapid progress at the airport to the extent of undertaking an hour's flight in the company of her husband after her sixth weekly treatment session. By extending her local flights and visits to the airport, she was comfortable about a flight to Europe at the end of her twelfth visit. According to both the patient and her husband, she accomplished this with far greater ease than either of them had expected.

Her progress in treatment had been temporarily marred after her third treatment by an ambitious excursion onto the open balcony of the air terminal. The noise and proximity to the action upset her deeply, but reassurance on her next visit that she would indeed eventually be able to do an exercise on the balcony, because she was capable of imagining the sound and action floating over her, reestablished the favorable course of treatment. She enhanced her progress by allowing free rein to her imagination, which enabled her—because of the planes' design—to regard those of one airline (which she eventually chose to fly) as "cute with black noses," and those of another that she rejected as resembling sharks.

Discussion

1. The therapeutic progress of this patient cannot be considered without acknowledging her dramatic responses to suggestions made largely when she was hypnotized, but also when she was not in hypnosis. Her ability to disregard distracting thoughts and the even more obtrusive noise of a departing jet when involved in an exercise of hypnosis is noteworthy. She was immediately upset by disappointing experiences and just as rapidly reassured by positive events and comments. Attention should be drawn, too, to the extent that she had been persuaded by her mother's terror of planes to assume an identical fear, until her husband began to encourage her to change.

2. Her interest in undertaking a second flight and her preparation for a third, despite the reported terror of the previous journeys, also raises a question about how convinced she herself was about the panic she experienced. She seems to have recognized that it was generated from within her, and different from the deeply felt terror that one feels realistically when danger is clearly situated in the environment and is in no way embellished by one's imagination, e.g., when threatened with a loaded firearm. It is as if, at some level during her panic states, some awareness of reality persisted.

3. In considering the specific role of hypnosis in her treatment, it should be remembered that she had come specifically for treatment with hypnosis, and was in no way ready to engage in a program of traditional psychotherapy. We must question what her expectations of hypnosis did for her progress in treatment, and what part they played in the therapeutic outcome.

CHAPTER 7

Clinical Behavior
and Hypnotizability:

PART III

In pursuit of a broader understanding of the association between clinical behavior and hypnotizability, we turn now to an examination of patients with puzzling physical symptoms that are poorly explained in pathophysiological terms. Such clinical pictures are generally categorized as hysterical. With the use of that term we are immediately reminded of the conviction of Charcot and then Janet that experiences in hysteria and hypnosis are identical, apart from the former being spontaneous and the latter induced. As stated earlier, the critics in their enthusiasm appear to have rejected not only their interpretations but also their observations. Janet (1901, 1907) described, in great detail, the rapid response of hysterical patients to ideas of pain, discomfort, or disease, and compared their reactions to the marked suggestibility of the hypnotized subject. Even disagreeing with the full extent of Janet's assertions, as one observes the ease and rapidity of the hypnotic response in individuals with marked trance capacity, one has difficulty believing that such a skill would fail to have important clinical consequences, much as would be the case with other unusual skills or deficits. For example, it is generally acknowledged that unusual intellectual skills or limited intellectual ability will both have an effect on how pathology manifests itself and on how it is most effectively modified.

Because of the flexible meaning and imprecise use of terms such as hysterical, conversion, and hypochondriasis, it is useful to note that the clinical problems to be discussed in this chapter include that dramatic, florid, and unexplained symptomatology that commands the attention of the clinician, and directs it to the disabling entities of pain, dysfunction, or limitation of movement. Although these generally defy anatomical or physiological understanding, they tend to be the focus of the clinical interviews, regardless of whether they are described by the patient with concern or with indifference. This differs in many ways from the generally masochistic impression created by patients with hypochondriasis where the prevailing affect is depression, the attitude to the illness one of gloom, and the demanding symptom a long-standing, uninterrupted delusional preoccupation with ill health.

When marked hypnotizability occurs frequently in association with the florid and puzzling symptoms, we cannot avoid questioning what the relationship is. As it is more than likely that individuals who have an unusual trance capacity will respond in terms of this capacity not only following a formal hypnotic induction procedure, we may reflect upon the consequences of such a response should it occur spontaneously and in the context of the doctor–patient relationship. Such a kind and helping authority relationship encourages a passive and regressive response in the patient, while a variety of complex—and from the patient's point of view —quasi-magical procedures are carried out. This situation, loaded with expectancy, is particularly well suited to produce hypnosislike events. Because the physician and the patient both share the need to find an organic explanation for the symptom, a large number of inevitably leading questions are asked in an effort to uncover the nature of the organic pathology. Quite apart from the leading questions, the medical context itself provides a variety of verbal and nonverbal cues that communicate the physician's expectancies and concerns about the patient's illness. It is difficult to ignore the profound suggestive effect likely to be exerted by such cues, often amplified and distorted by the patient's anxiety. Under circumstances such as these, where an altered state of consciousness facilitates the distortion of perception and memory, repeated discussions of puzzling symptoms might take place. It is too much to believe that the symptoms of such individuals fail to be modified by the explicit and implied suggestions provided by the situation, by the questions and explanations exchanged, and by the procedures carried out. It is to be expected that after having had several medical encounters, such patients present with a progressively more complicated picture of physical complaints.

In the cases to be described, where the puzzling nature of the symptoms and the marked hypnotizability are apparent, the possible influence of the medical investigative and therapeutic procedures is difficult to escape.

CASE HISTORY VI
Lower Back Pain

A thirty-three-year-old white married mother of two children was referred for a psychiatric evaluation because of her puzzling and disabling physical symptoms. These included pain in her lower back and lower limbs that had started precipitously while she was cleaning house. She felt something "give" at the time, and then experienced a pain in her lower back on the right side, radiating down the right leg. Bed rest produced no prolonged benefit and after radiological investigation the pain had shifted to the left side and radiated down the left leg. It continued in this uncertain way, and despite negative objective findings she underwent a surgical investigation of her lower back, at her insistence, a little more than a year after the initial trauma. The surgical exploration of the lumbosacral area revealed no abnormal findings, and the vertebral bodies L4, L5, and S1 were fused.

At the time the psychiatric consultation was requested she was still complaining of lower back pain radiating mostly to the right leg and foot, with intermittent pain in the left flank and left leg. The pain was variously described as burning, tightening, or knifelike. Apart from some limitation of movement in the affected areas and spasm in the back muscles, there were no objective findings on physical examination and no consistent sensory changes. Evidence of a neurological lesion was equivocal at best. Some degree of nerve root irritation was considered to be a likely explanation, but it was strongly suspected that important psychogenic factors in addition were contributing to the problem.

In the psychiatric interviews she was bright and related well. While describing her symptoms and the lack of consensus among the surgeons who had been consulted, she moved rapidly to a discussion of the strained relationship in her marriage, and of how her husband withdrew from her into his work when she complained of her symptoms. It soon became clear that much of significance had occurred since the time of their marriage eleven years previously to account for this. She had been twenty-two at the time, he three years older. Their courtship had proceeded rapidly, motivated more by persuasive drift to marriage at the end of the college senior year than by any deeper feelings or understanding in their relationship. She taught school while he completed his courses in law school, after which time he became increasingly involved in his profession. The subsequent arrival of their two children had kept her busily occupied until the younger began to attend nursery school. At that point her dissatisfactions with her life and her marriage surfaced. She held her husband responsible for their sparse and unsatisfactory sexual relationships because of his problem with premature ejaculation, and she objected to his preoccupation with his work. She learned computer programming in order to keep busy, and having made remarkably good progress, was soon acting as a consultant. The greater her involvement in her work, the more intensely preoccupied he became with his. It was against this background that the injury to her back had taken place.

He had remained unconvinced that her symptoms were really bothersome, recognizing that in some way she was seeking more attention from him. He would tell her that she was only as crippled as she needed to be, and from his discussions with her doctors, he felt justified in accusing her of having been foolishly persuaded by the surgeon to undergo an ill-advised operation. Their mutual lack of concern for each other had led to each of them entering an extramarital relationship and then punitively disclosing the information to the other. Their commitment to their children eventually led to their seeking marriage counseling. The patient herself admitted to feeling bound to her marriage by her obligations to her children, and fearful of leaving it because her incapacitating back symptoms would hamper any plans for a major change in her life-style.

She described spending roughly half of each day in a reclining position. To make the sitting or standing position bearable she was using diazepam (valium), 5 mg, three times a day. Because traveling about had been medically prohibited, she had turned her attention and directed her talents to a long-standing interest in graphic art, which she worked at in a studio at home. She had been able to impress a publishing house sufficiently well to have them offer her small but steady contracts.

The psychodynamic understanding of this case report is helped to some extent by information regarding her family and past history. She was the elder of two siblings, with an unmarried brother five years younger. Her relationship with him was warm and supportive. Her father in his sixties was a pharmacist who had interacted with the members of his family primarily as a provider of remedies when they experienced the mildest of discomfort. He was constantly attentive to their needs and considerably more so than his wife. The patient felt herself withdrawing from him as a young girl because she considered his physical attentions too sexual. Her mother was described in negative terms and the relationship between mother and daughter had been a consistently troubled one. She was seen by the patient as constantly carping and reprimanding. In the current marital crisis her only comment to the patient was that under no circumstances was she to think of divorce.

Clinical Course

Despite the lack of convincing neurological evidence throughout the investigation of her symptoms, the patient had great difficulty accepting the explanation that her emotional problems might have contributed to her physical discomfort. She was especially provoked by her husband's use of the term "psychosomatic" to describe her problem. Although her dissatisfaction with the course of her life and her marriage had been under fairly constant examination in the weekly marriage counseling sessions of the previous few months, her symptoms had remained unchanged. While it was apparent that there were many forceful psychodynamic issues that complicated their relationship and that must have contributed to how she dealt with her symptoms, the alleviation of the pain and muscle spasm was thrust into the foreground as the most urgent goal in the psychotherapy. In this regard she was accepting of, and interested in, the idea of exploring the potential role of hypnosis.

Her response to an induction of hypnosis was dramatic and impressive. Not only did one arm levitate on the suggestion that it would do so, but the other arm rose, too. She responded well to the posthypnotic suggestion that her lowered arm would rise at a given signal, as she did to the challenging suggestion that she would not be able to unclasp her fingers, regardless of how hard she tried to do so.

She was able to achieve some degree of immediate improvement in the experience of her pain by concentrating on numb and tingling feelings permeating and surrounding the painful areas. She learned to practice this exercise in self-hypnosis at home, and could by means of it achieve temporary relief. She found herself able to distort perception in her legs without even touching them with her fingers, which had previously been used in the earlier exercises as the source of tingling sensations. She also found after a few weeks that she could induce the feeling of numbness or tingling in her legs without first going through the procedure of inducing hypnosis. Both she and her husband became convinced that hypnosis was of considerable help in temporarily relieving her discomfort. After about six to eight weeks she had reduced her pain medication to one tablet in two or three days, and she found herself able to spend a whole day at her art without having to lie down. At one stage she became almost euphoric, while experimenting during an exercise at home, on discovering that she could not only cause pain to fade out but could also have it increase by her concentrating on it.

Psychotherapy with heavy emphasis on hypnosis continued at weekly and then fortnightly intervals for about four months. By that time, although not free of her symptoms, she was able to cope with her home and her work, and continued with her husband to examine their marriage in interviews with a marriage counselor. She claimed that one of the major gains from her contact with hypnosis was that she no longer feared the painful symptom, which she realized she could worsen or mask to a large extent. At times hypnosis was an especially unusual experience for her. When she herself could "let go" completely, she could feel herself becoming very deeply involved in a global distortion of perception, which she referred to as semi-orgasmic. She was able to achieve this both during exercises at home and occasionally during the exercises in interviews.

At this time, almost two years after her last psychiatric visit, she continues to progress satisfactorily. She has maintained a six-monthly contact with the neurologist who had referred her initially for the psychiatric evaluation. The neurological findings continue to be minimal and the question of further surgery has been ruled out. The marriage has improved some with the development of more considerate attitudes in the relationship. She recently won an important award for her artwork.

CASE HISTORY VII
Posttraumatic Symptoms

A thirty-four-year-old history professor was referred for a psychiatric evaluation because of persistent and troublesome symptoms that could not be explained on a purely organic basis. The problem had started seven years previously when he was involved in a minor automobile accident. His stationary car was hit and he immediately became aware of pain in his neck and scapular region. Following that, he experienced weakness and pain in his left arm for a period of about three years despite fusion of the fourth, fifth, and sixth cervical vertebrae about eighteen months after the accident. Improvement had not followed immediately on the surgery but did occur well over a year later, at which time he returned to work after a prolonged period of unemployment. The following year he was slapped on the back of the neck by a colleague, and immediately suffered a return of the symptoms, excruciating neck pains that radiated to the left shoulder and left upper arm. The symptoms fluctuated for a few months but then became so severe that he could no longer teach, and when first seen psychiatrically had not worked for two years.

Immediately prior to the referral, he had spent a brief period in the hospital where he had undergone neurosurgical and special diagnostic investigations with a view to possible further surgical intervention. The diagnosis of nerve root pathology in the cervical and lumbosacral regions was under consideration. The examination had revealed very limited movement of his neck, weakness in both hands (more marked on the left), and an inconsistent sensory deficit in both upper and lower right limbs. No purely objective signs had been elicited. A cervical myelogram had been negative as were electromyographic studies and nerve conduction time studies. X-rays had revealed good fusion at the interspace C5 and 6 and an electroencephalogram had been within normal limits. He had walked out of the hospital before all proposed investigations were completed, upset by the numerous studies and the uncertainty of surgical success. Psychiatric consultation was then requested as a result of the largely negative objective findings and the unexpected nature of his departure from the hospital.

When he was seen in the initial interview, his head and neck were supported by an orthopedic collar. His speech was somewhat slow, studied, and unemotional. He recounted the history of his symptoms as described above, and complained of recurrent dull pains in his neck that radiated to both shoulders and down his left arm to the wrist. He reported the use of a combination of analgesics and tranquilizers for symptom relief. While discussing how upset he had become by his symptoms, he spontaneously referred to the occurrence of "lapses" over the previous six months, during which he would lose touch with his surroundings for periods of about ten seconds. He found that his mind wandered inexplicably at those times, but he had no recollection of what his thoughts had been once the lapses had ended. Both his wife and mother told him they could recognize the presence of the episodes because of his vacant stare when they occurred. The normal electroencephalogram, referred to above, had been done in an attempt to explore the nature of the symptom.

Inquiry into his family and past history revealed that he was the oldest of three siblings. His father had died of cancer when the patient was seventeen. His mother was living and in her sixties. He reported an ambivalent relationship with both as he described the intense pressure on him to excel academically. This he had done by graduating from high school at the age of sixteen and obtaining his doctorate at the age of twenty-one. He married at the age of twenty-seven to a musician two years younger than he. They had no children and had become the target of considerable family pressure, partly as a result of that, but also because of the

persistence of his symptoms. His relatives believed he ought to be receiving more efficient medical help. He complained that he and his wife coped
poorly with both his mother's and his mother-in-law's interference in their
lives.

His marriage had been under considerable stress since the time of the
automobile accident, his wife having become impatient with the stubborn
nature of his symptoms and he having grown depressed. At one stage he
had attempted suicide because of the disheartening state of his marriage
by ingesting about twenty barbiturate capsules. He had seen a psychiatrist
at that time but had refused continued treatment.

He had worked very little during the two and a half years since the
neck trauma that had led to a return of his symptoms. This had depressed
him, as had the unhappy state of his marriage and his increasing yet
ambivalent dependence on his wife and his mother for direction and
advice. He appeared eager for help, and it was equally apparent that he
was in need of a treatment program that included active intervention. At
the time of the psychiatric consultation, longer-term uncovering therapy
was contraindicated by the urgency of the reality issues: the unresolved
insurance claims, his prolonged disability, and the vulnerable state of his
marriage.

He was interested in exploring the possible use of hypnosis and
responded immediately and dramatically to the induction procedure of the
Eye Roll Levitation Method. He scored maximally on the levitation and
posthypnotic responses, and had amnesia for the signal to terminate the
posthypnotic suggestion even though he had obeyed it with precision.
In a subsequent experience of hypnosis he was totally incapable of separating his clasped fingers when told he would find it impossible to do so, and
was unable to see the hour hand on a clock face when it was suggested to him that it would disappear. His response to hypnosis was immediately employed in helping him to produce a numb feeling in and around
the painful areas, which was helpful in screening out the hurt from the
pain. He was taught to induce the trance by himself without the assistance
of a second person, and after practicing at home for a week, was very
pleased with the relief he obtained. He claimed greater comfort in his arm
than he had had for the previous seven years.

Clinical Course

He was seen at weekly intervals for about four months. The interviews were spent partly on considering the critical issues that awaited resolution and partly on revising and strengthening the hypnotic techniques.

After six weeks he had reduced his use of pain medication by a third, and at the end of four months of treatment was taking only an occasional tranquilizer. His symptoms were clearly improving but his circumstances, in his own words, continued to be "chaotic." Toward the end of the treatment period he resolved to settle his insurance claims, and to move with his wife to a distant location removed from the pressures of their numerous relatives.

In the discussions about his ability to distort perception and to respond to suggestions, he volunteered information about himself that bore a close resemblance to the personality traits of somnambules, initially described by Spiegel (1974) and reported above. He referred to his remarkable memory, which tended to overawe others, and to his own longstanding recognition that he lacked common sense despite his high intelligence. He had known, too, for years, that he could engage in conversation and simultaneously be solving an entirely unrelated and difficult problem in his head.

When considering his so-called "lapses" that had appeared during the months prior to the psychiatric evaluation, and that grew more frequent during one period of his therapy, he became aware of their taking place at times when he was especially ill at ease. He discovered them happening when he was bored or angered by the company he was in, and recognized their escape value. He recognized that his skill in being able to concentrate on more than one mental task at a time might in some way be related to his ability to have his mind wander almost at will. He subsequently reported that as he learned to speak up in the large family circle with greater confidence, the lapses diminished in frequency.

The treatment ended when he moved from the area, feeling more hopeful and confident of his ability to deal with his problems. The last report from him a year later revealed that he had continued to experience relief from his symptoms by practicing the self-induced trance at least once daily. He then also requested the name of a therapist whom he could approach for further psychiatric treatment for his personal problems.

COMMENT

The uncertainty of the neurological data in the first of these two cases precludes our knowing the precise extent of the influence of the psychological factors. Whether they merely aggravated her reaction or contributed to the symptoms in a major way remains unknown. However one chooses to categorize the problems of both these patients, their impressive responses to hypnosis cannot easily be ignored. One assumes that whatever accounts for their marked hypnotizability also exerted an effect on their clinical behavior, and on their reactions to the surgical procedures.

We must also ask what hypnosis, specifically, won for the progress of treatment. In both instances it helped resolve the most pressing problem, namely, the demanding symptom, and helped shift the focus of attention to the context of the symptom and to some of the prevailing psychodynamic forces. In the first case, the marriage counselor was able to proceed with less hindrance; and in the second, the patient moved to a new environment and concluded there that he needed help to resolve his personal and marital problems.

Again the question of whether or not hypnosis was a face-saving device for these patients must be raised. I suspect that even if it were, finding that they had the ability to distort perception and to worsen the pain by concentrating on it was a highly reassuring and helpful experience for them. As a consequence, they recognized not only their ability to contain the symptom, but their contribution to its development in the first place.

CHAPTER 8

Hypnotizability and the Treatment of Phobic Behavior

In the seven cases reported in chapters 5, 6, and 7, I have emphasized the similarities between the clinical symptoms and hypnotic behavior. Further suggestive evidence of their relatedness lies in the frequently episodic nature of the clinical picture, at times strange and dramatic; its limited duration and tendency to recur; its inaccessibility to logic; its tendency to run its course autonomously; and when intense, its near-total absorption of the patient who becomes disconnected from his other experiences and activities, although at some level continues to be aware of them. In addition, all the patients reported were highly hypnotizable.

I am not suggesting that the clinical and hypnotic states are equivalent or identical, or that a patient experiencing the one cannot escape the other. I am, however, drawing attention to the characteristics shared by them, and to the finding that access from one to the other is facilitated.

In order to investigate the rich variety of clinical behavior reported more effectively, the focus of our attention must necessarily, initially, be narrowed down to one or two of the symptoms. Among the clinical pictures described, phobic behavior most invites further consideration. The primary reason is that it tends to occur more frequently than the other diagnostic categories. While hysterical fugues and multiple personalities, colorful as they are, have been less commonly reported in modern psychiatric practice than they were at the turn of the century, phobias have been recognized with increasing frequency. Marks (1969) reports the presence of phobic symptoms in about 20 percent of psychiatric patients, and the

occurrence of phobic disorders or phobic states (where the phobia domi-
nates the clinical picture) in about 3 percent of out-patients. Furthermore,
because of the increasing attention given to the clinical picture associated
with phobias in the past decade or two, the entity has become more
clearly defined and hence more easily identifiable. For the purposes of the
work reflected in this book, I have followed the definition of a phobia suggested by Marks (1969):

> A phobia can thus be defined as a special form of fear which (1) *is out
> of proportion to demands of the situation,* (2) *cannot be explained or
> reasoned away,* (3) *is beyond voluntary control,* and (4) *leads to avoid-
> ance of the feared situation.*

In addition, because of the relatively circumscribed nature of the clinical
problem, the therapeutic outcome is easily assessed.

Attention to phobic behavior is also encouraged by its dramatic
aspects. Those afflicted are at the mercy of their fears, which are poorly
understood and even ridiculed by unsympathetic relatives and friends who
not infrequently see the situations as foolish, trivial, and even manipula-
tive. Unlike psychotic patients, who draw more compassion from the
onlooker because of their total helplessness to deal with their delusions or
hallucinations without a great deal of support and assistance, the phobic
patient is often assumed (despite his pleas to the contrary) to be able to
pull himself together; and under special circumstances is in fact able to do
so, only to succumb to his problem when the exigency has passed. An
extreme example was cited by Kral (1952), who described the disappearance or improvement of phobic symptoms in concentration camp victims
threatened with extermination if they were unable to work, and the rede-
velopment of their former symptoms several months after liberation when
the danger had passed. Neurotics can compromise more than psychotics
when reality demands it, but what separates the phobic patients into a discrete group among the neurotics is the highly obtrusive nature of their
complaints, and the overwhelming character of the symptoms when they
occur. The incapacity of phobic patients is often offset by the embarrassed
sense of humor with which they learn to defend against the ridicule of
their fellows, and by their own recognition that they should have more
control over the problem than they reveal. Sudden shifts do occasionally
occur, in fact, with symptoms unexpectedly improving for no apparent
reason, only to worsen again, unavoidably, when attention is directed to
their absence or without recognizable cause.

As in hypnosis, then, the person with phobias has to defend himself
against the accusations of his critics. Phrases such as suggestible, overly
imaginative, pretending, or dramatizing are as likely to be used in describ-

ing phobic patients as they are in referring to hypnotized subjects. This has added to the incentive to understand more about the relationship between the two. It has also encouraged the exploration of the relevance of marked hypnotizability in the clinical context of fears and phobias, and the extension of the use of hypnosis in the treatment of phobic symptoms. The traditional uses of therapeutic hypnosis as a means of symptom removal by direct suggestion, or as an adjunct to exploration and uncovering techniques, appear to have made little impact on the course of phobic behavior. The combination of imaginal desensitization and hypnosis has been more effective, and Glick (1969, 1970) has reported the poorly understood enhancement of behavior therapy when combined with hypnosis in the treatment of phobias. Circumstances have therefore invited an investigation of the topic, and have paved the way for the testing of other methods utilizing hypnosis. The following few cases illustrate the usefulness of good hypnotic responsivity in allowing an acceleration of deconditioning procedures, and the effectiveness of emphasizing the importance of the hypnosis, as opposed to that of the deconditioning, in patients who are easily hypnotizable. Closer consideration of the therapeutic procedures used in the cases to be reported suggests that their effectiveness derives from providing the patients with coping mechanisms previously not available to them. By helping them to create, in their imagination, the experiences that are most fearsome and in some instances terrifying to them, the therapist enables the patients to become familiar with previously stressful situations under the comfortable and reassuring circumstances of the therapy session. Learning how to produce such subjective experiences on their own, subsequently, the patients gain a sense of mastery over the imagined situation. This then enables them to approach the reality with greater confidence, and to transfer the sense of success from the imagined to the real achievement.

CASE HISTORY VIII

Fear of Dentistry

A personable, successful, and highly intelligent young man in his mid-twenties requested hypnosis to help him overcome his fear of dentistry, which had prevented him from properly attending to the care of his teeth for years. His first unhappy experience with dental care was at about the age of nine years, when he started a series of weekly visits to his dentist. He found he reacted strongly to the drilling, which he then learned to tolerate only by groaning throughout the procedure, to the consternation of the dentist. That unfortunate man complained good-naturedly to the school administration responsible for the dental program of the professional burden he bore because of the patient and his younger siblings, who responded no more kindly to the drill than did he. His last visit to the dentist had been four years prior to his present request for assistance, and apart from that emergency treatment for an infected impacted wisdom tooth, he had successfully avoided a dentist's office for ten years. The last visit was marked by his having to be held down by two people. When he was eleven years old, the decision was made that he would receive no further injections of procaine hydrochloride (Novocain) because he experienced the same degree of pain with the use of the drug as without it.

In discussing his experiences relating to dentistry, he described the intense effort he would have to make in the dentist's chair to suppress the urge to shout. While talking about it, he could feel his muscles stiffen, especially those in his neck. He recounted that he could usually turn off feelings of anxiety related to other situations, but had not been able to do so in this regard. Increasing toothache had prompted him to seek help at this time. He had planned on arranging a dental appointment several weeks ahead, and had noticed an increase in pain, immediately after he thought of setting up the appointment. He realized that he would almost certainly disrupt the treatment unless he had learned beforehand how to cope with his anxiety. His attitude toward planning for the future had developed from almost two years of insight-oriented psychotherapy. It was on the recommendation of his therapist that he sought symptom relief via hypnosis. His therapy had dealt with several aspects of his life, including his attitudes to his work, and his family, but had in no way focused on his fear of dentistry. He was the oldest of four siblings with whom he had a comfortable relationship. His parents were in their mid-fifties and well. At the time of his treatment with hypnosis he was moving toward the conclusion of his postgraduate work in the behavioral sciences. He had been happily married for a few years to a young woman engaged in work similar to his. They had no children.

An investigation of his experience with hypnosis revealed that he had participated in a class experiment several months previously, and had had a moderately good response. His trance capacity was assessed using the Hypnotic Induction Profile (HIP). His score was 3+ on the 5-point scale from 0 to 4. The quality of his response was very good. On emerging from the test, which was an induced hypnotic experience, he *volunteered* the comment that the trance had characteristics that were similar to his spontaneous experiences in the dentist's chair. When asked to elaborate on this, he referred to subjective feelings that were difficult to describe, and to a sense of depersonalization in both circumstances in which it felt as if his head were separated from and above his body. He extended the comparison of the two situations by describing how he had been totally preoccupied with the subjective sensations in each, namely the sensation of weightlessness in the levitated arm during the trance, and the sense of fragility in his teeth when in the dental chair. He felt, too, that the feelings on emerging from the trance were similar to those he had experienced at the end of his visit to the dentist; it was like becoming aware again of other things that then became surprisingly clear. Some months after his treatment, his responses were assessed on the Harvard Group Scale. His score was 11 on a 12-point scale.

Clinical Course

On his second visit he was able, in hypnosis, to produce a tingling feeling in his fingers and hand, which he transferred to his mouth and jaw. He then rapidly learned to induce the trance himself, and to develop the numb feeling in his mouth. Combining the principle of the hierarchy used in imaginal desensitization (Wolpe, 1958) and hypnosis, he also learned to relax, in self-induced hypnosis, as he produced visual images of the increasingly stressful stages of his progress from the point of leaving home to sitting in the dentist's chair having his teeth drilled. He undertook to practice the self-hypnosis and relaxation accompanied by the envisioned stages, at least once daily, until he had accomplished his goal of successfully visiting his dentist.

The hypnosis was self-induced by adhering fairly closely to the routine described by Spiegel in the HIP (Spiegel and Bridger, 1970). While sitting comfortably in an armchair, our patient would roll his eyes up, then slowly close his eyelids. He followed this by inhaling deeply, holding his breath briefly, and then exhaling slowly and fairly completely; after that he permitted himself to relax totally from the top of his head all the way down to his toes, and to imagine that he was drifting, floating, or gliding. When this had been accomplished, he concentrated on his hand and forearm, permitting first movement sensations and then light feelings to permeate the area. When feeling light, the hand and forearm were then encouraged to float into the upright position, at which point he concentrated on the tingling and numb feeling in his fingers, which he then transferred to his mouth. While intensifying that numb feeling, he prepared himself to relax completely while he began to entertain the visual images of the steps leading to having his teeth drilled. He was able to remain completely calm and relaxed throughout the procedure, and when he was satisfied that he had mastered the event in his mind's eye, he brought himself out of the experience on the backward count from three to one, opening his eyes and confidently expecting that he would feel comfortable and relaxed, that he would have a feeling of well-being, and that the usual sensations and control would return to his hand and his forearm. The duration of the entire exercise was about ten minutes, occasionally less, sometimes more.

Confident of his intention to practice the self-hypnosis, he arranged an appointment for his dental treatment for a month ahead. He then coped well with an experience of about six dental visits that included cleaning, drilling, and root-canal work. He reported his successful encounters in two phone calls before his third visit to me, after an interval of over three months. At that time he discussed in greater detail some of his previous anguish, and his recently developed mastery of the situation.

Additional Comments

He described how, as a youth, he had grown to despair of ever being able to take adequate care of his teeth as he had found himself evading the routine dental visits arranged by his school program. He had hated to hear dental work discussed by his friends, and recounted how on occasions when he ran his tongue over his teeth to detect tender or painful sites, he would immediately be able to stop the sensation of pain by thinking about the dentist. He continued this practice until fairly recently, and would engage in that behavior at special times, such as when driving his car or having to wait for traffic light changes.

He recalled his childhood visits to the dentist, and the increasing intensity of his anxiety as the day approached. By the time the appointed hour arrived, he would find himself totally absorbed by the anticipated anguish of the experience and unable to pay attention to any other matter. He described the event associated with the treatment of his impacted wisdom tooth as a nightmare from which he felt he ultimately emerged, when it was all over, in a manner similar to the feeling of coming out of the trance. Describing his behavior during that episode and others, he recalled his inability to respond to any conversation, and remembered his total preoccupation with every move made by the dentist, and with the possible painful effects of each instrument as it was lifted and applied to his teeth. He had experienced intense fear that his teeth would crumble under the impact of any harsh attention or pressure.

Comparing his more recent successful experiences with those of the past, he described how in place of the experience of helpless vigilance, he felt like an adult who was able to control the nature of the event. He felt able to look at what was happening and to examine the details with a curiosity that he had not dared to show previously. He was especially struck by finding that the local anesthesia was effective. He had been told when young, and had believed that he had an immunity to the anesthetic agent because he experienced severe pain in his teeth during the dental work, regardless of whether the anesthetic agent had been used or not. During his recent treatment he learned to recognize the anesthetic effects of the procaine as they developed in his mouth. It would seem that he had been so convinced as a youngster that he would experience pain that he did, despite the chemical anesthesia. He felt greatly relieved that he had been able to withstand all the recent procedures without embarrassing himself in front of the dentist and his assistants, who, he was convinced, would not have understood the nature of his problem had it emerged.

CASE HISTORY IX
Flight Phobia (2)

A single woman in her mid-thirties, employed as a secretary to an airline executive, requested hypnosis to overcome her fears of planes and elevators. Although she had flown fairly extensively with her parents when younger, the fear of flying had commenced about five years prior to her seeking help, and had worsened. She attributed her fear to a feeling of being trapped and unable to leave the plane once it had taken off. She was not aware of a distinct fear of crashing, but described feeling that a disaster was imminent, and that she ought not to be there. Despite the increasing discomfort associated with flights, she had continued to take trips; some were related to her work, but most of them were to visit her parents. Her last trip had been one month prior to her initial interview, and she planned two further trips within the following few months.

Referring to the experiences in some detail, she described the extent of the discomfort and the panic. She found the initial period, including the takeoff, the worst. Despite her attempts to improve matters by securing an aisle seat and taking a few drinks, she generally found that the trips were ruined by her total preoccupation with her fears. She trembled, became increasingly tense, buried her head in her lap, and felt desperate. She was frequently approached by flight personnel who offered to help her. Once the elevation and flight plan had been announced by the pilot, she felt slightly reassured, but continued, wretched, until she sensed the preparations for landing. She knew, then, that the trip was nearly over. She expressed surprise that the situation worsened with each additonal trip she took. She had hoped that by facing the experience repeatedly she would be able to overcome it. Despite her counterphobic strategy she was obliged, on occasion, to forego the free flights associated with the work that she did.

Although she reported an uneasiness in elevators since the age of ten or eleven when she would pay regular visits to her dentist, this had grown into an experience of near-panic proportions during the three years prior to her request for hypnosis. She found that her life was now hampered by her anxieties. She refused to ride alone in an elevator, and on occasions requested strangers to go up to the higher floors with her, rather than remain alone for the latter part of the ride. She was reassured by the presence of an elevator operator. She recognized the extent of her disability on one occasion when she found herself walking to her eighth-floor apartment rather than riding in the elevator. Her father tended to regard her problem as an oddity that she would outgrow, but her mother, herself fearful of flying, had encouraged the patient to seek more active treatment.

In addition to her fear of flights and elevators, she was anxious about traveling on streetcars and driving in tunnels. She was uncomfortable when the streetcar went underground, but was usually not overwhelmed by it because she knew that by pulling the emergency cord she could, under extreme circumstances, bring the vehicle to a halt and escape from it. Disliking relatively lengthy travel in tunnels, she occasionally chose the alternative and longer route when driving her car. Although she frequently persuaded herself to drive through the tunnels, she was aware of a distinct sense of relief when she could see the light at the other end. She admitted choosing the aisle seat in a theater, and avoiding shows on Fridays and Saturdays because of the crowds. The dominant theme pervading her fears appeared to be that of claustrophobia.

Her parents were in their mid-sixties, her father a successful physician and her mother a devoted housewife. Aware of her ambivalence toward them, she was able to share her feelings about them with her three older siblings, and was keen to avoid any therapeutic investigation of issues relating to them. Her motivation for seeking help was to obtain relief from her troublesome symptoms. She had graduated from college, enjoyed her work, and was reasonably contented with the social and sexual aspects of her life.

She had been exposed to hypnosis a year previously when she had experienced a single quit-smoking session involving hypnosis. She had been surprised at the extent of her response at the time, and especially pleased with the fact that she had not smoked a cigarette since then. Her score on the Hypnotic Induction Profile was 3, and on the Harvard Group Scale she scored 8, both of which indicate a high level of hypnotizability.

Clinical Course

The treatment strategy sought to combine the principle of the hierarchy used in imaginal desensitization (Wolpe, 1958) and the use of hypnosis. Because of her high hypnotizability, ten stages were readily decided upon, and she was encouraged to work, when hypnotized, from the least noxious visual image to the most disturbing one. The former was the picture of her packing her suitcases and the latter was of the engines roaring on the runway as the plane was about to take off with her aboard. The intervening stages included being driven to the airport, alighting at the terminal, checking in her baggage, sitting in the departure lounge, walking down the ramp and entering the plane, settling in her seat, the cabin being closed and pressurized, and taxiing to the end of the runway.

In hypnosis, she was directed to think of the first stage (packing her suitcases) for a period of thirty seconds, or until she experienced anxiety, whichever was the shorter. The succeeding thirty seconds were devoted to relaxing completely before the image was again evoked. When she was able to experience three thirty-second periods devoted to the first visual image without experiencing any anxiety, work began on the next. She signaled the onset of her anxiety by lifting her index finger, whereupon the therapist immediately directed her to discontinue the image and relax. In this manner, and within six sessions, she was able to tolerate the repeated image of herself aboard a plane as it sped down the runway to become airborne.

Between the weekly sessions she was encouraged to practice, at home, frequent self-hypnosis exercises that accentuated the feelings of relaxation. She was given permission to re-create, in her practice sessions, the visual images that she had worked on and mastered in the previous treatment sessions, but was dissuaded from trying to visualize the stages of the hierarchy that had not yet been covered with her therapist.

Between the third and the fourth treatment sessions, she undertook a short flight that had been arranged well in advance. Although she had, by then, mastered the imagined stages only up to and including the picture of herself walking down the ramp and stepping onto the plane, she coped with the flight most successfully. She had been able to relax completely in her seat, and did so without having to depend on the ritual of self-induced hypnosis. She was greatly encouraged by the experience, readily worked through the subsequent stages of the hierarchy in her treatment sessions, and subsequently undertook a longer trip, with equal success.

CASE HISTORY X
Fear of Childbirth

A young woman well into the third trimester of her first pregnancy was referred by her obstetrician for hypnosis to cope with her overwhelming fear of the delivery. She recounted that she had been frightened as an adolescent by reports of the agony of childbirth and by her mother's recounting the fearsome details. She admitted that although she had been frightened by the prospect when she first learned that she was pregnant, she had decided "to keep it all in." She explained that she feared becoming afraid because when she did she would feel worse than before, with a feeling "like shock, with shortness of breath, shaking, and perspiration." She had dismissed the frightening thoughts of her delivery from her mind until she recognized that her due date was imminent.

She described other fears, including that of planes, since a turbulent flight to Europe three years previously. She reported being very frightened on that occasion and attempting two years later to overcome her anxiety by taking another flight, which disturbed her even more. She reported feeling that there was no escape from that experience, and in addition to the feeling of breathlessness and helplessness mentioned above, she described a light feeling in the whole of her body, like a floating feeling, at that time. She claimed to have had such an experience on a few occasions when she felt considerable panic, at which times she had also felt detached from her body, and as if she had had no limbs.

Her major concern at the time of her referral was to learn to deal with her delivery. She also spoke of wanting to learn to overcome her fear of flying at a later date, but the immediate problem was the birth. She had been married for almost two years to a sales representative three years her senior, who had learned to fly during his military training. He flew as a pilot about once a month, and was eager for her to share this with him. She was the only child of a marriage that had dissolved when she was less than a year old. She had had little contact with her father, now in his mid-fifties, but seemed to be fairly close to her mother, whom she saw frequently and described as nervous and suggestible like herself. Although apparently fairly bright, she had decided during her freshman year against continuing at college, and after doing secretarial work for a few years she had married.

She had never experienced or witnessed hypnosis previously, but was very interested in using it to cope with her immediate problem. She related warmly and well immediately, and although apparently very fearful of the delivery, was able to joke some about the late date of her request for help, and about the fact that she could no longer postpone facing the event that was now about to take place.

She scored very well on the Hypnotic Induction Profile, achieving a rating of close to 4. On the Stanford Hypnotic Susceptibility Scale she scored 8, but claimed that had she not been as heavy and close to term as she was, she would have moved from her chair to another, in accordance with the posthypnotic suggestion contained in the protocol. In any event, her response to hypnosis was at least in the category of high, if not very high.

Clinical Course

The total clinical encounter with her covered two sessions. Because of the advanced state of her pregnancy, and because she was clearly very responsive to hypnosis, the therapeutic program was initiated in the first interview. During the second interview, in addition to reinforcement of the program, the Stanford Hypnotic Susceptibility Scale was administered to confirm the clinical impression of her high responsivity.

The treatment strategy commenced with directions to her, in hypnosis, to relax completely and to experience a wonderfully pleasant sensation of floating. She was then asked to think about going into labor while enjoying the floating sensation, and to describe what she believed would be the most comfortable way of experiencing the contractions necessary for the birth of her baby. She chose to experience the anticipated contractions as a feeling of heaviness in her lower abdomen. She was then directed to imagine having waves of heavy feelings in her lower abdomen, which sensations would represent the work to be done by her uterus as some of her muscles contracted and others relaxed in order to permit the passage of her infant.

When she claimed that she could, in fact, feel the sensation of heaviness, she was instructed in how to induce hypnosis in herself and to re-create the experience of complete relaxation, of floating, and of feeling heavy in her lower abdomen. She was directed to practice the self-induced hypnosis for a period of about ten minutes two or three times each day. She was also advised, in hypnosis, that she could approach her delivery, confident in the knowledge that she would be able to induce the relaxed hypnosis when her labor started, and that she would be able to experience the contractions as a feeling of heaviness in her lower abdomen. With that feeling of heaviness that she, herself, could create, she would be able to screen out any feeling of pain during her labor.

During her second visit three days later, after the Stanford Hypnotic Susceptibility Scale had been administered, her experiences with the self-induced hypnosis were discussed. She reported favorable progress and success in being able to produce the distorted perception, and was again encouraged to imagine how readily she would be able to screen out the hurt of her contractions by concentrating her attention on the feeling of heaviness.

Two days after her second visit she entered labor, and with the mildest reminder from her obstetrician, who had been apprised of the treatment strategy, of her ability to create the sensations that she chose, she mastered the event, and was delighted with what she herself had been able to accomplish.

Comments

It is of interest to note that she had readily convinced herself that she was terrified of her pending delivery, and was subsequently equally readily persuaded by her experience of relaxed hypnosis and perceptual distortion that she would be able to cope with it. Her good response to hypnosis was used to prepare her for her labor by rapidly exposing her, in her imagination, to anticipated sensory experiences of parturition that were only mildly uncomfortable and that she could control. This was done on the assumption that she was capable of perceiving the sensory experience of parturition as agonizing, if that was what she expected, or as merely mild discomfort, if she could be persuaded that was possible. The experience of the exercise suggested repeatedly that it might be.

Although she had had no previous experience of childbirth, she was led to believe from stories she had heard that it was terrifying. From her description of her reaction to her first very unpleasant plane flight, we know that she was capable of rapidly becoming panic-stricken. Because panic was, for her, associated with perceptual distortions, we can assume that these aggravated the flight experience and contributed in some measure to her determination to avoid further trips. Left to her own devices, it is probably also safe to assume that she would indeed have panicked at the onset of labor and satisfied a self-fulfilling prophecy. The pain of the contractions would have been compounded by the frightening and inescapable feelings of depersonalization. By leading her through an experience of perceptual distortion that she herself produced, she was helped to recognize how much of the experience she could create and control.

Her almost total denial of the threat of her delivery until her obstetrician pronounced it imminent is perhaps further evidence of her unusual ability to distort perception.

CASE HISTORY XI
Stagefright

A thirty-five-year-old professional singer was referred for hypnosis, to lessen her fear of public performances, and to enable her to reach the high notes that she knew she was capable of doing when relaxed. The problem had bothered her for about ten years, and had interfered increasingly with her career. She found that she was comfortable singing in a choir, but because of the tension and tremulousness associated with solo perform-ances, she had backed away from many job opportunities, fearing that she would not be able to perform as well as she should. Although the intensity of the symptom had fluctuated somewhat, it had led to progressively greater disappointment with herself when she found that she was becoming tense at the mere mention of a solo performance. She considered that to be absurd.

In answer to direct questions, she also described a fear of heights and of flying, which had started suddenly five years previously and which had now reached uncomfortable proportions. Although she had become dis-tressingly anxious when she visited a friend in a twenty-fifth-floor apart-ment, and had avoided plane trips for almost five years, she preferred at this time to concentrate solely on the problem that directly involved her career. She claimed that she might return at a later stage for help with her flight phobia, which had appeared for the first time during a trip she had been forced to make, under the pressure of very distressing personal cir-cumstances that she preferred not to discuss. She reported that she had had no problem with flying prior to that time, and had flown frequently.

She was referred for therapeutic hypnosis by her husband's therapist who had seen them both, on occasions, in brief spells of couple-therapy. She had raised the possibility of hypnosis with him because she knew of his interest in it, and because she had been exposed to it in college courses. From her experience with it she knew that her response to hypno-sis was good.

Those aspects of her past personal history that she was prepared to disclose in the total of four interviews devoted to evaluation and treatment led to very little psychodynamic clarification of her problem. Her intention was clear. She wanted symptomatic relief in an area that was circum-scribed but highly important to her.

She was an only child and had had a good education in fine schools. Her parents had encouraged her in her chosen career, as had her husband, who was about the same age as she. They had been married for ten years. He was working toward a doctorate in engineering while she pursued her career in music. They had no children by choice.

Her response on the Hypnotic Induction Profile was between 3 + and 4. On the Stanford Hypnotic Susceptibility Scale she scored 10, failing only to hallucinate the fly or to follow the posthypnotic suggestion.

Clinical Course

The treatment strategy was based on her marked response to hypnosis, and on the assumption that she would be able to make rapid strides because of it. In the first treatment session, marked relaxation was achieved in hypnosis, and she was then instructed in how to induce the trance herself and how to practice an accompanying relaxation exercise. She was then, while still in hypnosis and deeply relaxed, encouraged to imagine the anticipated details of her next performance, reassured as she did so by the memories of past successful performances. The emphasis throughout was on her ability to relax and to approach her solo performances with confidence. She was directed to practice the exercise twice daily for a period of about ten minutes on each occasion, and to use it in anticipation of any performances, including her own private practice sessions, singing lessons, and public rehearsals. She was also directed, in hypnosis, to caress the side of her face when confronted by an immediately anxiety-provoking thought or situation, if a fuller exercise was precluded by the circumstances. In this manner the achievement of relaxation, possibly associated with some trance characteristics, was paired with the simple procedure of a face caress.

In her second interview, about two weeks later, the exercise was adjusted and refined, and a general outline was worked out for constructing similar exercises for future anxiety-arousing performances. She was very satisfied with the effect of her newly acquired mastery, and subsequently reported a successful solo performance. However, she did not return at a later date for help with her acrophobia.

Comments

It can be assumed that the immediate development of her plane phobia following a single episode of distress associated with flying was related to her marked hypnotizability, in a manner similar to that discussed in the previous case history.

She had been referred for the relief of a single symptom that was attended to. In whichever way that phobia was related psychodynamically to other problems was not explored. It was assumed that after ten years the symptom had a life of its own. A precaution against arbitrarily depriving her of a symptom still psychodynamically essential to her was provided by linking the treatment procedure to her willingness to spend time and energy on the practice of an exercise.

CASE HISTORY XII
Phobias and Temporal Lobe Epilepsy

A twenty-nine-year-old man applied for psychiatric help to overcome a number of fears. These included a fear of being trapped in closed spaces such as elevators or planes, of being caught in heavy traffic, and of being stranded in open spaces. He sought help at this time on the urging of his wife, who was with him when he selected a considerably longer route to the airport in preference to traveling through a mile-long tunnel at rush hour. He had minimized the extent of his disability in previous discussions with her, feeling embarrassed to have anyone know too much about it. When faced with having to go through any of the feared situations, he preferred to be alone lest his behavior reveal the high level of his anxiety. He admitted that in addition to his wife's insistence that he seek help, he, too, had noted that his fears had worsened recently and were hindering his activities.

Closer examination of the fears revealed the markedly disabling extent of his panic states at times. On these occasions he had felt his pulse quicken, and had become aware of intense perspiration and nausea. This had occurred on being stranded between floors in an elevator, and also when caught in heavy traffic. In defense of his previous preference to diminish the importance of his problem, he claimed that despite the discomfort, he had, in the past, been able to control his fears. He had not been prevented from doing anything important that had to be done.

His very first episode of panic had occurred when he was about twelve years of age, and seems to have followed what was then considered to be his first attack of petit mal. He recalled being alone in a boat, rowing away from the shore of a lake, when suddenly he felt very confused and disoriented. This was associated with intense panic, and he found himself rowing vigorously back to shore as rapidly as he could. Medical investigation at that time led to the diagnosis of petit mal, and a regimen of anticonvulsant medication that has persisted, with modifications, to the present.

He recalled some fear associated with flying during subsequent years, but no further panic until about seven years later when he was a college freshman. He related his fears, then, to a sense of being trapped or stranded in the situation, and of being unable to extricate himself. He had found himself swept into a state of intense anxiety approaching panic as soon as he had become aware of the enforced confinement associated with being in a plane or elevator, or when he had felt himself cut off on a boat that was a considerable way out. Having experienced with increasing frequency the episodes of quickened pulse, sweating, breathlessness, and nausea at about the age of nineteen, he decided to avoid sailing, and to take fewer plane trips. His last flight had been five years prior to this consultation requesting assistance.

For several years he had avoided heavy traffic whenever he could, fearing his reactions in a traffic jam. He had also preferred walking up eight flights of stairs rather than risk being stranded in an elevator caught between floors. He generally avoided the mile-long tunnel to the airport for fear of a traffic holdup while in it, and usually rationalized his avoidance to himself and to his wife. When under pressure or in the company of others, he forced himself to travel through the tunnel. The event that had precipitated his request for treatment was one in which, despite the pressure of time, his fear of the crowded tunnel had led him to take the much longer route and arrive late at the airport. He was embarrassed not only by experiencing his symptoms in the company of others, but even by having to discuss them.

It was clear from his history that in addition to the resurgence of his fears and panic states over the previous ten years, he had also experienced an increase in the seizure activity that had been diagnosed as petit mal in his youth. This had been especially noticeable during the previous two years, and had led to further neurological investigation and an altered regimen of medication. He described the seizures as episodes lasting from seconds to minutes in which he would feel confused and disoriented, while objects around him would develop very clear outlines. He generally rubbed his face reflexly during such episodes, which were followed by twenty to thirty minutes of an uneasy and nervous feeling. He claimed to remember most, if not all of the details of these events, and on only two occasions was there a suggestion of a partial loss of consciousness. Members of his family and those who knew him well claimed that they could recognize the occurrence of his seizures by the blank stare on his face at those times. More recent investigations had resulted in a change of diagnosis to that of temporal lobe epilepsy, with an electroencephalogram showing paroxysmal left temporal discharges detected with the aid of nasopharyngeal leads. His medication had been adjusted to include a combination of phenylhydantoin and phenobarbital, with only minor improvement. The seizures still tended to occur about once or twice a month, and according to the patient, were episodes of confusion and disorientation, quite different from the episodes of fear and the phobias that led him to seek psychiatric help. He conceded that his avoidance of the feared situations might at times have been caused by his fear of seizures occurring if he were captive in a plane, elevator, or traffic jam.

Some of the symptoms he reported in recent months seem to have been neither episodes of confusion, which characterized the seizures, nor phobic events. They were mainly strange sensations induced by his looking at busy scenes containing many contrasts. For example, while working on a boat in the marina, he suddenly noticed the innumerable colors and shades of the other hulls. These appeared to be temporarily sharper and more vivid than usual. Although this was associated with a light-headed feeling, he felt he was thinking quite clearly, and was able to dispel the strange sensations by closing his eyes or looking at the sky. The experience lasted about a minute, and despite his claim that he was thinking clearly, a friend who was with him reported that he looked "spaced out." That night, while looking down a row of coats in his closet, he again became aware of the vivid contrasts between the dark and light colors. The strange feeling associated with that experience was almost, but not quite, disorienting. For a split second it felt as if he were not there. He became anxious that he would lose consciousness, but did not. He also became aware of a very rapid pulse rate. By looking away he lessened the impact of the experience, which persisted nevertheless. Returning his gaze to the rack of clothing intensified the strange feeling and the anxiety. It lasted for about a minute. On two subsequent occasions, while shopping and surveying rows of boxes and clothing, he had similar experiences, which he was able to terminate only by leaving the stores. He continued on those occasions to feel light-headed for about half an hour. He was on his own at those times, he claims to have remembered all the details of the events, and he seems not to have drawn any attention to himself from passersby. Yet a further episode, similar in nature to these above, was apparently precipitated by his closely examining the intricate engine of his car.

The precise nature of these visual experiences, and their relationship to what he considered to be his more usual temporal lobe seizures associated with disorientation and confusion, are of interest. It is not unreasonable to assume, however, that they, too, are linked to the temporal lobe pathology, even though they differ from his stereotyped version of his seizures. They were precipitated by circumstances in the environment, provocative because of the intricate visual patterns they thrust before him. An alternative explanation is that the visual apperception would have occurred when the temporal lobe discharge occurred, regardless of what he was inspecting at the time. The association of phobic anxiety, depersonalization, and temporal lobe epilepsy has been described by Roth (1959); and Frankel (1975) has reported how episodes of perceptual distortion appear to have been precipitated in a highly hypnotizable and phobic man when he moved from a shaded environment into a brightly illuminated one, or vice versa. As the association is not clearly understood, I would like to return to a consideration of the issue at the end of this case report.

The patient's past personal history revealed little of significance. He came from a large family, and had been well supported by their warmth and interest in him as he grew up. Although the seizures were a matter of common knowledge, he was embarrassed by his phobic fears and secretive about them. He described a good relationship with his siblings and his in-laws. He graduated from college, and had made impressive progress at work. At the age of twenty-nine years, he had achieved executive status. He appeared to have a good marriage. His health, apart from his major complaints, was also complicated by mild hypertension.

He made it clear in the initial evaluation of his problem that he found the discussion of his fears very embarrassing. He was uneasy about the prospect of a lengthy uncovering and insight-oriented treatment, and specifically requested symptom relief by the quickest possible means. When the availability of therapeutic hypnosis was mentioned, he became interested and enthusiastic. He was a pleasant man who related warmly, in a somewhat low key.

His responses to the scales measuring hypnotizability were interesting. On the Hypnotic Induction Profile his performance was average and he scored 2. On the Harvard Group Scale he rated himself 6. Observer rating of that same performance during the taped instructions was 10. When questioned subsequently on why he had circled the negative responses in the booklet when his experiences had been obviously positive, he appeared to be very mildly confused and seemed not to grasp fully the importance of the task, or the significance of the questions. Because of his apparent marked responsivity during the administration of the scale, it was thought that he might still have been in trance when asked to fill out the answers in the booklet and during the subsequent discussion. Accordingly, the Stanford Hypnotic Susceptibility Scale Form B was administered a week later, whereupon he scored 11. The one item he failed was that involving the posthypnotic suggestion to stand up.

Clinical Course

Because of his impressive response to induction procedures, and because of his motivation to obtain relief from his symptoms as rapidly as possible, the treatment strategy was based on having him imagine, when hypnotized and relaxed, that he was experiencing the very situations that he had been avoiding. Each situation was dealt with and mastered in a separate session. For example, he was directed in one session, once hypnotized and deeply relaxed, to imagine the steps involved in approaching a tall building that he had cause to visit fairly frequently. Once in the lobby he was encouraged to imagine, while he continued to be hypnotized and deeply relaxed, how he summoned the elevator, entered it, and rode to the thirteenth floor. He was able to remain calm throughout the whole imagined experience. He was then instructed in how to induce hypnosis himself, and to repeat the imagined succession of steps during his practice two or three times daily at home. He was also advised to practice shortly before he left his home on the day he intended visiting the building, and was given the suggestion that at any time in the feared situation he caressed the side of his face, he would be able to relax completely, and would reactivate the confidence he had gained in his last practice session. The following week he coped successfully with an elevator ride to the thirteenth floor, having practiced energetically, and using the face caress to calm himself when he felt the anxiety build up as he entered the elevator.

Subsequent sessions were then individually devoted to thinking about flying, sailing, and driving in heavy traffic, all of which situations he then successfully negotiated. It should be remembered that he had neither sailed nor flown for several years prior to the treatment. He was also encouraged in subsequent sessions to think, when in hypnosis and deeply relaxed, about his distorted visual perceptions and other seizure activities. The purpose was to help him cope with them with a minimum of panic. After a few months he reported no further seizures and an absence of strange feelings related to visual stimuli. The period is too brief to be considered significant, but is nonetheless worthy of note, and the clinical progress worth watching.

COMMENT

As stated above, it is difficult to ignore the association of depersonalization and phobic anxiety. Roth (1959) proposed that the syndrome constituted a new form of neurotic illness, and emphasized its most consistent feature as being the combination of depersonalization with a characteristic form of phobic anxiety. Among his cases was a high proportion of obsessional, hysterical, depressive features and vasomotor disturbances, and the histories of some revealed episodes of psychotic behavior. He drew attention to the fact that in 40 percent of his 135 cases with depersonalization and phobic anxiety, there were features reminiscent of disturbances of temporal lobe function, but the incidence of abnormal electroen-cephalograms, when these were recorded, was not significantly different from that in a control group of patients.

Roth lists an impressive variety of depersonalization experiences among his patients, and a number of overwhelming fears of collapsing, or of losing consciousness or control and appearing foolish or ridiculous in front of others. Many of these resemble the experiences reported by patients in the case histories of this book. After a consideration of the pre-cipitating factors in his patients, their previous personalities, their family background and personal development, he suggests that the phenomenon is linked to some dysfunction of the mechanisms regulating awareness. He adds that depersonalization or dissociation of consciousness, which often follows acute stress, may be suspected of playing a purposive role when short-lived, in that it probably helps to prevent the individual from being overwhelmed by emotion. In the light of that, he recommends that the neurosis involving depersonalization and phobic anxiety may be viewed biologically as the maladaptive prolongation of a protective response. He makes no mention of hypnotizability and the mental mechanisms involved in spontaneous trance. It is, however, but a short step from his position to include them.

This is especially relevant in the context of this book where two patients reported thus far (the patients in Cases III and XII) have shown depersonalization and phobic anxiety, in addition to marked hypnotizability and features generally associated with temporal lobe dysfunction. It will be recalled that in Case III markedly disturbed visual perception and panic occurred suddenly and very often in a phobic and highly hypnotizable woman when she drove her car, or even when she anticipated driving it on occasion. I have also reported elsewhere (Frankel, 1975) how episodes of perceptual distortion and panic appear to have been precipitated on occa-sion in a highly hypnotizable and phobic man when he moved from a shaded environment into bright lights, or vice versa. Electroencephalog-raphy performed on him subsequently revealed a temporal lobe focus. He had no other positive neurological findings.

The precise relationship of depersonalization, phobic anxiety, marked hypnotizability, and symptoms reminiscent of temporal lobe dysfunction is obscure, and beyond the scope of this book. However, their appearance together in three cases in a relatively small series, and Roth's allusion to a situation that is similar (even though he makes no reference to hypnotiza-bility), prompted this digression. A wide range of behaviors has been included under the rubric of temporal lobe dysfunction. Benson and Gesch-wind (1976), Margerison and Corsellis (1966), and Blumer (1975), among others, have described a list of varied behavioral acts ranging from those lasting a split second to those that continue for considerably longer periods. The acts are described as auras, ictal manifestations, or postical activities that can and do occur in isolation or independently of seizure discharge. From the clinical material described above, we may assume that some very similar events are reproducible under hypnosis in markedly hypnotizable individuals. In addition to obtaining an electroencephalogram whenever temporal lobe dysfunction is suspected from a description of unusual symptoms, an assessment of the patient's hypnotizability will assist in the ultimate understanding of the mechanisms at work in both temporal lobe epilepsy and marked hypnotizability, and any possible relationship between the two.

CASE HISTORY XIII
Fear of Dogs

A twenty-six-year-old man, trained as a school counselor and psychologically very aware, was referred, at his request, for therapeutic hypnosis for his disabling fear of dogs. He complained that when he encountered dogs, especially strange animals, he experienced a panic that froze him to the spot until the creatures moved away. At those times he became aware of his increased heartbeat and rapid respiration, he could feel the cold sweat on his body, and he was especially sensitive to spatial relationships linked to an acute appreciation of the distance between himself and the animal, and the relative positions of his wife and other people around him.

Some animals evoked the panic response more dramatically than others. German shepherds and Doberman pinschers were especially fearsome, as were small irascible dogs and older ones. Animals belonging to his friends or people he liked were more easily tolerated. Dogs in the company of the casual and shabbily dressed were almost acceptable, whereas those in the well-kept grounds of established suburban residences were usually very frightening. He was able to report these distinctions with some mirth as he was fully aware of their possible meaning. Having himself struggled with considerable rebellion against the Establishment during his high school and college years, he recognized the symbolic significance to him of animals associated with the counterculture, and those owned by the Establishment. On the other hand, dogs encountered on their own in the woods or relatively deserted places were particularly threatening, because he perceived them as answerable to no one, and governed solely by their aggression.

He dated his fear of dogs to his early childhood, with very vivid memories of his maternal grandfather warning him, at the age of four years, to stay away from dogs because they bite. He remembered the incident, and his pleasure when touching the wet nose of the dachshund that he was warned to steer clear of. He recalled that shortly thereafter his father had brought home a small brown mongrel puppy that the patient enjoyed until it was removed at his mother's insistence because it messed.

He remembered thereafter being almost constantly wary of the presence of dogs. At times he was able to grow accustomed to the animals he came across in the homes of his friends, but was generally rarely completely relaxed in their presence. At one stage in his early teens, a close friend who ultimately studied veterinary science was instrumental in exposing him to many animals under circumstances so relaxed that his confidence grew. That lasted for about a year. Since then, however, the anxieties had returned, and as an adult he had been embarrassed by having to take circuitous routes to avoid areas that he knew were frequented by dogs. Calling on friends known to keep dogs was barely tolerable; visiting people for the first time became an ordeal on discovering dogs in their homes, or on being met by strange dogs on the front path. His first inclination was to remain rooted to the spot until the animal had left him. He had had to depend heavily on his wife's reassurance on such occasions, to avoid following his inclinations and making a fool of himself. Generally the panic receded sufficiently after a few minutes to enable him to attend to the social situation, but it seemed to hover at the periphery of his awareness throughout the entire time he remained there. Interestingly, he reported that he had never, ever, been bitten or harmed by a dog.

He was the youngest of four siblings, raised in a warm but somewhat inflexible household. He described a comfortable relationship with his parents, now in their late fifties, but recognized that he had had considerable difficulty growing up, in coping with authority figures and conforming to regulations. He claimed he was rebellious at high school and a social activist at college. He had, nevertheless, done well academically, and was working toward a higher degree at the time of his request for treatment, while employed full-time as a school counselor. He had married a young woman of his age, who was furthering her own career in education.

He reported having been in therapy with the school psychologist throughout his years in high school, and having had insight-oriented weekly therapy for two years while in college. He had developed a considerable understanding of himself and of his problems, and even had some distance on his phobia. He could joke when describing it, but felt totally incapable of ridding himself of it even though he had benefited markedly from his therapy in other ways. He was especially interested in using hypnosis therapeutically to deal with the problem. His score was 3 on the Hypnotic Induction Profile, and 8 on the Harvard Group Scale.

Clinical Course

His total treatment covered six sessions. He was familiar with the principles of imaginal desensitization and hypnosis, and expressed a preference for combining hypnosis with an imagined graded exposure to dogs. He feared that the anxiety generated by thinking immediately of an encounter with a Doberman pinscher in the woods would be too disturbing for him. Accordingly, a hierarchy of twelve different experiences with dogs was readily drawn up, commencing with the least anxiety-provoking and finishing with the most noxious. The first picture involved meeting a familiar dog in the company of its owner. Intermediate steps included, among others, seeing an unfamiliar dog at a distance in the street, seeing a dog barking on its own territory, and having a dog come growling down the driveway of a house as he passed by. The final and most threatening picture was imagining meeting a stray Doberman pinscher in the woods, at dusk.

The desensitization procedure was begun only after hypnosis had been induced and he had been taught how to relax completely under such circumstances. This was accomplished in the first interview. He was taught how to induce self-hypnosis, and encouraged to practice it at home, in order to learn how to achieve complete relaxation. In the second session, the initial steps of the hierarchy were approached, progressively, in hypnosis, as the procedure of imaginal desensitization was followed. He was asked to imagine the picture under consideration for periods of thirty seconds, alternating with intervening thirty-second periods of complete relaxation and calm. Any signal from him while imagining the hierarchical step that communicated any anxiety led to an immediate instruction to discontinue that mental picture and to return to thirty seconds of complete relaxation. Only after he had successfully completed three successive thirty-second periods devoted to imagining the same scene, without anxiety, did we proceed to the next picture on the hierarchy.

It was recommended to him that in addition to practicing the self-induced hypnosis and relaxation at home between sessions, he should, in his practice exercises, repeatedly imagine the steps of the hierarchy that he had already successfully negotiated in the sessions. He was also advised, when hypnotized, that caressing the side of his face in any anxiety-producing encounter with dogs would reactivate the relaxation skills acquired in his last exercise and help him to achieve a calm confidence.

After the first session of desensitization, when only the first four items on the hierarchy had been covered, he found himself having to reassure two small children in the presence of an unknown large German shepherd. He was delightedly surprised at his ability to relax after stroking his face, and at the ease with which he asserted himself to protect and comfort the children. In yet another social situation after his fourth session, he had experienced the onset of a panic when a large and unknown dog, a boxer, appeared on the scene. He calculated that he was distant enough to be able to practice a brief exercise lasting about twenty seconds, before the dog could reach his chair. He sensed immediate relief in his breathing, and in his pulse rate as he concentrated on the feeling of relaxation and buoyancy. This enabled him to rise and move in the direction of the animal, dealing confidently and comfortably with the social situation as he went.

Subsequent reports refer to his increasing confidence and satisfaction in being able to go as he pleases without having to plan to avoid an encounter with dogs. He claims to have discovered what he had long suspected: that he himself had written the fear-ridden script he had previously repeatedly enacted.

Comments

As discussed in the comments on Case IV above, the therapeutic role of hypnosis in this instance is not entirely clear. The patient was well motivated to work with hypnosis, and it presented a useful therapeutic vehicle. It also permitted him very clearly to take the therapeutic hour with him to the symptom, which can be said of most procedures used effectively in the treatment of phobias.

It is usually impossible to know with any certainty what in the mix of treatment is primarily responsible for improvement. The patient himself believed it was learning that he was able to control his anxiety that made the major difference.

CHAPTER 9

Relationship of Phobic Behavior, Hypnotizability, and Conditioning

The six case histories in the last chapter reporting treatment of phobic behavior illustrate, quite well, common characteristics. Although none of these patients can be described as severely disabled, they were all prevented by their neuroses, in some way, from participating fully in what they were obligated or wished to do. The casual observer was likely to suspect neither the extent of the episodic disability nor the extreme discomfort of the panic they were compelled to experience under fairly pedestrian circumstances. Even in reporting their problems they too, at times, had some distance on them, as they shared their amused embarrassment at the exaggerated nature of their phobic responses. More serious discussion of the symptoms, however, revealed how real they were. Regardless of their irrational nature, the fears were impermeable to logic under ordinary circumstances, and the events that would precipitate them were energetically avoided or denied where possible. All the patients reported were highly hypnotizable, and in one instance markedly so. While these cases were selected for their variety, general interest, and relatively straightforward clinical course, they are not unique.

The treatment strategy in each of the cases included the use of hypnosis in combination with an accelerated form of imaginal desensitization. Even the last case, which required six treatment sessions, was conducted in less time than the routine deconditioning procedure. The assumption behind the strategy was that these patients would learn more rapidly in hypnosis than under ordinary circumstances, and indeed they did. It was as if hypnosis provided the mechanism for persuasion to prevail, and for the introduction of a different reasoning embracing optimistic expectations not previously possible. The assumption, in fact, went further. Because of the comments spontaneously reported by some patients that their exposure to hypnosis and the experience of their symptoms were similar, the treatment procedure regarded them as related events, and utilized hypnosis to create the analogue of the symptom. The essential difference was the fact that in hypnosis the experience was a controllable and reassuring one. What was experienced previously and outside of hypnosis as an event that was fearsome to live through, or even to think about, was reenacted imaginally in hypnosis. This event was achieved in the imagination by rapidly moving through a brief series of steps leading up to it. The procedure conducted under calm and relaxing circumstances led, within minutes on some occasions, to a comfortable familiarity with what had formerly been threatening.

Let us now pursue the relatedness of the clinical experience and hypnosis. It is difficult to disregard the clinical finding, described in the earlier case reports, that highly hypnotizable patients have a propensity for experiencing spontaneous trancelike events. As all the patients described in these case reports of phobic behavior had high hypnotizability ratings, it can be assumed that they were also capable of spontaneous trance experiences. The hallmark of hypnosis is the perceptual distortion referred to repeatedly in these pages. The panic of the phobic patient is fraught with such distortions. We are in no position to describe the events of the hypnotic trance and panic as identical, but they have much in common, and could be.

Phobias are understood, in psychodynamic terms, as the symbols of repressed, displaced, and projected unconscious, unacceptable wishes and feelings. The frequency of depersonalization and other evidence of distorted perception associated with phobic behavior means that dissociation is frequently part of the mechanism involved. We will seriously consider the postulate that in order to protect the equilibrium of the personality, an even more anxiety-provoking situation is created, namely, the sudden and panicked experience of dissociation with its accompanying perceptual distortions. The term "maladaptive defense" is particularly apt under these circumstances, a concept considered by Roth (1959) and already reported in these pages.

How often the anxiety of panic proportions precedes the distorted perception in addition to being a sequel to it raises an interesting question with no readily available answer. Marks (1969) reports the onset of phobias as being frequently associated with or precipitated by a feeling of panic. In other words, the phobic behavior we have been considering above appears to involve spontaneous dissociation that could be part of a defense against overwhelming anxiety, leading to an even more overwhelming situation that in turn promotes further dissociation. We will have considerable difficulty trying to differentiate this specific dissociation from that attained under the conditions created by a hypnotic induction procedure.

An interesting relationship between hypnosis and phobias has been pursued by others. Glick (1969, 1970) commented on the beneficial combination of hypnosis and imaginal desensitization in the treatment of phobias, and suspected that there was something specific about the use of hypnosis in the treatment of phobias. Horowitz (1970) reported on the effective use of hypnosis in the treatment of snake phobias, and Marks *et al.* (1968) have reported on equivalent results using suggestions under hypnosis, and desensitization procedures. I have reported elsewhere (Frankel, 1974) on the possible association of the capacity to experience trance and the genesis of phobic behavior, and in association with Orne (Frankel and Orne, 1976), have reinforced that hypothesis by accumulating some of the supportive data. Until recently the evidence has been largely anecdotal.

STUDY OF HYPNOTIZABILITY AND PHOBIC BEHAVIOR

To support the notion that phobic experiences could be related to hypnotic events, that they both employ the same mental mechanisms, and that phobias were attributable in part to the occurrence of spontaneous trancelike events, we needed evidence of greater hypnotizability among phobic patients than among a comparable group. In the study about to be described, we utilized the hypnotizability ratings on consecutive phobic patients applying for treatment at the Beth Israel Hospital who were interested in the possible use of hypnosis in their treatment program.

Since normative data based on volunteer college student populations are hardly appropriate for comparison, a specific control group of patients was needed. Ideally, such a group of individuals would be seeking to be hypnotized for treatment purposes, but not in order to modify psychiatric symptoms. Accordingly, routine hypnotizability ratings on individuals seeking help by means of hypnosis to quit smoking seemed a suitable control. Such individuals were comparable to phobic patients in that they shared the motivation to succeed in hypnosis, but were not otherwise within the spectrum of psychiatric patients as usually conceived.

Procedure

A series of twenty-four phobic patients who applied for treatment privately or at the clinic, and who were interested in the possible use of hypnosis, were tested for hypnotizability either on the Stanford Hypnotic Susceptibility Scale or the Harvard Group Scale individually administered, and compared with a similar number of patients tested in the same manner who applied to the Clinic for Therapeutic Hypnosis for help in quitting smoking.

Results

The mean score of the twenty-four phobic subjects was 8.08 on a twelve-point scale of hypnotic susceptibility. The mean score of twenty-four smokers was 6.08. The difference was significant beyond the .01 level (two-tailed). This is shown in Table 1.

Table 2 shows the distribution of high, medium, and low scores among phobics and smokers. This type of analysis shows that among both the phobic and the smoker groups, hypnotizability was skewed upward, as one might anticipate in a highly motivated, volunteer group. However, while among the smokers 30 percent were essentially nonresponsive, show-ing scores of a 0–4 on a twelve-point scale, *not a single nonresponsive individual was seen in the phobic group.* This difference is not only highly

Table 1

Hypnotizability and Symptomatology

Age *	Phobics			Smokers				
	N	$\overline{X}$	SD	N	$\overline{X}$	SD	t	p
All Ss	24	8.08	2.12	24	6.08	2.98	2.68 = .01 2-tailed	
40+	4	6.00	.82	7	7.14	1.86	1.40	
39−	20	8.50	2.06	17	5.65	3.28	3.10 < .01 2-tailed	

* It is worth noting that the mean age of the phobics was slightly lower than that of the smokers, and since hypnotizability tends to decrease in older individuals, the differences in scores become even more pronounced when only patients under thirty-nine are compared.

Table 2

Distribution of Hypnotizability in Different Groups

		Phobic	Smoker	
	Hi (8–12)	14	9	
HGS	Med (5– 7)	10	8	X^2 (Hi vs. Lo) = 5.73
	Low (0– 4)	0	7	(2-tailed) $p < .025$

significant, but the total absence of truly low responders among the phobic group suggests a phenomenon of great clinical relevance.

Within the phobic group, patients were divided into those reporting multiple phobias and those complaining of only a single phobia. On Table 3, seventeen patients reported more than one phobia whereas seven had only one. The mean score among the former was 8.53, whereas that among patients with a single phobia was seven. This difference is significant beyond the .05 level (two-tailed) and supports a further link between the occurrence of phobic symptoms and hypnotizability.

Discussion

The findings reported above lend strong empirical support to the view that phobic patients show a tendency to the same kind of mental functioning that is involved in responding to hypnotic induction. They also suggest that individuals who develop phobic symptoms must have the capability of manifesting the kind of cognitive functioning that characterizes the hypnotized individual.

Before proceeding, we need to consider these findings in the context of the work of others who have examined the possible relevance of high hypnotizability, and how it might correlate with psychiatric illness or personality structure. It will be remembered that systematic work in the past

Table 3

Hypnotizability and Number of Phobias

	N	$\overline{X}$	SD
Multiple phobia	17	8.53	2.24
Single phobia	7	7.00	1.41

$t = 2.01$ $p = .05$ (2-tailed)

two decades has shown that the ability to enter hypnosis is normally distributed in the normal population (Hilgard, 1965), and that an individual's ability to enter hypnosis shows remarkable consistency over time and can appropriately be viewed as a stable trait (Morgan, Johnson, and Hilgard, 1974). It will also be remembered that, surprisingly, hypnotizability has not been shown to be associated with any of the usual tests of personality (Shor, Orne, and O'Connell, 1966) and that even with extensive clinical interviews it was very difficult to predict an individual's response to hypnosis (Hilgard, J.R., 1970).

Superficially, the findings in our study reported above might appear to contradict the well-documented observations of these other workers, until it is recognized that their observations were largely within the normal population, and our findings derive from a different population—that of individuals seeking psychiatric help. This may help explain the apparent paradox between the lack of identifiable personality attributes associated with high hypnotizability within a normal population, and the relative ease with which the hypnotizable individuals reported by us were recognized. Our findings are also in line with Gill and Brenman's observation (1959) that hypnotizability is higher among normals than among any clinical population, but that among *patient populations* hypnotizability is most pronounced among hysterics.

CONDITIONING PROCEDURES AND HYPNOSIS

If all or most phobic patients are indeed moderately responsive to hypnosis, what might be said about the hypnotic relevance of the relaxation procedures and repetitive phrases used in the techniques of imaginal desensitization? It does not seem unreasonable to raise questions about what, in reality, is the effective mechanism in the impressive results of deconditioning in phobic patients. In the deconditioning process with its emphasis on the content and arrangement of the hierarchy the essential therapeutic lever; or might the hypnotic responsivity be playing a large, even if unrecognized, role in leading to the patient's altered behavior? From the clinical experience with the phobic patients discussed above, and the effectiveness of their experiencing the trance and the encouragement while in it to imagine the feared situation, I had begun to suspect that even when hypnosis was not formally induced in imaginal desensitization, hypnotic responsivity was probably being tapped. The question was whether the relaxation procedures and repetitive phrases included in the desensitization program did not contribute to producing a trance or trancelike state in phobic patients who were all, as shown above, at least moderately hypnotizable. In the circumstances this is best described as covert hypnosis. While I was musing on the difficulty, inherent in clinical studies, in establishing with certainty what therapeutic mechanisms are responsible for improvement, Cautela's recent and interesting publication (Cautela, 1975), in which he grasped the initiative on behalf of conditioning therapy, appeared. He was asking the same question of hypnosis that had been asked of conditioning—namely, do hypnotherapists claim to be carrying out one procedure, while in effect they carry out another? In other words, does the technique of hypnotherapy, under some circumstances, depend far more than hypnotists realize on conditioning procedures that go unrecognized? Cautela compares hypnotic treatment procedures employing imagery with what he describes as covert conditioning. The concept of covert conditioning is based on the conjecture that if overt punishment is successful in inhibiting positive responses, perhaps aversive stimuli presented in imagination only would have the same effect. The main assumption underlying the covert conditioning procedures is that stimuli presented in imagination *via* instructions affect covert and overt behavior in a manner similar to stimuli presented externally; i.e., if an individual is asked to imagine a noxious stimulus just after he has imagined a response, the probability of the response will decrease. For example, if an obese person is directed to imagine that he is nauseated and vomits while thinking of eating a delicious pastry in a bakery, his enthusiastic response to bakeries will diminish in the future. Also, if a pleasant or reinforcing stimulus is presented to a subject just after he has imagined a response, then we can expect the probability of the response to increase in a manner similar to the effects of external reinforcement.

Referring to the fact that imagery has been used by hypnotherapists both to facilitate hypnotic induction and to treat maladaptive behaviors, Cautela proposes that the successful treatment results of the hypnotherapists might, in part, be due to their unwitting use of this covert conditioning procedure. He illustrates his point by describing posthypnotic suggestions in which patients are to think of the word "scar" each time they pick their faces; imagine revolting scenes every time they bite their nails; and imagine that they are getting nauseated when they take a drink. He speculates on the possibility that the acknowledged use of covert conditioning by hypnotherapists would increase the probability of successful treatment results, and considers it likely that the hypnotic induction procedure itself may serve to facilitate covert conditioning. His presentation is persuasive.

Returning now to the topic of phobias, of the four procedures described by Cautela as available for changing response probability—

namely, punishment, positive reinforcement, negative reinforcement and extinction—the one he believes most relevant to the treatment of *phobias* is covert positive reinforcement. This procedure entails first accustoming the patient to imagining pleasant, reinforcing scenes of his own choosing by having him repeatedly practice at doing so. The scenes are then called to mind periodically by the therapist during the office session, as the patient proceeds to imagine each step of the way in his move toward the feared object. Because of the very pleasant feeling accompanying the reinforcing, imagined scene, the customary relaxation procedures are considered to be unnecessary.

The similarity between this last mentioned deconditioning procedure and a situation in which hypnosis is induced to permit the patient more vividly to create the image of the feared situation under comfortable circumstances is very clear. The two events might even be indistinguishable apart from the inclusion of the formal hypnotic induction procedure in one, and the imagining of pleasant scenes in the other.

We might digress here for a moment to acknowledge again that hypnosis is what the patient experiences, not necessarily what the hypnotist instructs him to do. This will remind us that for highly hypnotizable subjects, repeatedly imagining pleasant scenes can readily lead to a hypnotic trance even when a more formal induction procedure is lacking. If the findings are valid that few, if any, phobic patients score low on the hypnotizability rating scales, and the hypothesis reasonable that phobic behavior and spontaneous trance behavior are related, then the occurrence of a trance in the context of the covert positive reinforcement procedure, spontaneously and in the absence of a formal induction, must be a possibility. Were such a trance to occur, and were the patient to produce images of the feared situation while in it, he might well be creating an analogue of the phobic experience referred to previously in these pages, and in this way be reliving a previously frightening event under more reassuring and controlled circumstances. In this manner the covert conditioning is being enhanced by the addition of a covert trance, and the same useful advice employed by Cautela in recommending that hypnotherapists modify their treatment by acknowledging and openly employing covert conditioning is applicable. Behavior therapists would probably be more successful in achieving their goals with phobic patients more rapidly by the overt use of a hypnotic induction procedure. Cautela does recommend the consideration of this, but not for the reasons that I have mentioned.

There can be little doubt that any further understanding of the relationships touched on in this section will stem only from further studies not from additional theorizing. The effectiveness of the various treatment forms in dealing with phobic behaviors demands careful investigation, and a highly important component of the methodology is likely to be a measurement of hypnotizability on all the subjects and controls. The outcome of such studies is not solely of interest theoretically. In practical terms, if the phobic patient's hypnotic response is ultimately considered to be the effective therapeutic lever, then a carefully planned hierarchy is redundant and hypnosis is of the essence. Where the hypnotic response is unimpressive and therefore unimportant, the traditional procedures of imaginal desensitization should take precedence.

CHAPTER 10

Therapeutic Failures

The following two cases are included because although the treatment for phobias outlined above is effective in many cases, some patients do not improve with it. Judgments in retrospect are generally easier, even if more sobering, than prognoses. The histories suggest that any method of therapy, including therapeutic hypnosis, is likely to succeed only when it is the right treatment, at the right time, and can mesh with the psychodynamic forces at work in the clinical picture. With therapy, it is as difficult to be certain about the causes of failure as it is to be certain about the reasons for success. Although both patients were motivated to respond well to hypnosis, neither were strongly motivated to work toward ridding themselves of their symptoms or changing their life patterns. Sifneos (1972) in his work with short-term psychotherapy, has drawn attention to the importance of positive motivation for therapy to succeed.

CASE HISTORY XIV
Persistent Flight Phobia

A twenty-seven-year-old salesman was referred for an opinion regarding the value of hypnosis in the treatment of his fears and phobias. He had been treated with both tranquilizers and antidepressant medication without improvement; and had been seen briefly in insight-oriented psychotherapy but found to be unsuitable because of his apparent inability to talk much about his personal life or his feelings.

His history revealed that he had developed an intense fear of flying within recent years, and that although he had forced himself to fly on one occasion four months prior to seeing me, he had found it very stressful. He was also unhappy about members of his family taking plane trips. Prior to his flight four months before, he had not flown for almost two years. He attributed his fear of flying to a fear of death, for himself and for his close relatives, which had been on his mind fairly constantly for a year or two. A closer examination of his concerns with death revealed some preoccupation with the claustrophobic aspects of interment, which had bothered him occasionally since his first years in college, and fairly constantly recurring fears and fantasies about the death of his parents, especially his father. The primacy of the preoccupation with his own interment and his father's dying became apparent only in the eighth interview. In sessions prior to that time, the emphasis had been on his fear of death as a result of flying. Despite the obvious distress apparent even in thinking about flying, he maintained on several occasions that if he had to fly, he knew he could.

He was the only child of a very successful New England stockbroker whom he admired, loved, and wished to emulate. He felt close to both his parents, rarely mentioned his mother, and talked of how he enjoyed spending much of his leisure time in his father's company, discussing business matters. After graduating from college he had worked in his father's business for a few years, and had then left to gain experience in other organizations. He was barely in touch with his deeper feelings about his father, but did recognize a degree of competitiveness on his own part, and a keen desire to succeed in business to an even greater extent than his father had done, and at an earlier age. He also conceded after several interviews that he was often frustrated by his father's comments that he, the patient, was in too much of a hurry to achieve his goals.

He had had a comfortable school and college career, and had worked reasonably well, achieving average grades. He claimed that he wished to be constantly in control of himself and of his feelings, as was his father. He had always dressed extremely well and formally in an era when this had become the rare exception, and had never permitted himself to display his anger or his distress in public. He had had several superficial friendships but no close friends either at school or at college.

Two years prior to his referral for treatment he had married a woman his own age who worked as a travel agent. They had no children. Because of her job she had access to, and had made frequent flights. He admitted his envy of her because of this, and although he had accompanied her on an occasion four months prior to his initial visit (referred to above), he felt distinctly inferior to her because of his problem. The marriage was under stress because of his withdrawal emotionally, and because she objected to his frequent and lengthy visits to his parents' home. For several months he had spent his evenings watching television to divert his attention from his unpleasant thoughts about death and flying. Sexually he was inhibited, very controlled, and not nearly as active as she had wished him to be. Despite his overriding preoccupations and concerns, he had attended to his work regularly and successfully, and had made considerable strides. The onset of his symptoms was difficult to relate chronologically to any specific events, but appears to have been associated with the period that he worked for his father.

He was a good-looking man, impeccably and conservatively dressed, extremely polite, and very formal in his manner. His character style was markedly obsessive-compulsive and narcissistic. He seemed reasonably intelligent, and had a remarkable capacity to persist in the face of difficulties. He had almost no awareness of his conflict regarding his parents, nor of the extent of his angry feelings toward them and toward his therapy.

Hypnosis

Having reached a stalemate with his previous therapist who referred him, he arrived, claiming to be interested in the use of hypnosis in his case, and in the initial interview scored between 3 and 4 on the Hypnotic Induction Profile. The rating on each phase was consistently high. On his subsequent visit he scored 11 out of a possible 12 on the Stanford Hypnotic Susceptibility Scale, failing only item 4, by being able to raise his arm more than one inch in ten seconds after having been told it would be too heavy to lift. His high ratings were an encouragement to consider therapeutic hypnosis in his case, despite the poor response in his previous treatment.

As he indicated that he wished, particularly, to be helped with the flight phobia, a hierarchy consisting of ten items, each approaching closer to the final step of sitting in the plane and flying, was drawn up on his third visit. He claimed to be interested in mastering the flying because he recognized it as the most accessible of his fears, and believed that by overcoming it he would experience a greater confidence in tackling his other problems. He considered his fear of flying as especially humiliating. He was taught to induce self-hypnosis and to relax during that exercise. He was also encouraged to practice the exercise two or three times per day for about ten minutes on each occasion, between his visits.

Clinical Course

He made good progress on the hierarchy during his sessions, and by the fourth session devoted to working with it, he was able to imagine himself flying comfortably in the plane, in a totally calm and relaxed state. He had, however, complained that he was having difficulty achieving the state of relaxation in his exercises at home. This aspect was given special attention during the session.

On his next visit, which was the eighth of the total number of visits, he claimed that although he was more capable of achieving relaxation in his exercises at home, he had practiced only four times in a period of two weeks. His plan to achieve in vivo some measure of what he had already accomplished with the imagery had been thwarted by his inability to concentrate on his exercise in a departure lounge at the airport because of the noise. He spent much of that eighth interview discussing his claustrophobic fear of coffins, and his concerns about his father's death. He then presented them as overriding preoccupations whenever he was not busy working, discussing business with his father, or watching television.

The subsequent event was a phone call from his wife, interested, but distraught because she felt excluded by him from being in any way helpful. She was urged by me to discuss her phone call to me with him.

Although he talked on his next visit about the fact that his fearful preoccupations were interfering with his marriage, he was still keen to continue his struggle with the problem without his wife's help. He claimed to be very fond of her, and had tended to demonstrate this by spending considerable sums of money on expensive gifts for her.

The subsequent five visits were devoted, in part, to strengthening his ability to relax in the exercise, and to drawing up plans for gaining real experience in some of the earlier steps on the hierarchy. He also talked of the possibility of his taking a short flight, and of having his wife accompany him on one of his therapy visits. A large proportion of each interview, however, was devoted to his concerns about succeeding, and about how he wished he could be less controlled and generally more relaxed. The gentlest probing in questions led to his changing of the subject, and despite his repeated assertion that he was keenly interested in flying and in preserving his marriage, neither the plans involving his wife nor those that included regular practice between sessions eventuated.

He then called to cancel two appointments because he had become involved in an ambitious business venture. He was to call to arrange for a subsequent appointment as soon as he knew what his timetable would be, but he never did.

Discussion

It is apparent from the history that this man had had difficulty in most of his relationships, solving the problem eventually by becoming emotionally involved with virtually no one in his life other than his father. This was complicated by his counterdependence and his competitiveness, and was associated with a passive-aggressive quality and an inability to accept help from men in authority. In therapy he seemed to refuse to share very much of his history or emotional experience. Quite apart from his character problems, he appeared to be struggling with fairly severe depressed feelings, and gave the impression that if not for his very rigid obsessive-compulsive defenses he might have shown more severe psychiatric symptoms.

His exceptionally good scores on the hypnotizability scales remain somewhat of a challenge. With his need to discredit authority figures, it is surprising that he scored as well as he did. His behavior on being tested was convincing, and in no way suggested that he was merely complying with the requests. Similarly, his responses to the procedures in imaginal desensitization followed a model course. He claimed, by the end of the fourth treatment session, to be completely relaxed and calm while imagining that he was on a flight. It was immediately after that stage that his confused motivation appeared to interfere with his execution of the treatment program. Some doubt remains as to whether the failure of treatment was due to spurious hypnotizability scores (because disturbed patients are generally not very responsive to the hypnotizability scales he was tested on), or due to strong psychodynamic forces in him compelled to resist any recommended means of improvement, or both.

CASE HISTORY XV

Persistent Fear of Dogs

A twenty-five-year-old mother of two small children was referred for the treatment of phobias. She complained of several fears that had started about the time of her marriage five years previously, but was especially phobic about dogs, which she carefully avoided. She was also fearful of cats, of riding in elevators, and of being attacked. Although initially gradual in onset, her symptoms had kept her relatively housebound in recent years. She had become dependent on her husband to take her shopping and to attend to the laundry, as both these chores entailed her having to leave her apartment and confront the neighborhood dogs. Because of her fears of being attacked, she insisted that her husband be at home with her after nightfall. As this interfered with his work schedule, the problem came to a head.

In discussing the nature of her fear of animals, and of dogs in particular, she described a fear of being jumped upon by the creatures.

Although she could tolerate a cat being in the same room as herself, she had not permitted a dog to come closer to her than ten feet since the symptoms had begun. On the rare occasions when she had succeeded in forcing herself to make trips to the stores or the laundry, she had lessened her sense of fearfulness by turning her mind to the praise her husband would shower on her for braving the situation. By deliberately thinking of other things, she had, on occasion, been able to forget about her fear of dogs. When one approached, she would move quickly into the closest building, and had even sat in stange cars at times. Finding an acquaintance or friend nearby to talk with had also helped her to remain where she was until the animal had passed by. When in the fearsome situation, she experienced feelings of hunger, palpitations, tachycardia, and perspiration. These would continue until she felt safe.

She recalled having been pushed over by a dog when five or six years old, but did not remember having been hurt at the time. She claimed she was pursued by a collie at the age of ten. She ran, slipped and fell, and to her surprise found that the animal walked away when she lay without moving for a while.

Beginning about eighteen months prior to her initial consultation with the clinic, she had attended weekly private psychotherapy for almost a year. Although she gained considerable confidence from her visits, she developed no understanding of the nature of her symptoms. She was able to move about somewhat more freely for a while, but decided against returning to her previous therapist when the problem relapsed, because of the expense.

Regarding her personal history, she was the youngest of four siblings, and her parents were living and well. As a small child she had felt close to her father and was considered his favorite. As she matured, she had felt a growing disgust as she recognized the extent to which her mother controlled him. She had been ignorant of sexual matters until her mid-teens, and although shy, had managed to attend college in a midwestern state, a considerable distance from her parents' home. She had married at the age of twenty to a man two years her senior. He was a college graduate and well thought of by his employers. They had two small daughters, the elder two and one-half years old and the other not yet six months. Although she had become sexually unresponsive after the first birth, her interest had returned since the arrival of the second child. She attributed this to her nursing of the new infant, which had allowed her to feel "more of a woman." She made no reference to the association, but it appeared that her phobic symptoms had worsened toward the end of her pregnancy and since the second birth.

Evaluation

She was considered to have a characteristic phobic neurosis, precipitated initially by her marriage and aggravated recently by the stress of pregnancy, childbirth, and having to care for two small children. Although somewhat helpful, her course of psychotherapy had produced only a limited improvement. Both she and her husband were reluctant to commit themselves to a lengthy and expensive second term of therapy. She, especially, claimed to be interested in getting relief for her symptoms, which were interfering with her marriage and her husband's advancement at work. When hypnosis was offered as a possible adjunct to therapy, she was interested, and agreeable to it. Her response to hypnosis on the Hypnotic Induction Profile was 4. Her experiences in the test were consistently impressive, and indicative of a good reaction to the induction procedure. On a subsequent occasion she failed to achieve a negative hallucination, but was unable to separate her clasped fingers when told that she would be unable to do so. From her behavior she appeared to be at least a highly hypnotizable person.

Clinical Course

She was seen in a modified program of imaginal desensitization augmented by hypnosis, for a total of five treatment sessions at roughly two-weekly intervals. The frequency of the visits was influenced by her commitments to her schedule at home, and the expenses of babysitters and travel. The program commenced with directions in how to achieve self-hypnosis. She was to practice exercises lasting about ten minutes and involving self-induced hypnosis and relaxation, three times a day.

In her second treatment session, the deconditioning process was initiated by utilizing a strategy that she had helped to evolve. She was to imagine herself observing a dog in her yard, through a sliding glass door. The dog was to be brought, by degrees, from a distance of about fifty feet to within ten feet of the door. At that point she was to begin opening the door an inch at a time, ultimately stepping outside to approach within touching distance of the dog. All the steps of the hierarchy were to be undertaken in hypnosis. Within the second treatment session she was able to imagine the dog ten feet from the door, which had been opened about nine inches. She was to continue practicing the exercise of self-hypnosis at home, three times a day. She was expected, in these exercises, to concentrate primarily on achieving a sense of complete relaxation and comfort. She could, if she continued to feel relaxed and so inclined, also imagine the steps of the hierarchy that had been covered in the treatment sessions, but she was strongly advised against going beyond that point on the hierarchy.

At the third treatment session she reported that her daughter's schedule had interfered with her exercise routine, and that she was embarrassed by practicing in her husband's presence. She had, therefore, done the exercises only once a day, and had achieved a good trance on only four occasions. She had done the laundry on the previous day, however, and admitted that she had felt the need to bring a gift to the therapy session to compensate for her poor record since the last meeting. She was then able, during the session and in hypnosis, to imagine that the door was two feet ajar and that she had moved out toward the dog, close enough to touch him. She then described him as "cuddly and cute, with a wagging tail."

In the fourth treatment session she complained that the self-induced exercises at home had become so intense that she had become anxious about them. When the meaning of this comment was discussed with her, she talked of her concern about being a generally undisciplined person, and of her fear that she would not be able to persist with the program of exercises. She admitted that she had not even done a daily exercise since the last visit, as she had recognized that the end point would involve her having to confront real dogs. She then became tearful and complained that she had always to do things for others. She had undertaken this treatment primarily for her husband. She reported that she much preferred to spend the time with him in the evenings instead of doing the exercises. This had provoked him to anger, and they had argued. He had formerly offered to leave an interesting sales job with attractive prospects to earn more at a construction job, in order to have her return to her private therapist. She had insisted that he was not to follow that course, and had agreed to the hypnosis treatment in the clinic to prevent it. Aware of her commitment and feeling obligated to continue, she acknowledged she was angry.

After having considered these factors, she dried her tears and then admitted that she had visited a pet shop and had admired the puppies through the window. She claimed that she was quite comfortable while looking at them, and that she intended going into the store on the next occasion that she was in the neighborhood. She also conceded that she had been able, during the exercises that she had previously practiced on her own at home, to imagine herself approaching the dog and patting him, and being completely comfortable while doing so.

On her fifth and final visit, she appeared bright and particularly well groomed. She had visited the pet shop and had accomplished her Christmas shopping on her own. She had encountered several dogs in the street, and had been able to ignore them, as if they "were trees." She claimed to be surprised that she had progressed this far, and that she felt comfortable with it.

While in the hypnotic trance during that visit, she was able to feel relaxed while imagining herself patting the dog and walking with him. She was confident that she could increase her exposure to confrontations with the neighborhood dogs. She did not feel the need for a further appointment at that time, but undertook to report her progress by phone, or by letter, within the ensuing weeks. In answer to her request, she was given the assurance that she could call for an appointment should she deem it necessary.

Six months elapsed before the arrival of a letter, which reported very satisfactory progress. She claimed that she had shopped on her own, and that she had been attending to her laundry herself. She also reported that she had invited her in-laws to visit with their dog plus a litter of puppies, and was eagerly awaiting their arrival. The second part of the letter was written a week after the first. In it, she expressed doubts about herself and her progress. She re-emphasized that she had indeed attended to her shopping and her laundry, and that she was able to cope with the neighborhood dogs fairly comfortably. She reported, however, that when away from home she was sometimes anxious in the presence of strange but friendly and frisky dogs. She claimed that if her phobia were improved, this should not bother her. Nevertheless she was fairly confident that she would cope with the visit of her in-laws, and their puppies.

The next report of her progress came from her husband about eighteen months later. Her symptoms had relapsed, and the marriage was threatened. She had refused her husband's request that she ask for an appointment. Six months later still—that is, two years after her letter—she telephoned to report that the two-year period had been a very unhappy one. Her husband had been interested in another woman, but the rather lengthy episode was now ended. She was feeling better and was thinking about acquiring a dog.

Discussion

This history was heavily punctuated with psychodynamically significant aspects. It is difficult to escape the sexual symbolism of the fearsome dogs that might jump upon her, and the rather confused and guilty relationship with her husband, whom she regarded more like a father than a spouse. Her marked dependence on his approval, his concern, and his attention contributed in no small measure to the secondary gain from her symptoms. This markedly affected her motivation to get well, and is reflected in her obvious ambivalence toward treatment and her progress. Despite the acknowledgment of her anger at one point in the treatment, her more usual pattern was a considerably more passive-aggressive one.

Despite the wealth of psychodynamic clues, and her high hypnotizability rating, both traditional psychotherapy and the treatment with hypnosis failed. At no point in the clinical course was there an unequivocal and lasting improvement in the symptom. If it appeared to be easier in one area, it was worse or no better in another. If it happened to improve some, this was not maintained. The conflict in the marriage, both explicit and implied, and the unresolved Oedipal issues, seem to have been at the root of the problem, as were her poor motivation to deal with them, her passive-aggressive style, and our inability to change any of them.

Hypnotizability and Related Physical Symptoms

I would like to return to a consideration of physical symptoms and the relevance of high hypnotizability in that context. It will be remembered that among the first seven case histories reported in the earlier chapters were two patients with incapacitating physical complaints. They had both undergone surgery to the spine with little benefit, and continued to struggle with the effects of their poorly understood diseases. Reference was made to the fact that their persistent and puzzling physical complaints bore a resemblance to the physical sensations that can be created as effects of hypnosis; it was emphasized that both people were highly hypnotizable, and the occurrence of spontaneous trance was considered a factor in the etiology of the clinical picture. The case history that we will now examine in some detail extends over many years from puberty to menopause; the treatment program differs from the earlier two cases of physical symptoms in that it lasted for a few years, and the psychotherapy and hypnosis were in the hands of the same therapist.

CASE HISTORY XVI

Multiple Symptoms

Psychiatric consultation was requested on a forty-eight-year-old divorced mother of two teen-age sons because of her persistent and puzzling symptoms. She complained in general terms of being able to function neither physically nor "as a human being." More specifically she talked of periodically aching pains in her muscles, joints, and bones; occasional swelling of the joints at those times; feelings of being cold and weak; and ultimately involuntary crying when she felt her body folding. Capitulation, in tears, sometimes led to an improvement in her condition. The present bout of symptoms had been in evidence for approximately two months since the onset of a viral illness diagnosed as flu; but it was, according to her, merely another in a long succession of similar episodes that had started during her adolescence, worsened during her years at college, and had persisted, unabated, since then. She had been given few firm diagnoses throughout the thirty years of her troubles, but many tentative theories and innumerable medical preparations that she had continued to administer to herself in varying doses, some with the help of her family physician, and some on her own prescription because she believed they helped her. They included among other items, neostigmine, thyroid, amphetamine with amobarbital (never exceeding two tablets per day), vitamin preparations, calcium, diazepam, antihistamines, and more recently, steroids. They all tended to provide some relief at varying times, but apparently not very consistently. Food, warmth, and bed rest were frequently helpful as were one or two drinks.

The periodicity of the symptoms was difficult to establish, but it was clear that they were often precipitated by viral infections, that they lasted from days to weeks at times, that they were less apparent in the summer months, and that the present episode being more severe and more enduring than many had led to her present admission to the hospital for further investigations. She had been admitted to the hospital fifteen years previously for intensive study at a time when she was so disabled by the symptoms that she spent almost a year in bed. Diagnoses considered at that time included myopathy, arthritis of rheumatoid nature, lupus erythematosis, and phosphorylase deficiency. On this occasion, neurological disease having been ruled out, endocrine disorder and allergic reaction were added to the list. She had never been given a definite and lasting diagnosis. Her health during childhood had been marred by occasional migraine headaches, and not inconsiderable abdominal pain and vomiting, which was finally relieved by a surgical procedure at the age of thirteen years, to relieve what she described as "constricting bands in the vicinity of the stomach."

She was a tall and impressive woman, highly intelligent and talkative, and in the initial interview considerably more revealing about her physical symptoms than about her personal life and feelings. She had been described by the medical resident staff as "fascinating and difficult to follow at times, possibly because of her intelligence." She was viewed by them as seductive in a narcissistic and intellectual way, if not sexual. She informed me early in the interview that she had seen two well-known psychiatrists several years previously, each for about two years, but had felt she derived little benefit from the treatment and had discontinued it.

Much of the information concerning her personal and family history emerged later in subsequent interviews, only after hypnosis had been used to provide her with some relief from her physical symptoms. Some of those interviews were augmented by hypnosis as a vehicle for reaching otherwise inaccessible memories. Interviews with members of her family and some of her friends, all at her request, added to the information.

She was the oldest of three siblings. She had a sister still living whom she liked but saw only occasionally, and had lost her only brother, six years younger than herself, from a malignant illness five years previously. She and he had been close, although there had been disagreements prior to his terminal illness. Her parents had died within a few years of one another, around the time of her brother's death. This had led to considerable grief and sadness, in addition to considerable responsibility for settling the estates. Although raised and still living in New York, she had family ties firmly planted in New England, with a background dedicated to duty and hard work. Her father, several years older than her mother, had been a highly successful man, warm and interesting, but deeply committed to his professional career and rarely involved emotionally with his family and their problems. She claimed to have felt very close to him when he was available. She had both loathed and admired her very critical and argumentative mother, who had been totally rejecting of all the children while she pursued her career as a concert artist, conforming very little to social demands. The patient considered her parents' marriage a poor one. She was raised by a series of nannies, occasionally coming under the influence of an interested and kindly grandmother, whom she had loved.

Although rarely praised for it, she had done well as school, and graduated from college with honors. After working in public relations for a few years, she married a man about her own age recently graduated from law school. The marriage had been emotionally unsatisfactory from the start, but produced two very bright and talented sons who, at the time she was first interviewed, were eighteen and sixteen years old. Her husband had been totally incapable of sustaining her in her grief when the three close members of her family had died within three years. Despite his competence in legal matters, he had offered her no help whatsoever in the reorganization of the legacies. He had, instead, withdrawn increasingly, his moods culminating in a severe depression and his insistence on leaving the home.

Against the background of her own unfulfilled emotional needs, she was left to raise two adolescent sons, having little confidence in her ability to set legitimate and constant limits. When helped to do so, she could talk about her emotionally deprived childhood and her predominantly sad and lonely adult life. Despite opportunities for a second marriage, she remained constantly alert to the possibility of such an arrangement adding responsibilities and demands with little assurance that she would gain what she desperately needed; to be taken care of in addition to caring. She spent a considerable portion of her time away from home, participating in committee work related to philanthropic ventures. Despite her unusually imaginative approach, and the high regard of many with whom she worked, she often felt she lacked the credentials to be doing the kind of work she was involved in. When confronted by opposition, she had great difficulty deciding on whether she should meet it with aggression and assertiveness, or passivity and acquiescence. She not infrequently vacillated, creating confusion among others and dissatisfaction with herself for being inconsistent.

She offered no information regarding the severity of her physical symptoms at the times of her intense emotional stress, and any attempts to relate important events in her history to a recrudescence of symptoms were unsuccessful. Only during the course of therapy was some chronological association between current stress and complaints about physical symptoms recognizable.

Hypnosis

Because of the interesting history of puzzling symptoms, and the eagerness of her current physicians to offer her some relief other than by adding to her medication, the subject of hypnosis was introduced in the very first interview. Although she had had no previous experience or knowledge of the topic, she was interested in experiencing it. It must be stated that at the time of the initial consultation, massive building operations were underway in the neighboring lot outside of her window. Despite the incessant thumping of a pile driver, she responded immediately and remarkably well to the Hypnotic Induction Profile, with a score of between 3 and 4 on all the phases. On a subsequent occasion she was unable to separate her interlocked fingers when challenged to, but could not experience negative hallucinations when encouraged to do so. Several months later she scored 10 on the Harvard Group Scale (maximum score is 12).

In discussing her response to the first induction procedure in that very noisy situation, she talked excitedly of how readily she seemed able to exclude the environment when she was unable to cope with it. She recognized that she generally paid a price subsequently for doing so, but claimed to be incapable of preventing it. She proceeded to speak of blocking out memories, frequently involuntarily, and of how there were large patches of her life in her senior year of high school and in college that she remembered not at all. She added that at times, her head felt as if it were divided into sections, and that whole sections involving large blocks of experience were then unavailable to her. After taking one or other of the medications that she depended on, the previously unavailable section would seem to return. She talked of often being able to recognize the intentions of others, and of something like clairvoyance in her relationships.

During a subsequent meeting with her, after an induction procedure designed to help her relax and block out the painful feelings in her fingers and joints, she reported a "foggy" feeling that persisted after the trance. She likened it to wool separating the top of her head and her feet from the rest of her, and compared it with feelings she had had premenstrually when coming down with a cold. She continued to describe how she had no sense of herself, that she felt vague, and that this would ordinarily be frightening to her had it not happened frequently before. She referred to two distinct parts of herself that at times failed to mesh, which resulted in her "getting stuck between levels as if between gears." She admitted that she had not spoken of this to others, not even her doctors, for fear of scaring them into hasty conclusions that she was very odd; and that she had jocularly attributed the experiences to a wrong combination of astrological signs to satisfy both her imagination and her sense of humor.

She then described the conflict between assertiveness and passivity, already referred to above, but in terms that conveyed the impression that she functioned like two different people when following one or other character style. She claimed that while being assertive, for example, she could have no idea at all about what it felt like to be otherwise. It was as if she were totally absorbed by and committed to being someone totally different at those times from the person she would be were she passive. She felt, too, that she usually had little or no control over which style she adopted. She might present one aspect of herself on one occasion, and then on another under similar external circumstances have no clear idea of how she had behaved previously. This confused others because they found her unpredictable, yet very determined and "quixotic." There were times when she felt "out of it" because she was caught between the two tendencies, unable to proceed in either direction.

In pursuit of the origins of her skill in blocking out unpleasantness, she recalled that as a child she had learned an exercise in correct posture that involved inhaling in a manner that would make the vertebrae separate. She claimed that in doing so she would feel herself float away into the state where she could block out the abdominal discomfort that led ultimately to surgery at the age of thirteen.

On two subsequent occasions after trance induction during interviews, she again had problems cutting off the dissociated feelings. Once she was mildly spatially disoriented for about half an hour, and at another time she failed to respond to the signal that was to interrupt the sensory distortion in her arm. She claimed not to have heard it, and only after a repeated induction procedure with repeated emphasis on the cutoff signal was she able to regain her normal state of comfort. Although resistance is known to manifest in this way, those events can also be interpreted as evidence of her deep involvement in the dissociated state, rather than as an indication of resistance to the therapist.

Clinical Course

With no clearer understanding of the pathophysiology possibly underlying her physical symptoms, her doctors had discharged her after about ten days in the hospital, on the understanding that she would maintain a contact with her family physician, and travel from out of state at weekly intervals for a while, to determine what she could gain from a combination of hypnosis and psychotherapy. The contract between us was that we would use hypnosis in the therapy to help her diminish or block out the physical pain and discomfort, but that we would also try to apply it in other ways in order to learn more about her reported capacity to block out reality, both purposefully and unwittingly. She also agreed with me that it might be helpful if we understood more about her past, but indicated that she had been discouraged by her previous experiences with psychotherapy. I suggested that we both keep an open mind on the matter, although we recognized that I favored the assumption that her symptoms, though largely physical, were related to her marked hypnotizability, and she leaned strongly toward a physical etiology, however obscure. She was nonetheless impressed by the amount of physical relief she had obtained by distorting her perception of pain, when in hypnosis.

We met at weekly intervals for about four months, and thereafter at monthly and then less frequent intervals for a few years. Despite the long distance she had to travel, usually by air, she never failed to be punctual for her appointments. The initial visits were devoted to exercises in entering and emerging from hypnosis, and to distorting perceptions in the affected joints when hypnotized. She was encouraged to experience a variety of sensations in and around the painful areas, ranging from a feeling of numbness in order to screen out the pain, to accentuating the discomfort in order to recognize that she could control it. She was also instructed in the use of self-hypnosis, and encouraged to practice entry into and exit from the trance at least a few times daily, between visits. Despite some initial uneasiness about the procedure, she gradually grew comfortable with the notion of marked hypnotizability and with her use of it.

After a couple of months she claimed to be feeling a general improvement in the frequency and severity of the physical discomfort, and was clearly pleased with the relief that self-hypnosis exercises provided. She no longer felt governed by the discomfort, and began to introduce considerably more material into the interviews, related to the challenge involved in raising her sons who were traveling through the most provocative stages of adolescence and early adulthood. She had also become increasingly more concerned about the prospect of a second marriage, and discussed that, too.

In describing some of her personal and social problems, she became aware of her constant inclination to exclude troublesome issues from her thoughts by forgetting about them. In fact it became clear, as we proceeded, that she tended to dwell on her physical complaints not infrequently when she was particularly bothered by obstacles in her personal life. With encouragement to concentrate on the situations and circumstances that were more painful than her joints, she was ultimately able to concede that she had in the past used the trance unwittingly to escape both physical *and* emotional discomfort. She had also, by now, developed a comfortable familiarity with entry into the trance and exit from it under controlled circumstances, and had thereby learned more easily to recognize the early signs of any unwitting move into trance. At these times she would induce a trance purposefully, and then concentrate while in it, on the problems she realized she was trying to evade.

Although she clung to her belief that underneath it all was probably some obscure organic pathology to account for at least some of her symptoms, she had begun to embrace the notion that even her physical complaints could, at times, be due to her responsiveness to ideas and suggestions. She conceded that her understanding of that had eased her sense of guilt somewhat, when challenged by the members of her family that she, herself, created her physical symptoms. In her commitment to some underlying organic pathology in addition to whatever else was troubling her, she was stoutly supported by her medical advisers who, at no stage, were prepared to state emphatically and clearly that there was no organic foundation to her problems. This, even though it was impossible for them to agree on any organic pathology. It became clear, too, that her large pharmaceutical inventory had been augmented from time to time by trials of new medication prescribed by her doctors, who were constantly enthusiastic about trying to help her and concerned about the uncertainty of their diagnoses.

By the end of the second year in treatment, she felt she was more in touch with her feelings, both sad and angry; in keeping with her usual counterdependent style, she was eager to try to cope more on her own. Meetings subsequently became less frequent, occurring only at two- to three-month intervals. Some of the problems she then chose to discuss were partially attributable to her, but many were not of her making. Her physical symptoms, less troublesome, were dealt with largely by means of the trance and the perceptual distortion it enabled her to achieve. She learned to guard against her tendency to flee unpleasant matters by using the trance constructively and assertively, to concentrate her attention on the conflicts.

Formulation and Comments

She was primarily a sad and depressed person with unresolved feelings of anger, and a poor sense of identity. This can be largely explained by the constant rejection from most of those who meant much to her, and the complex series of mothering figures in her early life. Forced, early, into a counterdependent position, she ultimately found herself overwhelmed by the demands of her restless teen-age children; and her conflict over remarriage centered, too, on whether it would supply some of her emotional needs or merely add to her responsibilities. Her eagerness to escape the unpleasantness of her conflicts meshed well with her remarkable ability to dissociate. With this she was able to flee into another role, or into a massive physical complaint that had been poorly understood to begin with, and had grown increasingly complex with the passage of time and considerable medical attention. With her degree of responsivity, it is difficult to ignore the impact on her symptoms, whatever their original cause, of the innumerable medical comments, questions, and recommendations that must have accumulated over the years.

It should be clear from the case history that hypnosis was not *the* treatment but only an important—perhaps even necessary—additional procedure that provided her with a crucial kind of learning experience, namely, that she was, indeed, able to exert control over her distressing symptoms. It should be remembered, however, that without a clear understanding of the context in which the symptoms occurred and of the secondary gains associated with them, any measurable improvement would hardly have been feasible. The importance of an adequate psychiatric evaluation as early as is possible in a program that aims to use hypnosis in this fashion cannot be overemphasized. By teaching her how to obtain some control over her symptoms by practicing on her own, deliberate entry into and exit from the trance, and by making her aware of her ability to distort perception, hypnosis was readily integrated with dynamically oriented psychotherapy seeking to establish and strengthen her coping mechanisms. Its usefulness was also reaffirmed for her by its value, at times, as an aid to recalling memories with which she had previously had difficulty; and by revealing to her one of the mechanisms contributing to her symptoms.

Further work will be necessary to confirm that such patients, manifesting the kind of psychopathology illustrated by the clinical material in this case history, do in fact have a higher hypnotizability rating than other patients with different types of problems.

Hypnotizability and Unrelated Physical Symptoms

Thus far, I have dealt only with the therapeutic use of the trance in clinical situations associated with a marked response to hypnosis, where it could be reasonably assumed that the response was, in some way, causally related to the symptoms. The trance was used therapeutically to create the symptoms or a facsimile of them, thereby increasing the patient's familiarity with the trance experience, on the assumption that the clinical picture was initiated by the occurrence of a spontaneous trance. In this way, a coping mechanism was added to the patient's repertoire.

Clinical experience, however, attests eloquently to the fact that hypnosis can also be very usefully employed in the treatment of symptoms that are in no way causally linked to hypnotizability. This method, too, augments the individual's coping mechanism, by uncovering his trance capacity and adding to his ego strengths in teaching him how to use it, on his own, in self-induced hypnosis exercises. Quite apart from the feeling of near-exhilaration described by many patients when they first experience the hypnotic trance (which discovery itself carries its own advantages), being able to contribute to the success of one's own treatment program is a highly reassuring experience.

Innumerable clinical anecdotes reflect the frequent success of hypnosis induced by a therapist or self-induced, and those who use hypnosis generally recognize the therapeutic momentum that flows from the attainment of a hypnotic trance. The increased self-esteem attendant on success, and the associated sense of mastery become useful as leverage for more extensive achievements in other aspects of the patient's life, and in his therapy. This aspect of therapeutic hypnosis was captured by Spiegel and Linn (1969), who, referring to a "ripple effect," pointed to the advantages of using a consultant psychiatrist in ancillary hypnosis for the removal of symptoms for that very reason.

Whatever the theoretical objections to symptom removal, a few practical issues have become clearly apparent from the clinical experience of recent decades. Regardless of the contribution by emotional factors to physical symptoms, and of the extent to which psychological conflicts might be resolved in treatment, rarely does traditional psychodynamically oriented psychotherapy, on its own, effectively lessen physical symptoms. This might relate to the difficulty patients have in accepting emotional problems as the underlying cause of their symptoms, or it might result from the propensity of symptoms to be perpetuated by habit, learning, secondary gain, or their own momentum. Whatever the cause, the record of success is poor. It has also long been recognized that coercive suggestions in hypnosis, in the absence of an appreciation of the prevailing psychodynamic forces and secondary gain from the situation, might lead to the advent of depression. Commenting on the fact that some therapists have claimed excellent results with symptom removal while others insist that such efforts are quite ineffective and dangerous, Schneck (1965) concludes that both assertions are probably exaggerated. He presents the psychodynamically highly convincing statement that symptoms essential for the maintenance of psychological equilibrium will not be eliminated with ease, regardless of how neurotic that equilibrium might be. He comments further that it would be only fair to concede that even though long-term psychotherapeutic and analytic efforts may be helpful in promoting favorable personality change, specific symptoms sometimes stubbornly persist.

Experienced clinicians (Meares, 1960; Spiegel, 1967) go to great lengths to ensure the availability of adequate emotional support for patients with whom they propose to work toward symptom removal, and also time enough for interacting with the patients in order to provide that support. Dramatic single-encounter cures are not encouraged. On balance, it is probably correct to assert that a cavalier attitude toward the removal of symptoms linked to some degree of psychogenesis is as misguided as one that prohibits the practice totally. Using hypnosis in an ancillary role to lessen or remove symptoms, while attending simultaneously to the psychodynamic context in which the symptoms arose and in which they are being maintained, appears to be a reasonable compromise. The following case history (Frankel and Misch, 1973), reporting on the use of hypnosis in a case of long-standing psoriasis in a person with character problems, attests to the feasibility of this approach.

Psoriasis is primarily a chronic skin disease, lesions of which are characterized by an unusual or abnormal increase in epidermal tissue and a greatly accelerated rate of epidermal turnover. The lesions are usually discrete erythematous papules and plaques covered with white scales. The cutaneous disease may be extensive and even generalized to the extreme of total skin involvement. While specific systemic and environmental factors are known to influence the disease, improvement or exacerbation of lesions may spontaneously occur without discernible cause. Even though progress has been made, psoriasis is yet to be understood and specific therapy is still awaiting discovery and development (Van Scott and Farber, 1971).

Medical publications for several years have referred to the importance of psychological factors in the precipitation, aggravation, and improvement of skin conditions. Whereas there has been an avoidance in more recent years of linking specific personality types and emotional reactions to particular skin diseases, the significance of emotional factors in psoriasis has been described by several authors, including Wittkower (1946), Obermeyer (1955) and Farber, Bright, and Nall (1968). The therapeutic value of psychotherapy and hypnosis, however, has been reported in relatively few instances; virtually none seem to have been published in the English language in the past few years. Among the reports appearing previously have been those by Kline (1954, 1958), Luthe and Schultz (1969), and Bethune and Kidd (1961). In most of the cases reported, the use of hypnosis and sensory imagery appears to have been beneficial, with partial improvement in others. The sensory imagery encouraged in those patients was selected at random and involved the development of a feeling of change in the skin, or a feeling of temperature change and/or constriction or expansion of the psoriatic lesions, with apparently no specific purpose in view other than the accomplishment of different or comfortable healthy skin sensations. In the case to be reported, the sensory imagery was precisely selected in an attempt to replicate a real-life experience that had been beneficial in the past. There is no effective way of measuring the possible value of this specifically chosen imagery, but it seems, if any imagery involving the skin would be helpful, that this method would have an added advantage because of the very therapeutic association with the past.

CASE HISTORY XVII
Psoriasis

A thirty-seven-year-old, unmarried man with a lifelong history of severe, socially restricting psychological symptoms and psoriasis of twenty years duration, raised the question of the possible value of hypnosis in the treatment of his skin condition with his psychotherapist in June of 1970. He was referred for the assessment of his trance capacity, and scored 2 on the Hypnotic Induction Profile. He was able to report the course of his skin condition over several years, having observed it carefully and intelligently, and knew that direct sunlight and the warmth of the summer months, even when associated with extensive perspiration, were therapeutic as opposed to the cold and snow of the winter, which aggravated the old lesions and were associated with new ones.

His recognition of the beneficial effects of direct sunlight and summer warmth is shared by many people suffering from psoriasis. Not only are the lesions aggravated in many instances during the winter months, but the patients themselves are also severely distressed by the symptom of chilliness when the psoriasis is extensive. The generalized subepidermal vasodilatation and capillary proliferation permit excessive loss of body heat.

The patient had neither sought nor tried new skin remedies for a few years prior to his request for hypnosis. He had ceased visiting dermatologists, and had continued to use only a cosmetic ointment on exposed parts when the lesions were very severe. Though skeptical, he was interested in a trial of hypnosis; in itself an important factor for a person with his problems and life-style, as will become apparent in the history that follows.

Three years previously he had sought psychotherapy for his increasing sensitivity to the opinions of others, and for what he himself referred to as his "delusions of self-reference." In his first job as a junior accountant, in 1966, he had first become aware of immobilizing concerns about the criticisms of his colleagues. He changed his job and yet remained equally anxious. He believed he heard uncomplimentary comments, and soon became unsure about whether or not they referred to him. There is little to suggest that he was hallucinating; he had the insight to question his own suspiciousness and whether or not his underlying psychopathology and near-paranoia would interfere with his career. Aware, too, of his inability to relate well to women, he wondered whether working closely with several female bookkeepers might not have added to his anxiety. He began psychotherapy at that time and had continued to see his therapist at regular intervals since.

At the time of the patient's request for a trial of hypnosis in the treatment of his psoriasis, he had been receiving psychotherapy for three years; the paranoid features were less in evidence and his obsessional defenses had been re-established, but his concern about the psoriasis was obstructing any further progress in the psychiatric treatment. The goal of hypnosis here was symptom removal. Psychiatric exploration under hypnosis was neither intended nor practiced in his case. Any adverse impact of the hypnotic procedure on his near-paranoid inclination was immediately minimized by the technique (described more fully below), in which the control of the procedure was handed back to him in the very first hypnotic encounter. This was accomplished by encouraging and assisting him to achieve the hypnotic state by means of self-hypnosis. He was accompanied to the first hypnosis interview by his therapist in whom he had implicit trust.

The patient was the second of four siblings, raised in a household where maintaining appearances and stoically accepting discomfort were cardinal rules. He attended school in a rural area where, because both of his parents were on the teaching staff, he felt under considerable pressure to be a model pupil, and he performed reasonably well. He regarded his parents as fiercely independent, often angrily so, and his mother as someone who gave very little of herself. At the time of his younger brother's birth, when the patient was fourteen years old, he and his older brother were sent to live with his maternal grandfather because his father's elderly and invalid mother had moved into their already cramped household. He had little or no communication with his grandfather, an unfortunate circumstance that was aggravated after his older brother's departure for college. Childhood and adolescence were painfully lonely and isolated, apart from one relationship that he recalled with fondness and obvious warmth. This was his friendship with the local choirmaster, a conservative, unmarried man who showed considerable interest in him. Their association continued into the first two years of his college life, after which time they were separated by his leaving to enlist in the Army Medical Corps because, in his opinion, his academic performance was unsatisfactory. Shortly after enlisting in the Army his psoriasis began, and within two years had become severe and widespread, involving his face, scalp, all four limbs, and trunk, apart from his shoulders and upper back. The Army doctors implied at the time of his discharge that he would simply have to learn to live with the condition.

After leaving the Army, the patient completed the remaining year of college and then studied accountancy. Throughout the years his social contacts had been few and isolated. His only heterosexual relationship was with a woman many years his senior whom he met in the course of his work, and who ultimately seduced him. Their associations were limited to occasional weekends when he traveled many miles to where she lived and worked. His only friends were her friends whom he met with her on those weekends.

His course of psychotherapy had been associated with a lessening of anxiety, and his interpersonal problems at work had become less painful. His overwhelming obsessional defenses and intellectualizing, however, seemed to obstruct further progress after the first two years of treatment. He had maintained his improved status by means of a heavy reliance on the regular contact with his therapist. Referring more frequently to the socially crippling aspects of his psoriasis, he eventually requested hypnosis for the treatment of his skin condition.

Clinical Course

The patient was a tall man, somewhat portly, with a fair complexion. On his initial visit for hypnosis his suit buttoned with difficulty and seemed a size too small; his trousers ended well above his ankles. His speech seemed studied and somewhat halting, which added a pedantic quality to the general impression he created. After the initial induction and test of trance capacity using the Hypnotic Induction Profile, he was encouraged to re-enter the trance state and indicate that he was experiencing a floating sensation by permitting his hand and forearm to levitate. Further evidence of his concerns about passivity and the transference was his preference (declared with an insightful explanation by him in the second hypnosis session) for holding his wrist and hand extended rather than limp during levitation.

In the trance state he was asked to imagine himself basking in the sun with the warmth of the sun on his shoulders and upper back. He was encouraged to picture the sunlight reflected directly on those parts of his body, creating a feeling of pleasurable and warm comfort in that whole area. It was then suggested that he could permit the pleasant sensations to spread to involve the contiguous areas of the skin until more of the surface of the trunk, limbs, head, and neck were involved. The trance lasted about fifteen to twenty minutes and included instructions on how to induce the hypnotic state and the imagery on his own. He was also directed to practice this exercise of trance induction and imagery for a few minutes, five or six times each day. Arrangements were made for a return visit a few weeks later.

No prognosis about the efficacy of hypnosis in his case was offered. He was told that some success had been reported by other workers, but that his success would probably depend in large measure on his capacity for hypnosis and his preparedness to utilize it. He was to continue his weekly psychotherapy with his therapist, but would also see me at less frequent intervals to permit a reinforcement of the technique and to discuss questions relating to the hypnosis and the psoriasis, should they arise.

On his second visit for hypnosis he reported a greater ability to relax than he had anticipated; and on the third visit he reported with great surprise and excitement a considerable strengthening of the imagery that he had been able to achieve in his practice at home. He attributed this to the suggestion at the previous visit that he should enjoy the sensations of relaxing, floating, and very pleasurable warmth on his skin. He regarded this as especially effective because it was the first occasion he could recall when he had received unambiguous permission to enjoy a physical experience. He was clearly delighted with his success. On that third visit, he also reported what he thought was some lessening of the scaliness of the skin lesions and a lightening of the red discoloration. He added that he had been reminded during the previous week that his only friend in childhood, the choirmaster, had also had psoriasis, a fact that he had apparently suppressed or denied during the preceding years of treatment.

It will be remembered that his psoriasis began shortly after he left college and his choirmaster friend to enlist in the Army. The position that the older man had held in his life is probably best described as that of a father surrogate. Because the difficulty that he encountered in mentioning meaningful issues had been the hallmark of the previous years of therapy, his silence about his friend's psoriasis was not altogether unexpected. He had had ample opportunity to become aware of that man's skin condition, as they had spent long hours together in choir practice and in discussing music. Though the possibility of an overt erotic element in their relationship is of interest psychodynamically, it was not borne out in discussions about the friendship. He had mentioned his concern about homosexuality during the years of therapy, but had denied any homosexual interests or experiences. His academic exposure to the theory of psychopathology had linked passivity and paranoid thinking to homosexuality, and he was aware of both of these factors in himself. He created the strong impression, however, that to him homosexuality was a state of opprobrium rather than an emotional experience.

The patient also commenced in the third visit to discuss his resistance to relinquishing his psoriasis. He raised the possibility of a reluctance on his part to achieve an improvement in the condition by psychological means, as that might indicate that the condition was attributable solely to psychological factors. He became very aware, too, of the secondary gain from his condition, which had shielded him for years from attempting social interaction at which he felt inept and clumsy. We attempted, as much as was possible, to have him work through these issues in his weekly psychotherapy visits, keeping the nature of his approximately monthly hypnosis sessions with me more or less confined to issues of technique, enhancing the quality of the sensory imagery, and discussions about psoriasis.

By the fifth hypnosis session in mid-August of 1970, he reported that the psoriasis was better than before, and three weeks later he expressed the view that his improvement was incredible. He was practicing about six times per day, each exercise lasting from two to four minutes. He claimed at that time that he had lost twenty pounds in weight in the three previous weeks. Although attempts to lose weight by dieting five years previously had failed, he now found that by concentrating on doing so, he could reduce his feelings of hunger. He regarded the accomplishment of this feat as an unexpected bonus.

Because he was uncertain of his ability to maintain the level of his concentration and the quality of the imagery when the winter weather began, the patient preferred to continue with regular, even if infrequent, hypnosis sessions. By mid-January, despite heavy snow, which had been associated with a deterioration in his condition in the past, he was able to report a continuing improvement. The scaliness was considerably reduced in almost all the lesions and the red discoloration was less. The three or four new lesions that had developed were very unlike previous lesions. They were no larger than a dime in diameter and were paler and less scaly than the others. Previously, new lesions would occur over large areas of up to several inches, deep red under heavy scales.

In February, seven months after his first hypnosis session, he used such terms as "leprous" and "syphilitic" when describing the sense of his contagion that he had suffered for almost twenty years since the onset of his skin disease. He talked of the strange feelings he experienced with the new knowledge that a bleak destiny was not necessarily inevitable. He had felt a growing optimism, cautious until he had successfully negotiated the winter months, about ways in which he could more fully experience life. He was still fearful, though, that he might suffer a sudden relapse and lose the ground he had gained.

At that stage, the patient hesitantly granted a request to measure the skin temperature on the volar aspect of his right wrist. Using a Cary skin thermometer, we measured a temperature rise from $85.4°$ to $87.5°(F)$

from the commencement of the trance to the time immediately prior to its termination, a period of three minutes. He was subsequently disappointed and angry at himself for his failure to look at the thermometer reading himself. He believed that he was unwilling to verify the evidence that he might be able to intervene in the course of his disease. A further attempt a month later to measure the skin temperature on his chest interfered to such an extent with his ability to induce the trance that attempts to record the measurements were abandoned.

During the months of the spring and summer of 1971 the state of his psoriasis remained at the same satisfactory level of improvement. Where the lesions did disappear totally, e.g., on his lower legs, he noticed a yellowish pigmentation that he found somewhat disappointing. The remaining lesions on his body, hands, head, and neck continued to be minimally obtrusive. While not expanding, they had not disappeared entirely either.

Progress in Psychotherapy

Interpersonal problems, both at work and socially, had been a major focus of discussion in the therapy over the years. Initially, he had tended toward extreme interpretations of events that impinged upon him, either viewing himself as a passive victim of circumstance or harshly blaming himself. After two years of therapy, he had become somewhat more reasonable and realistic, both in acknowledging his own role in the conduct of his life and in viewing the part played by circumstance. This shift, however, had been only partial. He had also become somewhat more assertive and active in pursuing his own goals over the first two years, but his social isolation, apart from very minor shifts, had remained, the barrier of the psoriasis constituting his excuse. Subsequently, with the improvement in his skin, he became increasingly open in his psychotherapy, talking about his reactions in a much richer way and revealing vast areas of his feelings that, even though ambivalent, were considerably more differentiated than ever before. Concurrent with this, he had to deal with his first clear appreciation of his depression and sadness about the painful life he had lived. His previous detachment and denial of feelings gave way enough to permit much more meaningful discussions about himself and his circumstances.

Discussion

On examining the clinical history, it would seem that the spectrum of therapeutic gains can hardly be attributed solely to the directly beneficial effects of the altered sensations in the skin. We cannot overlook the surprise and sheer delight of our patient on his third visit when he first reported the very vivid experience of the distorted perception. For him it was the kind of unchallenged success he had rarely achieved. It should be remembered that his response to hypnotic induction, although measured only once, appeared to be in the average range, and that only after his second visit and considerable diligent exercising was he able to achieve some vividness in the sensory imagery. It was clear from his surprise at being able to produce the planned sensations, and from the delight he gained in the reassurance they provided, that this meant a great deal to him. The indirect benefits gained from the unambiguous permission he had detected in the previous interview, to enjoy a physical event, must be considered, too.

The importance of the psoriasis to his dynamic defenses was captured in his unwillingness to look at the thermometer reading and verify the evidence that he might in fact have been able to intervene in the course of his disease. His faithful exercising five or six times a day seems therefore like an uneasy contradiction, until one recognizes the all-embracing ambivalence that permeated much of his behavior. We might wonder to what extent he had continued to nurture, secretly, the hope that the hypnotic system would fail despite his compulsive and diligent exercising. He had frequently referred to his psoriatic "armor" protecting him from the threatening aspects of social encounters by forcing him into relative social isolation. Whether or not the unusual and novel experience of the trance had helped to topple the ambivalence is a matter for conjecture. Because of his delighted reaction to the treatment at that time, it is likely that it might have. On that third visit in which he recounted surprised success with the trance, he reported the first minor improvement in the skin lesions, and recalled for the first time in years that his only boyhood friend had also had psoriasis. Within days of that visit he had begun to lose the twenty pounds in weight, which attempts at dieting five years previously had failed to shift. In his therapy he began, at that time, to consider, even if ambivalently, new ways of encountering his other difficulties. He began to experience what he talked of as a "tentative optimism" about what might yet happen. This was, without exaggeration, the first evidence of brightness for over twenty years in a rather gloomy life. It is difficult to ignore the possibility that his achievement of the trance had added richly to his coping mechanisms, even though assuredly the trance itself had played no part in the etiology of his symptoms.

CHAPTER 13

An Unusual Trance

Benefit appears to flow from becoming aware of one's trance, even when this seems to be a limited skill. The following report of a case of writer's cramp suggests that even in these circumstances the trance can be valuable in providing a coping mechanism. The case is worth noting because the unusual self-rating, in hypnosis, of his own response, far exceeded any objective measurement of the response by an observer. In retrospect, the case history demonstrates that a great deal of therapeutic momentum was derived from the patient's feeling that his arm levitation was considerably more impressive than, in fact, it was.

Writer's cramp, first described over a century ago, is a condition in which incoordination of the small muscles of the hand appears when attempts are made to write. As the principle nerves and muscles are often intact, the condition is regarded as a functional disturbance of coordination. Although the symptom resembles conversion hysteria, the patients are generally described as tense, anxious, conscientious, striving, precise, and emotionally overcontrolled individuals. Electromyographic studies of patients suffering with writer's cramp provide evidence of high muscle tension in the total musculature of the involved limb (Von Reis, 1954). Patients generally attempt many different styles of writing in an effort to overcome the initial difficulties, involving them in bizarre writing postures that then become established as faulty habits.

In the treatment of the condition, psychoanalytic psychotherapy seems not to have been effective, whereas treatment programs including muscle relaxation, re-education, psychotherapy of a primarily supportive kind, and encouraging suggestions have been helpful (Crisp and Moldofsky, 1965). Both for producing rapid relaxation and for conveying repeated suggestions, hypnosis has been described as a method of choice (Pai, 1947).

CASE HISTORY XVIII
Writer's Cramp

A successful business executive in his mid-thirties, complaining of writer's cramp for over two years, was referred for psychiatric evaluation and hypnosis, if indicated. His symptoms had commenced while working in a hostile and challenging environment from which he was ultimately asked to resign. Although the symptoms were minimal at the time, they worsened after he left to develop a business of his own. He then also became aware of a tremor complicating the pen-holding operation, and a marked slowing of his writing ability. In attempting to compensate for the difficulty, he had developed the somewhat bizarre mechanism of extending his index finger when he wrote, evoking comments occasionally from those who witnessed it. The difficulty with coordination was, and had remained confined to his writing. Any anticipation of writing had made him immediately conscious of the problem, and aware of a tightening of the related muscles. He had been thoroughly investigated and cleared neurologically during the months following the onset of his symptoms. Tranquilizing medication had been totally ineffective in alleviating the problem. At the time of his referral more than two years later, he was convinced that his problem, which had remained unchanged, was primarily psychological in nature. He recounted the following facts in a markedly nonemotional style.

After graduating from college and spending three years on military duty, he had declined the opportunity of attending a school of business administration in order to join his father in a successful and growing business venture. However, setbacks for which he personally was in no way responsible, led ultimately to near-bankruptcy, and after ten years he left the firm to find another job requiring similar skills. After working for a few weeks, he noticed the hostility of his associates and superiors, who, he believed, were threatened by his more extensive business background and his competence. When after a few months he was asked to leave, he finally told them that their expectations of him had been beyond any person's capacity, and although aware of his anger at the time, he was pleased that he had been able to keep it under control in the final encounter. It was during the preceding months that his symptoms had first developed, when he felt he was being observed as he wrote out business documents. After leaving the firm he continued to feel angry at their attitude toward him, and frustrated by his inability to meet their challenges more successfully. Despite the very satisfactory development of his own business thereafter, he admitted his resentment at having had to work harder than others when employed in his father's business, of having had to leave that business because it was incapable of supporting the many family members in it, and of then having landed in a position that demanded more of him than he considered fair.

As mentioned previously, the history was presented in a highly intellectualized manner, precise, with little or no feeling. His life-style was obsessive-compulsive, and his appearance impeccable. He presented the story of his family and childhood with the firm assurance that there were "no real problems," and when reporting the death six years previously, by suicide, of an older brother, he repeatedly claimed that he had experienced little sadness at the time because there had been a ten-year gap in their ages, and not much interaction between them. Further attempts to explore his feelings regarding his parents and his marriage produced the same steady description of satisfactory, relatively uninvolved relationships. He admitted that he had occasionally recognized that he rarely felt things to the extent that he thought he should. However, he had continued to experience great difficulty with his feelings, and had little interest in pursuing a course of treatment designed to explore them while uncovering his past. He was highly motivated to rid himself of his symptom, and very interested in the use of hypnosis if this were available.

Clinical Course

His response on the Hypnotic Induction Profile was very limited. His score on each phase was low, with a consistent rating of 1. On a subsequent occasion he managed easily to separate his interlocked fingers when challenged that he would not be able to do so. The same induction procedure used in the Profile (namely rolling up the eyes, closing them, inhaling deeply and exhaling, concentrating on a relaxed feeling throughout the body, and then thinking of a lightening of the right hand and forearm until it floated off the arm rest) was then used to achieve and establish a sense of relaxation and calm throughout his body and limbs. In that situation, relaxation in his barely levitated right forearm and hand was again emphasized, and he was encouraged to feel comfortable and confident about his ability to write with his hand and forearm in that relaxed state (he wrote with his right hand) following the termination of the exercise. On opening his eyes, he wrote a few words of his choosing. Before the end of the exercise, he had been instructed in how to induce a similar state on his own, and encouraged to practice it at home for ten to fifteen minutes twice daily and to follow it with a writing task.

Because of his apparently limited response in hypnosis, the emphasis in the session had been placed on the achievement of relaxation as opposed to sensory distortion. As the prognosis with therapy was difficult to predict, we agreed to meet for six sessions and then review progress to decide whether further meetings were indicated. Because the nature of his work demanded frequent lengthy trips out of town, and because of his interest in practicing the exercises on his own, we arranged to meet at monthly intervals. A physiatrist was consulted for advice on motor exercises that would most improve the skills, and that could be incorporated into the exercise of relaxation. He concurred with the program of relaxation we had chosen, adding a brief series of elbow joint movements with tension of the muscles on flexion, and relaxation on extension, to be carried out just prior to the commencement of each writing practice.

Fairly elaborate attention was given by the patient to the writing materials he used in the exercises. He initially used a broad felt-tip pen and copied only the easiest samples from a manual of cursive writing, slowly graduating to the more complicated when he felt himself able to do so. He also introduced narrower pentips of harder texture until he was able to practice with a regular metal tip.

He worked at his exercise assiduously for five months, never less than twice a day. During his monthly visits to me, a small portion of the interview was devoted to some discussion of his past resentments, but the greater part was taken up with reports of his progress, with improving the technique involved in his exercises at home, and with the induction of hypnosis to reinforce the previous suggestions aimed at relaxation, comfort, and confidence in his ability to write.

He claimed a very satisfactory response at his second visit, and remarkable improvement in his ability to write by the fourth and fifth visits. Evidence of his progress was apparent after a few months when he attended a weekend course in advanced business methods and found that he coped admirably with the dictation and his lecture notes. His wife agreed with him that he had done remarkably well, and his writing samples confirmed it. He estimated on his fifth visit that 85 percent of his previous ability to write had returned, and the product initially modeled on the cursive writing charts had assumed its premorbid pattern.

He was especially pleased with his progress, and had made frequent reference in the interviews to his satisfaction with hypnosis, and to the good effects he was able to feel from it. As his arm levitation, when observed in the hypnotic sessions, appeared to be extremely limited, my assumption was that he was describing his achievements in relaxing well with the induction procedure. Although his arm, when levitated, was never more than an inch off the arm rest, the goals of therapy led me to encourage him with approving comments, and strengthen his confidence in his responses. It was felt, too, that the hypnotic induction procedure provided him with an ideal vehicle for attaining marked relaxation, and for the development of a highly organized and compulsive treatment program appropriate to his personal style. In the fifth treatment session, the hypnotic exercise was modified by the suggestion that he should try writing before he came out of it. This meant that he had to open his eyes while his right arm was still levitated, and then move it to take hold of the pen and write. All the previous exercises had been structured in such a way that he would end the relaxation exercise by returning his arm to the arm rest of the chair *before* opening his eyes to commence with the writing. On this occasion, when he opened his eyes with his arm still levitated, he reacted with considerable surprise. He had great difficulty accepting that his arm had been barely raised above the armrest. He had felt then, and on all previous occasions, that his forearm had made at least a 60° angle with the arm rest. It then became clear that his reference in the previous sessions to the good effects he had felt in hypnosis referred mainly to the feelings he experienced in his right forearm and hand, and not primarily to the relaxation, although this, too, had influenced his sense of achievement.

Discussion

Again, it is not possible to be certain about the mechanisms involved in a successful therapeutic result. The highly organized therapy ritual meshed well with his obsessive-compulsive life-style, and he clearly was highly motivated to relinquish the symptom.

Considering his behavior in terms of Shor's three dimensions of hypnotic depth (Shor, 1962), we are interested in knowing whether he was well motivated to fill the role of a good hypnotic subject, what his relationship with the operator was, and the extent of his actual capacity to experience the trance. In this context, we would have concluded that he was merely trying to please the operator had he permitted his forearm to rise impressively without any true feeling of lightness. However, in this instance quite the opposite was true: His forearm was minimally raised, never more than an inch above the arm rest, yet he had consistently felt when practicing on his own and in my presence, that the levitation achieved by him was of a superior kind. Although this is a noteworthy degree of perceptual distortion, his response is clearly different from that of the more usual, highly hypnotizable individual who perceives his arm as very light and permits it to levitate to the fullest extent.

What can we say about his impressive yet circumscribed distortion in the context of a generally poor hypnotic experience that he had initially recognized and acknowledged as poor? Perhaps that the unusual trance experience was successful in that aspect of it that was most relevant to the recovery of his symptoms, namely, perceptual distortion and relaxation in the hand that held the pen.

It is difficult to believe that his satisfaction with what he experienced, repeated with each practice-exercise, was not crucial to his enthusiasm and to the successful result he ultimately achieved. Although his general hypnotizability was limited, he was, under appropriate circumstances, capable of distorting perception to a considerable degree. As this is the characteristic by which we index the hypnotic experience, we must regard his hypnotic response as high though unusual, rather than low. Special profile scales (Hilgard, 1965) have been developed to rate these kinds of unusual responses more effectively. His performance attests to the complexity of hypnosis, and though different and unexpected, demonstrates how an experience of trance can be linked to increased confidence and a sense of mastery.

CHAPTER 14

Summary and Conclusion

We began by examining the controversial beliefs surrounding hypnosis from the time of Mesmer's discovery to the present, where diverse opinions still prevail. We were familiar by the end of the first chapter with the fact that the magnetic fluid of Mesmer was a myth; that the subject and not the operator was essentially responsible for the event of hypnosis; that the continued use of the sleep metaphor defies the electroencephalographic finding that hypnosis is not sleep; and that many of the "magical" and poorly understood somatic changes associated with hypnosis and reported in the clinical literature should be respected as evidence of a psychosomatic interaction, even though the nature of that interaction is not yet discovered. We had also learned that hypnotic control is really a very subtle two-way communication process; that expert opinions differ about subjects in hypnosis being compelled to carry out antisocial acts against their will; and that although there is a close relatedness between hypnosis and meditative states, they are generally not considered as equivalent.

We then moved to consider the obstacles in the path of the investigator working toward an understanding of the phenomenon. The artifacts complicating clinical and experimental findings were exemplified in a study demonstrating how the demand characteristics in a situation, rather than hypnosis, influenced the behavior of subjects; the difficulties in setting up adequate controls in hypnosis research were exposed; the use of the simulating nonhypnotizable control subject was discussed; and the importance of quantifying the hypnotic responsiveness of an individual by means of standardized and valid scales was explained. We learned that not all persons were hypnotizable to the same degree, that at least a fifth of the thou-

169

sands tested responded poorly or not at all, and that at the other end of the spectrum, 5 or even 10 percent of subjects are very highly hypnotizable. We also learned that a person's level of hypnotic responsivity is a relatively stable and enduring attribute, and that laboratory attempts to correlate hypnotic ability with the variables of sex, education, and items such as personality traits have not been successful.

By turning then to a consideration of a few specific theories regarding hypnosis, we became familiar with the three dimensions of hypnotic depth and were exposed to the importance of the trance as a separate aspect of the hypnotic experience; interrelated with the elements of motivation and the relationship between the operator and the subject, but nonetheless an aspect that can be examined on its own. The trance was viewed as an altered state of subjective awareness, and considered in the context of a suggested neodissociation theory. The essential characteristic of hypnosis was then described as the presence of perceptual distortion.

Armed with what can best be considered as an evolving basic science in hypnosis, we proceeded to examine its clinical uses, able to review some of the clinical literature in the light of our new knowledge. It was clear that hypnosis has, in recent decades, been applied clinically in two major ways; for symptom removal, and as an uncovering and interpretative technique. It became apparent that the many wide claims made for hypnosis in symptom removal have paid little heed to placebo effects or the results of demand characteristics, and in many instances hypnosis has been assumed to be present because the therapist had carried out an induction procedure. The experience of the patient was not often questioned for the subjective evidence of hypnosis. Furthermore, on reviewing the reports of hypnosis used in association with psychotherapy or psychoanalysis, the importance assigned to the relationship between therapist and patient and the latter's emotional involvement in that interaction has far outweighed the attention paid to the patient's experience of the trance.

With no intention of diminishing the relevance of the interaction between subject and operator, we have tried to reestablish the balance by concentrating our attention on the trance experience. From an examination of clinical reports at the turn of the century, and of seven clinical case histories, we could not fail to be impressed by the high hypnotizability of those patients, and by the resemblance between elements of their clinical syndromes and events that occur in hypnosis. The similarities supported the notion that under certain circumstances the trance could occur spontaneously in individuals who had a high or very high trance capacity. Because of the distorted perception accompanying such events, trance was experienced by the individuals as a fearsome or bothersome symptom.

Paying special attention to the relatively circumscribed field of phobic behavior, which was one of the clinical entities seen to contain elements resembling events in hypnosis, we affirmed that deconditioning procedures could be accelerated by combining them with hypnosis. Examining the case histories of six phobic patients, we saw how the hypnotic trance could be used to produce an analogous symptom in the office, which closely resembled the psychopathology most troublesome to the individual. If one produced the symptom and guided the patient to a degree of familiarity with the mastery over this very compelling but experimentally induced situation, the patient began to learn something about the shift in mental functioning that was involved in causing and in controlling his own psychopathological manifestations. At times the trance process helped the patient experience the feelings previously seen as frightening and ego-alien, as familiar, under control, and perhaps even as comfortable. A use of hypnosis such as this, instead of focusing mainly on the psychodynamic and motivational factors underlying the psychopathology, helped the individual to identify his propensity to respond with trance manifestations and to cope with the consequences of such a response.

In support of the notion that phobic experiences could be related to hypnotic events, we found evidence of greater hypnotizability among phobic patients than among a comparable group. This was provided by a study of twenty-four phobic patients whose scores were significantly higher than the controls, and among whom those with multiple phobias had a mean score significantly greater than the mean score of patients with a single phobia. Not a single nonresponsive individual was seen in the phobic group.

In another two phobic cases reviewed by us, despite the impressiveness of the hypnotizability ratings, no enduring improvement attended the treatment procedures involving hypnosis. The most likely reasons were resistant psychodynamic forces and inadequate motivation to change. We were reminded that no treatment program can depend solely for its effectiveness on one crucial factor. The total treatment situation is of paramount importance.

In a further consideration of physical symptoms, we examined two cases in which, although symptoms could not be causally related to hypnotizability, the trance mechanism became an invaluable means for the patients to establish mastery over their pathology. The last case demonstrated an unusual degree of perceptual distortion in the absence of a high general hypnotizability. Although somewhat exceptional, this is not unknown, and epitomizes for us the complex nature of the hypnotic response.

We have thus observed that developing trance capacity into a mechanism for coping is a third major way of using hypnosis clinically, and can be integrated into any psychodynamically sensitive treatment plan geared toward discovering a patient's assets.

What have we learned from trying to understand the trance as a coping mechanism? It is that in the psychodynamic theories we depend on to explain psychopathology and human behavior, the concept of dissociation has been given short shrift. There is no intention on my part to resuscitate all that was written nearly a century ago on the subject, nor to hurry the development of a neodissociation theory before its time. Attention, however, should be drawn to the impression that the clinical behavior in hysterical fugues, multiple personalities, conversion hysteria, and phobias, and their usually close association with high or very high hypnotizability, cannot be fully understood in the absence of a workable concept that permits one or more mental activities to function in a manner that is separated or dissociated from others.

Those who respond readily and well in hypnosis, and distort perception easily, most probably do so because of a marked ability to dissociate or carry out some mechanism of a similar nature. This mechanism, should it occur spontaneously, and at inopportune times, can lead to problems and disabling symptoms. On the other hand, we know it can also be an enjoyable and reassuring experience if it occurs with the assistance of the operator or at the behest of the individual himself. It can thus be said of marked trance capacity, as it can of other special gifts such as unusual physical aptitudes or intelligence, that training is generally needed to harness the skill and develop it in ways that are useful. For those clinicians interested in the concept, the first step will be to measure the hypnotizability of as many patients as possible, and to be especially watchful for patients where the clinical pictures resemble the syndromes described in these pages. This will not only enhance treatment procedures; it will also illuminate our understanding of hypnosis.

Bibliography

Ås, A., O'Hara, J.W., and Munger, M.P. The measurement of subjective experiences presumably related to hypnotic susceptibility. *Scandanavian Journal of Psychology,* 1962, *3,* 47–64.

August, R.V. Obstetric hypnoanesthesia. *American Journal of Obstetrics and Gynecology,* 1960, *79,* 1131–1138.

Bailly, J.S., *et al. Rapport secret sur le mesmérisme, ou magnétisme animal.* (Secret report on Mesmerism or Animal Magnetism). Paris, 11 August, 1784 (not published). Signed: Franklin (Chairman), Debory, Lavoisier, Bailly (Reporter), Majault, Sallin, d'Arcet, Guillotin, Le Roy. Reproduced in A. Bertrand. *Du magnétisme animal.* (On animal magnetism). Paris: J.B. Baillière, 1826, pp. 511–516. Reproduced in A. Binet and C. Féré. *Animal Magnetism.* French original, 1887. English translation, New York: D. Appleton and Co., 1888, pp. 18–25.

Banyai, E., and Hilgard, E.R. A Comparison of active-alert hypnotic induction with traditional relaxation induction. Paper presented at *26th Annual Scientific Meeting, The Society for Clinical and Experimental Hypnosis,* Montreal, Canada, Oct. 1974.

Barber, T.X. Hypnotic age regression: A critical review. *Psychosomatic Medicine,* 1962, *24,* 286–299.

Barber, T.X., and Calverley, D.S. "Hypnotic behavior" as a function of task motivation. *Journal of Psychology,* 1962, *54,* 363–389.

Barber, T.X., Spanos, N.P., and Chaves, J.F. *Hypnotism: Imagination, and human potentialities.* New York: Pergamon Press, Inc., 1974.

Benson, F.D., and Geschwind, N. Psychiatric conditions associated with focal lesions in the nervous system. In M. Reiser (Ed.) *American Handbook of Psychiatry.* New York: Basic Books, 1976.

Benson, H. *The relaxation response.* New York: William Morrow and Co., 1975.

Benson, H., Beary, J.F., and Carol, M.P. The relaxation response. *Psychiatry,* 1974, *37,* 37–46.

Bernheim, H.M. *Hypnosis and suggestion in psychotherapy: A treatise on the nature and uses of hypnotism.* French original of first part, 1884, second part, 1886; with a new preface, 1887. English translation by C.A. Herter, 1888. Reissued with an introduction by E.R. Hilgard, New Hyde Park, New York: University Books, 1964.

Bethune, H.C., and Kidd, C.B. Psychophysiological mechanisms in skin diseases. *Lancet,* 1961, *11,* 1419–1422.

Blumer, D. Temporal lobe epilepsy and its psychiatric significance. In F. Benson and D. Blumer (Eds.) *Psychiatric aspects of neurologic diseases.* New York: Grune and Stratton, 1975.

Bowers, K.S., and Bowers, P.G. Hypnosis and Creativity: A theoretical and empirical rapprochement. In Fromm, E., and Shor, R.E. (Eds.) *Hypnosis: Research developments and perspectives.* Chicago: Aldine Atherton, 1972.

Bowers, M.K., Brecher-Marer, S., Newton, B.S., Piotrowski, Z., Speyer, T.C., Taylor, W.S., and Watkins J.G. Therapy of multiple personality. *International Journal of Clinical and Experimental Hypnosis* 1971, *19*, 57–65.

Braid, J. *Neurypnology: The rationale of nervous sleep considered in relation with animal magnetism, illustrated by numerous cases of its successful application in the relief and cure of disease.* London: John Churchill, 1843. Edited version under title: *Braid on hypnotism: Neurypnology. A new edition edited with an introduction, biographical and bibliographical, embodying the author's later views and further evidence on the subject.* Edited by A.E. Waite, London: George Redway, 1889. Reprinted as: *Braid on hypnotism: The beginnings of modern hypnosis.* New York: Julian Press, 1960.

Bramwell, J.M. *Hypnotism: Its history, practice and theory.* London: Rider and Co., 1903. Reprinted 1930.

Breuer, J., and Freud, S. *Studies on hysteria* (original German edition 1893–1895) In J. Strachey (Editor and Translator) *The standard edition of the complete psychological works of Sigmund Freud. Vol. 2.* London: Hogarth Press, 1955.

Cautela, J.R. The use of covert conditioning in hypnotherapy. *International Journal of Clinical and Experimental Hypnosis,* 1975, *23*, 15–27.

Charcot, J.M., *Oeuvres complète* (Complete works) Paris: Aux Bureaux de Progrès Médical, 1886. 9 vols.

Conn, J.H. Is hypnosis really dangerous? *International Journal of Clinical and Experimental Hypnosis,* 1972, *20*, 61–79.

Crasilneck, H.B., and Hall, J.A. Clinical hypnosis in problems of pain. *American Journal of Clinical Hypnosis,* 1973, *15*, 153–161.

Crasilneck, H.B., and Hall, J.A. *Clinical hypnosis: Principles and applications.* New York: Grune and Stratton, 1975.

Crisp, A.H., and Moldofsky, H. A psychosomatic study of writer's cramp. *British Journal of Psychiatry,* 1965, *111*, 841–858.

Diamond, M.J. Modification of hypnotizability: A review. *Psychological Bulletin,* 1974, *81*, 180–198.

Du Maurier, G. *Trilby.* New York: Harper, 1895.

Ehrenreich, G.A. The relationship of certain descriptive factors to hypnotizability. *Transactions of the Kansas Academy of Science,* 1949, *52*, 24–27.

Ellenberger, H.F. *The discovery of the unconscious: The history and evolution of dynamic psychiatry.* New York: Basic Books, Inc., 1970.

Evans, F.J. Suggestibility in the normal waking state. *Psychological Bulletin,* 1967, *67*, 114–129.

Evans, F.J. Recent trends in experimental hypnosis. *Behavioral Science,* 1968, *13*, 477–487.

Farber, E.M., Bright, R.D., and Nall, M.L. Psoriasis: A questionnaire survey of 2,144 patients. *Archives of Dermatology,* 1968, *98*, 248–259.

Faria (Abbé de Faria) *De la cause du sommeil lucide ou étude de la nature de l'homme.* Paris: chez Mme. Horiac, 1819.

Frankel, F.H. The effects of brief hypnotherapy in a series of psychosomatic problems. *Psychotherapy and Psychosomatics,* 1973, *22,* 269–275,

Frankel, F.H. Trance capacity and the genesis of phobic behavior. *Archives of General Psychiatry,* 1974, *31,* 261–263.

Frankel, F.H. The application of hypnosis to psychotherapy. *Psychotherapy and Psychosomatics.* 1975, *25,* 20–25.

Frankel, F.H., and Misch, R.C. Hypnosis in a case of long-standing psoriasis in a person with character problems. *International Journal of Clinical and Experimental Hypnosis,* 1973, *21,* 121–130.

Frankel, F.H., and Orne, M.T. Hypnotizability and phobic behavior. *Archives of General Psychiatry,* 1976, *33,* 1259–1261.

Friedlander, J.W., and Sarbin, T.R. The depth of hypnosis. *Journal of Abnormal and Social Psychology,* 1938, *33,* 453–475.

Fromm, E., and Shor, R.E. *Hypnosis: Research developments and perspectives.* Chicago: Aldine Atherton, 1972.

Gidro-Frank, L., and Bowersbuch, M.K. A study of the plantar response in hypnotic age regression. *Journal of Nervous and Mental Disease,* 1948, *107,* 443–458.

Gill, M.M. Discussion of papers on hypnosis at the Annual Meeting of the American Psychiatric Association, Detroit, 1974 (unpublished).

Gill, M.M., and Brenman, M. *Hypnosis and related states: Psychoanalytic studies in regression.* New York: International Universities Press, 1959.

Glick, B.S. Conditioning: A partial success story. *International Journal of Psychiatry,* 1969, *8,* 504–507.

Glick, B.S. Some limiting factors in reciprocal inhibition therapy. *Psychiatric Quarterly,* 1970, *44,* 223–230.

Graham, C. Hypnosis and attention. Paper presented at *6th International congress for hypnosis,* Uppsala, Sweden, July 1973.

Gur, R.C. An attention-controlled operant procedure for enhancing hypnotic susceptibility. *Journal of Abnormal Psychology,* 1974, *83,* 644–650.

Haley, J. *Advanced techniques of hypnosis and therapy: Selected papers of Milton H. Erickson, M.D.* (Edited by J. Haley). New York: Grune and Stratton, 1967.

Hilgard, E.R. *Hypnotic susceptibility.* New York: Harcourt, Brace and World, Inc., 1965.

Hilgard, E.R. Dissociation revisited. In M. Henle, J. Jaynes, and J.J. Sullivan (Eds.) *Historical conceptions of psychology.* New York: Springer Publishing Company, Inc., 1973.

Hilgard, E.R., and Hilgard, J.R. *Hypnosis in the relief of pain.* Los Altos, California: William Kaufmann, Inc., 1975.

Hilgard, Josephine R. *Personality and hypnotizability: Inferences from case studies.* Chapter in E.R. Hilgard, 1965.

Hilgard, Josephine R. *Personality and hypnosis: A study of imaginative involvement.* Chicago: University of Chicago Press, 1970.

Hilgard, Josephine R. Imaginative involvement: Some characteristics of the highly hypnotizable and the non-hypnotizable. *International Journal of Clinical and Experimental Hypnosis,* 1974, *22,* 138–156.

Horowitz, S.L. Strategies within hypnosis for reducing phobic behavior. *Journal of Abnormal Psychology,* 1970, *75,* 104–112.

Hull, C.L. *Hypnosis and suggestibility: An experimental approach.* New York: Appleton-Century-Crofts, 1933.

Jacobson, E. *Progressive relaxation.* Chicago: University of Chicago Press, 1938.

Janet, P. *The mental state of hystericals: A study of mental stigmata and mental accidents.* With a preface by J.M. Charcot. Translated by Caroline Rollin Corson. New York: G.P. Putnam's Sons, 1901.

Janet, P. *The major symptoms of hysteria: Fifteen lectures given in the Medical School of Harvard University.* New York: Macmillan, 1907.

Kline, M.V. Psoriasis and hypnotherapy: A case report. *Journal of Clinical and Experimental Hypnosis,* 1954, *2*, 318–322.

Kline, M.V. Age regression and regressive procedures in hypnotherapy. In M.V. Kline (Ed.) *Clinical correlations of experimental hypnosis.* Springfield, Illinois: Charles C. Thomas, 1963.

Kline, M.V. *Freud and hypnosis: The interaction of psychodynamics and hypnosis.* New York: Julian Press, 1958.

Kline, M.V. The production of antisocial behavior through hypnosis: New clinical data. *International Journal of Clinical and Experimental Hypnosis,* 1972, *20*, 80–94.

Kral, V.A. Psychiatric observations under severe chronic stress. *American Journal of Psychiatry,* 1952, *108*, 185–192.

Krippner, S., and Bindler, P.R. Hypnosis and attention: A review. *The American Journal of Clinical Hypnosis,* 1974, *16*, 166–177.

London, P., and Cooper, L.M. Norms of hypnotic susceptibility in children. *Developmental Psychology,* 1969, *1*, 113–124.

Ludwig, A.M. Altered states of consciousness. *Archives of General Psychiatry,* 1966, *15*, 225–234. Reprinted in Tart, 1969.

Luthe, W., and Schultz, J.H. *Medical applications* (Second of 6 volumes, *Autogenic therapy,* edited by W. Luthe). New York: Grune and Stratton, 1969.

Mann, T. *Mario and the magician.* (Translated by Lowe-Porter). New York: Knopf, 1931.

Margerison, J.H., and Corsellis, J.A.N. Epilepsy and the temporal lobes: A clinical electroencephalographic and neuropathological study of the brain in epilepsy, with particular reference to the temporal lobes. *Brain,* 1966, *89*, 499–530.

Marks, I.M. *Fears and phobias.* New York: Academic Press, 1969.

Marks, I.M., Gelder, M.G., and Edwards, G. Hypnosis and desensitization for phobias: A controlled prospective trial. *British Journal of Psychiatry,* 1968, *114*, 1263–1274.

McGlashan, T.H., Evans, F.J., and Orne, M.T. The nature of hypnotic analgesia and placebo response to experimental pain. *Psychosomatic Medicine,* 1969, *31*, 227–246.

Meares, A. *A system of medical hypnosis.* New York: The Julian Press, Inc., 1960.

Mesmer, F.A. *Mémoire sur la découverte du magnetisme animal.* Geneva, 1774. With the *Précis historique écrite par M. Paradise en mars 1777.* Paris: Didot, 1779. English version: *Mesmerism by Doctor Mesmer: Dissertation on the discovery of animal magnetism, 1779.* Translated by V.R. Myers. Published with G. Frankau, *Introductory Monograph.* London, Macdonald, 1948.

Morgan, A.H. The heritability of hypnotic susceptibility in twins. *Journal of Abnormal Psychology,* 1973, *82*, 55–61.

Morgan, A.H., and Hilgard, E.R. Age differences in susceptibility to hypnosis. *The International Journal of Clinical and Experimental Hypnosis,* 1973, *21*, 78–85.

Morgan, A.H., Johnson, D.L., Hilgard, E.R. The stability of hypnotic susceptibility: A longitudinal study. *International Journal of Clinical and Experimental Hypnosis,* 1974, *22,* 249–257.

Obermeyer, M.E. *Psychocutaneous Medicine.* Springfield, Illinois, Charles C. Thomas, 1955.

O'Connell, D.N., Shor, R.E., and Orne, M.T. Hypnotic age regression: An empirical and methodological analysis. *Journal of Abnormal Psychology Monograph,* 1970, *76,* (3, Pt. 2).

Orne, M.T. The nature of hypnosis: Artifact and essence. *Journal of Abnormal and Social Psychology,* 1959, *58,* 277–299.

Orne, M.T. Hypnosis, motivation and compliance. *American Journal of Psychiatry,* 1966, *122,* 721–726.

Orne, M.T. On the simulating subject as a quasi-control group in hypnosis research: What, why and how. In E. Fromm and R.E. Shor (Eds.) *Hypnosis: Research developments and perspectives.* Chicago: Aldine Atherton, 1972a.

Orne, M.T. Can a hypnotized subject be compelled to carry out otherwise unacceptable behavior? *International Journal of Clinical and Experimental Hypnosis,* 1972b, *20,* 101–117.

Orne, M.T. Hypnosis. In G. Lindzey, C. Hall, and R. Thompson (Eds.) *Psychology.* New York: Worth Publishers, 1975.

Orne, M.T., and Evans, F.J. Social control in the psychological experiment: Antisocial behavior and hypnosis. *Journal of Personality and Social Psychology,* 1965, *1,* 189–200.

Owens, H.E. Hypnosis and psychotherapy in dentistry: Five case histories. *International Journal of Clinical and Experimental Hypnosis,* 1970, *18,* 181–193.

Pai, M.N. The nature and treatment of "writer's cramp." *Journal of Mental Science,* 1947, *93,* 68–81.

Prince, M. (1905) *The dissociation of personality: A biographical study in abnormal psychology.* New York: Longmans, Green and Co., 1930.

Puységur, A.M. Marquis de. Letter (on the discovery of artificial somnambulism) to a member of the Société de Harmonie. March 8, 1784. Reproduced in A. Teste (Ed.) *Practical manual of animal magnetism.* Translated from the second French edition by D. Spillan. London: H. Baillière, 1843.

Roth, M. The phobic anxiety—depersonalization syndrome (abridged). *Proceedings of the Royal Society of Medicine,* 1959, *52,* 587–595.

Rowland, L.W. Will hypnotized persons try to harm themselves or others? *Journal of Abnormal and Social Psychology,* 1939, *34,* 114–117.

Ruch, J.C., Morgan, A.H., and Hilgard, E.R. Measuring hypnotic responsiveness: A comparison of the Barber Suggestibility Scale and the Stanford Hypnotic Susceptibility Scale, Form A. *International Journal of Clinical and Experimental Hypnosis,* 1974, *22,* 365–376.

Sacerdote, P. The uses of hypnosis in cancer patients. *Annals of the New York Academy of Sciences,* 1966, *125,* 1011–1019.

Sacerdote, P. Theory and practice of pain control in malignancy and other protracted or recurring painful illnesses. *International Journal of Clinical and Experimental Hypnosis,* 1970, *18,* 160–180.

Sarbin, T.R. Contributions to role-taking theory: I. Hypnotic behavior. *Psychological Review,* 1950, *57,* 255–270.

Sarbin, T.R., and Coe, W. C. *Hypnosis: A social psychological analysis of influence communication*. New York: Holt Rinehart and Winston, Inc., 1972.

Sarbin, T.R., and Slagle, R.W. Hypnosis and psychophysiological outcomes. In E. Fromm and R.E. Shor (Eds.) *Hypnosis: Research developments and perspectives*. Chicago: Aldine Atherton, 1972.

Schilder, P.F., and Kauders, O. *Hypnosis*. Translated from the German by S. Rothenberg. *Nervous and mental disease Monograph Series*, 1927, No. 46. Reissued in P.F. Schilder, *The nature of hypnosis*. New translation by G. Corvin. New York: International Universities Press, 1956.

Schneck, J.M. *Principles and practice of hypnoanalysis*. Springfield, Illinois: Charles C. Thomas, 1965.

Schultz, J.H. *Das autogene training*. Stuttgart: Georg Thieme Verlag, 1932.

Schultz, J.H., and Luthe, W. *Autogenic methods* (First of 6 volumes, *Autogenic therapy*, edited by W. Luthe). New York: Grune and Stratton, 1969.

Sheehan, P.W. Hypnosis and the manifestations of "imagination". In E. Fromm and R.E. Shor (Eds.) *Hypnosis: Research developments and perspectives*. Chicago: Aldine Atherton, 1972.

Shor, R.E. Hypnosis and the concept of the generalized reality-orientation. *American Journal of Psychotherapy*, 1959, *13*, 582–602. Reprinted in Tart, 1969.

Shor, R.E. The frequency of naturally occurring 'hypnotic-like' experiences in the normal college population. *International Journal of Clinical and Experimental Hypnosis*, 1960, *8*, 151–163.

Shor, R.E. Three dimensions of hypnotic depth. *International Journal of Clinical and Experimental Hypnosis*. 1962, *10*, 23–38. Reprinted in Tart, 1969.

Shor, R.E., and Orne, Emily C. *The Harvard Group scale of hypnotic susceptibility, Form A*. Palo Alto, California: Consulting Psychologists Press, 1962.

Shor, R.E., Orne, M.T., and O'Connell, D.N. Validation and cross-validation of a scale of self-reported personal experiences which predicts hypnotizability. *Journal of Psychology*, 1962, *53*, 55–75.

Shor, R.E., Orne, M.T., and O'Connell, D.N. Psychological correlates of plateau hypnotizability in a special volunteer sample. *Journal of Personality and Social Psychology*, 1966, *3*, 80–95.

Sidis, B., and Goodhart, S.P. *Multiple personality*. New York: Appleton, 1905.

Sifneos, P. *Short-term psychotherapy and emotional crisis*. Cambridge, Massachusetts: Harvard University Press, 1972.

Spiegel, H. Is symptom removal dangerous? *American Journal of Psychiatry*, 1967, *123*, 1279–1283.

Spiegel, H. The grade 5 syndrome: The highly hypnotizable person. *International Journal of Clinical and Experimental Hypnosis*, 1974, *22*, 303–319.

Spiegel, H., and Bridger, A.A. *Manual for hypnotic induction profile: Eye-roll levitation method*. New York: Soni Medica, 1970.

Spiegel, H., and Linn, L. The "ripple effect" following adjunct hypnosis in analytic psychotherapy. *American Journal of Psychiatry*, 1969, *126*, 53–58.

Stevenson, J.H. The effect of hypnotic and posthypnotic dissociation on the performance of interfering tasks. Unpublished doctoral dissertation, Stanford University, 1972.

Sutcliffe, J.P., and Jones, J. Personal identity, multiple personality and hypnosis. *International Journal of Clinical and Experimental Hypnosis*, 1962, *10*, 231–269.

Tart, C.T. (Ed.) *Altered states of consciousness: A book of readings.* New York: John Wiley and Sons, 1969.

Tellegen, A., and Atkinson, G. Openness to absorbing and self-altering experiences ("absorption"), a trait related to hypnotic susceptibility. *Journal of Abnormal Psychology,* 1974, *83,* 268–277.

Van Scott, E.J., and Farber, E.M. Disorders with epidermal proliferation. In T.B. Fitzpatrick, K.A. Arndt, W.H. Clark, Jr., A.Z. Eisen, E.J. Van Scott, and J.A. Vaughan (Eds.) *Dermatology in general medicine.* New York: McGraw-Hill, 1971.

Vingoe, F.J. Comparison of the Harvard Group Scale of Hypnotic Susceptibility, Form A and the Group Alert Trance Scale in a University Population. *International Journal of Clinical and Experimental Hypnosis,* 1973, *21,* 169–179.

Von Reis, G. Electromyographical studies in writer's cramp. *Acta Medica Scandinavica,* 1954, *149,* 253–260.

Watkins, J.G. Antisocial behavior under hypnosis: Possible or impossible? *International Journal of Clinical and Experimental Hypnosis,* 1972, *20,* 95–100.

Weitzenhoffer, A.M. *General techniques of hypnotism.* New York: Grune and Stratton, 1957.

Weitzenhoffer, A.M., and Hilgard, E.R. *Stanford Hypnotic Susceptibility Scale, Forms A and B.* Palo Alto, California: Consulting Psychologists Press, 1959.

Weitzenhoffer, A.M., and Hilgard, E.R. *Stanford Profile Scales of Hypnotic Susceptibility, Forms I and II.* Palo Alto, California: Consulting Psychologists Press, 1963.

White, M.M. The physical and mental traits of individuals susceptible to hypnosis. *Journal of Abnormal and Social Psychology,* 1930, *25,* 293–298.

White, R.W. Two types of hypnotic trance and their personality correlates. *The Journal of Psychology,* 1937, *3,* 279–289.

White, R.W. A preface to the theory of hypnotism. *Journal of Abnormal and Social Psychology,* 1941, *36,* 477–505.

Wittkower, E. Psychological aspects of psoriasis. *Lancet,* 1946, 1, 566–569.

Wolberg, L.R. *Hypnoanalysis.* New York: Grune and Stratton, 1945.

Wolpe, J. *Psychotherapy by reciprocal inhibition.* Stanford, California: Stanford University Press, 1958.

Young, P.C. Antisocial uses of hypnosis. In L.M. LeCron (Ed.) *Experimental hypnosis.* New York: Macmillan, 1952.

Zamansky, H.S., Scharf, B., and Brightbill, R. The effect of expectancy for hypnosis on prehypnotic performance. *Journal of Personality,* 1964, *32,* 236–248.

Index

Académie de Médecine, 9
Académie des Sciences, 9
age
   hypnotic responsivity and, 30
   regression, 14, 27, 41–42, 67, 68
      case history of clinical use, 66–68
agnosia, 27
"alert-type" induction, 19
altered psychological state, hypnosis as, 35–39
altered states of consciousness (ASC), 39–40
alternate personalities, *see* Multiple personalities
amnesia
   hysterical, 48, 59
      case history, 66–71
      denial in negative hallucination and, 71
   posthypnotic, 41–42, 56
animal magnetism, 5–6, 7, 9–10, 47, 56
anxiety, phobic, 74–80, 85–88, 101–5, 105–8, 108–10, 111–13, 113–19, 119–22, 133–37, 137–42
   dissociation mechanism, 124–25
Ås, A., 30–31, 74
Atkinson, G., 30
attention, 10, 30
August, R. V., 50
autogenic training, 18, 48

Bailly, J. S., 9
Banyai, E., 19
Barber, T. X., 13–14, 15, 17
Beary, J. F., 48
Beauchamp, Sally, case of, 59
behavior, antisocial, 12–13
behavior therapy, 130
Benson, F. D., 118–19
Benson, H., 18, 48
Bernheim, Hippolyte, 11
Beth Israel Hospital, 125
Bethune, H. C., 155
Bindler, P. R., 30
Blumer, D., 118–19
bowel control, 48–49
Bowers, K. S., 30
Bowers, M. K., 60
Bowers, P. G., 30
Bowersbuch, M. K., 14
Braid, James, 10
Bramwell, J. M., 6
Brenman, M., 15, 51–52, 128
Bright, R. D., 155
Brightbill, R., 14

Calverley, D. S., 13–14
cancer, pain relief in, 49–50
capabilities, transcendence of normal, 8, 13–14
Carol, M. P., 48

case histories
    I Martha and Harriet, 60–65
    II Hysterical fugue, 66–71
    III A fear of driving, 74–80
    IV A marital crisis, 80–85
    V Flight phobia (1), 85–88
    VI Lower back pain, 91–94, 97–98
    VII Post-traumatic symptoms, 94–98
    VIII Fear of dentistry, 101–5
    IX Flight phobia (2), 105–8
    X Fear of childbirth, 108–10
    XI Stagefright, 111–13
    XII Phobias and temporal lobe epilepsy, 113–17
    XIII Fear of dogs, 119–22
    XIV Persistent flight phobia, 133–37
    XV Persistent fear of dogs, 137–42
    XVI Multiple symptoms, 143–51
    XVII Psoriasis, 156–62
    XVIII Writer's cramp, 164–68
catalepsy, 31, 56
Cautela, J. R., 129–30
Charcot, J. M., 10–11, 56, 89
Chaves, J. F., 15, 17
childbirth, fear of, 108–10
children, hypnotic responsivity of, 28, 30
clinical setting, use of hypnosis in, 45, 47–54
  diagnosis of hypnosis, 45–46
  psychiatric symptoms, 51–54
  physical symptoms, 48–50
  rating scales, use of, 46–47
Coe, W. C., 15, 37
cognitive strategies, 17
conditioning, covert, 129–31
Conn, J. H., 13
control of subject, 10, 11–13
Cooper, L. M., 28
Corsellis, J. A. N., 118–19
Crasilneck, H. B., 50
Crisp, A. H., 163–64

Davis–Husband Scale, 25
demand characteristics, 31–32, 59
dental surgery, 49–50

dentistry, fear of, 101–5
de Puységur, Marquis, 7, 9–10, 13, 56
desensitization, imaginal, 125, 128, 131
  case histories, 100–22, 123–24
  conditioning procedures, 128–31
Diamond, M. J., 27
dissociation, 11, 41, 124–25
dogs, fear of, 119–22, 137–42
dreams, 27
dual-factor theory, 35–39
du Maurier, G., 12

ecstasy and ecstatic visions, 56
Ehrenreich, G. A., 45, 55
Ellenberger, H. F., 11, 56
epilepsy, temporal lobe, perceptual distortion and, 114–18
Erickson, Milton, 54
Evans, F. J., 12–13, 14, 17, 19, 29
eye roll indicator, 47
Eye Roll Levitation Method, 47, 77

failures, therapeutic, 133–42
Farber, E. M., 155
Faria, Abbé, 10
fluid theory, Mesmer's, 7, 8–9
flying, fear of, 85–88, 105–8, 133–37
Frankel, F. H., 14, 48, 116, 118, 125, 155
Franklin, Benjamin, 9
Friedlander–Sarbin Scale, 25
fugues, 56, 58–59, 66–71

generalized reality orientation, 36–38
Geschwind, N., 118–19
Gidro–Frank, L., 14
Gill, M. M., 15, 51–52, 128
Glick, B. S., 101, 125
Goodhart, S. P., 70
Grade 5 syndrome, 71–72
Graham, C., 30
Guillotin, 9
Gur, R. C., 27–28

Haley J., 54
Hall, J. A., 50
hallucinations, negative, 62, 68, 87
hallucinations, positive, 41–42
Harvard Group Scale (HGS), 25, 26–27, 103, 107, 116, 121, 146

hierarchy, 103 107, 121, 131, 135, 139, 140
Hilgard, E. R., 11, 18, 19, 25, 27, 28–29, 30, 31, 40–42, 45, 50, 55, 128, 168
Hilgard, J. R., 30, 50, 65, 128
Horowitz, S. L., 125
Hull, C. L., 21
hypnoidal state, 49
hypnosis
   dimensions of, depth, 35–39
   experience, demonstration of, 23–25
   induction procedures, 22–23
   theories of, 35–42
   working guidelines, 42–43
hypnotic behavior, categories of, 26–27
hypnotic depth, 46–47
   dimensions of, 35–39
Hypnotic Induction Profile (HIP), 47
   and grade 5 syndrome, 71–72
hypnotic responsivity
   age, 30
   children, 28, 30
   clinical behavior and, 55–98, 99
   cognitive traits, 30
   complexity, factorial, 29–30
   desensitization, imaginal, and conditioning procedures, 128–31
   diagnosis in clinical context, 45–46
   distribution in population, 28–29
   experience, other hypnosis like, 30–31
   eye roll as indicator, 47
   Hypnotic Induction Profile (HIP), 47, 62, 71, 77, 84, 96, 102, 107, 109, 112, 116, 121, 135, 139, 146, 156, 165
   neurotics, 31, 55
   nonequivalence of hypnotic experiences, 29
   perception distortion, 48, 49–50, 75–76, 79–80, 114–17, 125
   personality traits and, 30, 71–72, 128
   phobic behavior and, 99–131
   and physical symptoms
      related, 60–63, 66, 91–94, 94–97, 143–151
      unrelated, 153–62
   playmates, imaginary, in childhood, 65
   psychiatry and, 51–54

hypnotic responsivity, *Continued*
   psychotics, 31, 55
   rating scales, 25–27, 46–47
   sex, 30
   stability of attribute, 27–28
hypnotic situation and responsivity to therapy, 51–54
hypnotic state vs. social interaction, 15
   neobehaviorism, 17–18
   psychoanalysis and, 15–16
   role theory, Sarbin's, 16–17
hypnotism, coinage of term, 10
hypnotist
   centrality of, 7
   omnipotence of fantasies, 15–16
hypnotizability, *see* Hypnotic responsivity
hysteria, 11, 56–57
   amnesia, *see* Amnesia, hysterical
   hypnosis similarity, case histories illustrative of, 55–98, 99

imagination, goal-directed, 17
induction procedures, 22–23

Jacobson, E., 18, 48
Janet, P., 11, 40–42, 56–58, 89
Johnson, D. L., 128
Jones, J., 57, 59–60, 64, 70

Kauders, O., 15, 38
Kidd, C. B., 155
Kline, M. V., 13, 53, 155
Kral, V. A., 100
Krippner, S., 30

Lavoisier, 9
lethargy, 56
Liébeault, Auguste Ambroise, 11
Linn, L., 154
London, P., 28
Ludwig, A. M., 40
Luthe, W., 18, 48, 155

magic of hypnotism, 8, 11–12
   capabilities, transcendence of normal, 11, 12–13
   control, 12–13
   somatic changes, 14–15
magnetic diseases, 56

magnetic fluid hypothesis, 7, 8–9
magnetizer, role of, 7, 9, 10
magnetizing, 6
Mann, T., 12
Margerison, J. H., 118–119
Marks, I. M., 99–100, 125
McGlashan, T. H., 19
Meares, A., 18, 49, 154
mental healing, 6
Mesmer, Franz Anton, 5–10, 13, 47, 169
methodology, 21–22
    conditioning, covert, 129–31
    controls and nonhypnotizable simula-
        tors, 32–33
    demand characteristics, 31–32
Misch, R. C., 14, 155
Moldofsky, H., 163–64
Morgan, A. H., 17–18, 28, 30, 128
motivation, 133, 142
    hypnotic responsivity, 37
    psychiatric hypnotherapy and, 51–52
multiple personalities, 56, 57–60
    Beauchamp case, 59
    comparison with other behaviors, 65,
        70
    demarcation between personalities, 65
    interviewer influence, 64–65
    Martha, case history of, 60–65
    playmates, imaginary, in childhood,
        65
    simulation, 60, 65
Munger, M. P., 30–31, 74
mystical experiences, 8

Nall, M. L., 155
neobehaviorism, 17–18
neodissociation theory, 40–42
neurosis
    hypnotizability, 55
    phobic behavior compared to, 100

Obermeyer, M. E., 155
obstetrics, 49–50, 108–10
O'Connell, D. N., 14, 30, 128
O'Hara, J. W., 30–31, 74
Orne, E. C., 25
Orne, M. T., 12–13, 13–14, 19, 29, 30,
        31–33, 46, 125, 128
Owens, H. E., 50

Pai, M. N., 164
panic
    phobia onset and, 125
pain relief, 49–50
perceptual distortion, 43, 48, 49–50,
        75–76, 79–80
    temporal lobe epilepsy, 114–17, 118
personality
    hypnotic responsivity and, 30, 71–72,
        128
    multiple, see Multiple personality
phobic behavior
    covert conditioning, 129–31
    dissociation mechanism, 124–25
    hypnotizability and
        case histories illustrative of, 74–80,
            85–88, 99–122
        genesis of phobias, 125
        studies, 125–28
    neurosis compared to, 100
    occurrence, frequency of, 99–100
    phobia defined, 100
    selfhypnosis and control of, 101,
        103–5, 107–8, 109–10, 117,
        121–22
    therapeutic failures, 133–42
physiology, 14–15
placebo response, 8, 19–20
posthypnotic suggestion, 12, 24, 27
Prince, M., 59
Progressive Relaxation, 18, 48
psoriasis, 154–62
psychiatry and hypnotherapy, 51–54
psychoanalysis, 15–16, 47–48, 51,
        52–53
psychodynamics, 50, 124–25, 133,
        141–42
    and unrelated physical symptoms,
        153–62
    see also Phobic behavior
psychosis, hypnotizability, 55
psychosomatic events, 14–15
    case histories, 91–98
        of longer duration, 143–51
    hypnotherapy, 48–50
    influence of medical and therapeutic
        procedures, 90
public performance, fear of, 111–13

rating scales, 25–27, 46–47
  see also Hypnotic Induction Profile
    (HIP), Stanford Hypnotic
    Susceptibility Scale, and Har-
    vard Group Scale
reality orientation, 36–38
regression
  age, 14, 27, 41–42, 66–68
  components, in hypnosis, 53
relaxation response, 8, 18–19, 48,
religious rituals, 8, 48
ripple effect, 154
role-taking, 16–17, 37–38
role theory, 16–17
Roth, M., 116, 117–18, 124
Rowland, L. W., 12
Ruch, J. C., 17–18

Sacerdote, P., 50
Sarbin, T. R., 14–15, 16–17, 37
Scharf, B., 14
Schilder, P. F., 15, 38
Schneck, J. M., 53, 154
Schultz, J. H., 18, 48, 155
selfhypnosis, 18, 48
  in therapy of phobic behavior, 101,
    103–5, 107–8, 109–10, 117,
    121–22
sex, hypnotic responsivity and, 30
Sheehan, P. W., 30
Shor, R. E., 14, 17, 25, 30–31, 35–39,
    51, 52, 74, 128, 167
Sidis, B., 70
Sifneos, P., 133
skin diseases, 154–55
Slagle, R. W., 14–15
sleep, 7, 9–10
Société Royale, 9
somatic changes, 14–15
  see also Psychosomatic events
somnambulism, 7, 9–10, 56–57, 58–59,
    71–72
Spanos, N. P., 15, 17
Spiegel, H., 47, 57, 71–72, 103, 154
Stanford Hypnotic Susceptibility Scale
    (SHSS), 25, 26, 28, 109, 112,
    116, 135

suggestibility, 17–18
  categories of behavior, 26–27
  posthypnotic, 12, 24, 27
  see also Hypnotic responsivity
susceptibility
  scales, 25–27, 46–47
  see also Hypnotic responsivity
Sutcliffe, J. P., 57, 59–60, 64, 70

Tart, C. T., 39–40
Tellegen, A., 30
temporal lobe dysfunction, phobic anx-
    iety and, 114–18
trance, 39–40, 52
  depth, 38–39, 53
  hypnosis compared to, 35, 37, 48
  panic events and, 124–25
  orientation, generalized reality and,
    36–37
  similarity to spontaneous experiences,
    30–31, 102–3
Transcendental Meditation, 18, 48
transference, 15–16, 38–39
  psychiatric hypnotherapy, 51–54

Van Scott, E. J., 155
Vingoe, F. J., 19
Von Reis, G., 163

Watkins, J. G., 13
Weitzenhoffer, A. M., 22, 25–27
White, M. M., 25
White, R. W. 35
will, control of, 10
Wittkower, E., 155
Wolberg, L., 47–48, 53
Wolpe, J., 103, 107
writer's cramp, 163–68

yoga, 18, 48
Young, P. C., 12

Zamansky, H. S., 14
Zen, 18, 48